De la Bibliothèque
Duhau de Bérenx

Billy Baldwin

Billy Baldwin

AN AUTOBIOGRAPHY

with MICHAEL GARDINE

LITTLE, BROWN AND COMPANY   Boston •   Toronto

FIRST EDITION

Photographs from Condé Nast Publications: Courtesy *Vogue:* Copyright © 1933 (renewed
1961), 1936 (renewed 1964), 1939 (renewed 1967), 1943 (renewed 1971), 1946 (renewed
1974), 1949 (renewed 1977), 1950 (renewed 1978), 1951 (renewed 1979), 1953 (renewed
1981), 1959, 1962, 1965, 1972 by The Condé Nast Publications, Inc.; courtesy *House &
Garden:* Copyright © 1979 by The Condé Nast Publications, Inc.

Library of Congress Cataloging-in Publication Data

Baldwin, Billy.
Billy Baldwin, an autobiography.

Includes index.
1. Baldwin, Billy.   2. Interior decorators—United
States—Biography.   I. Gardine, Michael.   II. Title.
NK2004.3.B34A33   1985   747.213 [B]   85–13011

BP

Designed by Patricia Girvin Dunbar

*Published simultaneously in Canada
by Little, Brown & Company (Canada) Limited*

PRINTED IN THE UNITED STATES OF AMERICA

To BILLY
and for
BABS

Contents

Acknowledgments

SCORES OF PEOPLE were helpful to me in the preparation of this book. I would especially like to acknowledge the following: Way Bandy, Anne Berruet, Jean-Charles Berruet, Sean Byrnes, Lydia Cresswell-Jones, Louise Dahl-Wolfe, Deelia D. Davis, Karen Dukess, Diana Edkins, Joe Eula, The Evergreen Foundation, Martha Gray, Paul Gray, Christopher E. Green, Michael Halpern, Horst, Ross Hunter, Virginia Greenleaf Koch, Mrs. Lewis Lapham, Walter Lees, Jacques Mapes, Michael Mattil, Ruth Mattiello, Mrs. Gaines McMillan, Mrs. Paul Mellon, Meredith P. Millspaugh, Andy Oates, Mrs. Jacqueline Onassis, Laura Pettibone, Joan Pollock, Roberta Pryor, William P. Rayner, Ray Roberts, Francesco Scavullo, Beatrice Simpson, Arthur E. Smith, Etheleen Staley, Katherine Stevens, Stuart Symington Taylor, Susan Tripp, and Woodson Wallpapers and Fabrics, Inc.

Foreword

AFTER BILLY RETIRED in 1973, he was approached by several publishers and writers who were interested in his memoirs. He refused them all and it seemed to me not for good reasons. I, like many of his friends, had urged him to write his autobiography or have it written. It did not occur to me that many years later it would be I who would write the story of his life. Consequently, the purpose of this introduction is to explain why this book came to be written, and how it was written.

On Nantucket Island in the fall of 1982 Billy and I were at a dinner party, and another guest, Eugenia Voorhees, suggested that I write the story of Billy's life. Because of our friendship it was not the first time that had been suggested by someone, but quite frankly I was not interested in doing so for many reasons.

The year before, my first novel had been published and this had encouraged me to finish writing a book that I had been working on for years. I did not need much more time to finish it, and I did not want anything to stand in my way, but I must admit that the major reason I was not interested in writing Billy's life was because of Billy himself.

I did not see how it would be possible to write about him without his total help and cooperation, and I knew that he could be quite arbitrary and forcefully subjective. I also knew that he was a perfectionist and that he would want to have the final say on every word written.

There was also the problem of what to write. I had no desire, nor the ability, to be a Boswell. *Billy Baldwin Decorates* and *Billy Baldwin Remembers* had been published, and a great portion of his life, philosophy, and career was to be found in those books.

Another drawback it seemed to me was that I would have to bombard Billy with countless questions, and because of his fragile health I was not sure he would be able to muster up the strength to answer them.

During the years of our friendship Billy had told me about his life, his career, the people who had been his friends, and those for whom he had worked. Many of these people and events he felt strongly about, and I did not think that it was possible that he would allow some of them to appear in the book.

Perhaps the most important reason I had for not being interested in writing Billy's life was that I did not think I could do the job.

Not so many days passed after the dinner party and I found myself having lunch with Billy. "Why don't you want to write the story of my life?" he fired at me. "If you don't do it now, it will not be done."

I must admit that the reasons I have listed did not quickly come to mind in answering him, and I glibly said that it was not true. "Good," he said. "We can work every day after lunch."

I was simply at a loss. It did not occur to Billy that I might not be able to do the job. He had decided that it was to be done and I was to do it. That was that. However, before I agreed, I wanted time to think about it, and I told him I'd give him an answer the next day. "Fine," said Billy. "And then we must begin."

I decided that since I'd been working on a novel for more years than I cared to think about, another postponement wouldn't make much difference, and I naïvely thought that if it appeared I could successfully write his life, I could finish the book in six months.

The next day I told Billy I was willing, and that afternoon we agreed to the following things before we began work.

Billy wanted the story of his life to be a celebration of that in his life which was amusing, interesting, positive, or enhancing, and he wanted the narration to be as straightforward as possible. I asked him how he thought the continuity of the book would be if those facets of his life were omitted that might not fit into one of those categories. "We will say everything or nothing," he said. "I will tell you everything, but I will also tell you what I do not want written about, and if you think that something I don't want written about is crucial and must be included; well then, your judgment will stand."

We decided that what had been published in *Billy Baldwin Decorates* and *Billy Baldwin Remembers* would not be retold unless it was necessary for the understanding of this book. For example: Billy felt that all he could say about Mrs. Wood had been said in a chapter entitled "The Years with Ruby Ross Wood, 1935–1950" from *Billy Baldwin Remembers*. Consequently, what is written about Mrs. Wood in this book appears if it is necessary to the reader for the sense of the book or if it has not been published before. The same procedure was followed for everyone else.

I thought very strongly that it would be necessary for someone to edit and verify the manuscript, and that it could not be Billy himself. He agreed, and it was with the greatest of good fortune that Beatrice Simpson, who was eminently suited for the job, agreed to do the task, but only after she, too, had a night to think about it.

Not so long after she agreed, Babs came to Nantucket to see Billy, and when we were all at dinner, it was she who suggested that the book be called "Billy Baldwin Celebrates." Billy loved it, and thereafter we all referred to it by that title.

Billy agreed that I should have all of his letters, papers, photographs, and scrapbooks for the project. He also arranged for me to speak to those who had been part of his life. It was astounding how his many many friends, without hesitation, helped me in any way that they could. His former partner and protégé, Arthur E. Smith, and his firm were invaluable in providing answers to my questions and in allowing me to go through Ruby Ross Wood's scrapbooks.

Billy agreed to be interviewed on tape. My taped interviews with Billy began on September 1, 1982, and went through December 6, 1982. We taped many days each week, and Billy faithfully told me the story of his life. It seemed to me that he answered thousands of questions and always with the greatest of patience.

Lastly, he agreed that he would not interfere in any way with the writing of the book, and that after he had finished speaking to me, with or without the tape machine, what I was to write, based upon our dialogues, would stand.

After we finished taping and I had worked on the manuscript for several months, it did not seem to me that I was going to be able to write the book. What I had written was stilted, dry, and awkward. Because most of the information in the book was personal, the use of the third person did not work, and Billy seemed to be a character who was carved of wood. I had almost made up my mind that I was going to have to tell Billy that I was not the person for the job, but before I did, I spoke to Babs and told her of my problem.

Babs asked me if I could write it using the first person, as if Billy were speaking himself. I felt doubly a fool — not only because it had not occurred to me, but also because I had taught English for years and one of the assignments that I always gave my students was to write an essay imitating the writing style of a famous author.

Billy's manner of speaking was extremely easy to imitate and reproduce because he spoke in hyperbole. It might appear to someone who never knew Billy that he contradicted himself. For Billy, everyone was the most attractive or charming, and every room the most ravishing. He viewed his world in terms of the best or the worst. If he said so-and-so was his best client or had the best taste, he did so for emphasis, because he meant it at the time he said it, and because it was simply his way of expressing himself. He was an intense man who was fascinated by his world. He adored the moment of the present and what he said at that time was true for him at that moment. He was absolutely a man of the present situation.

After working several months on the book using the first person, I sent what I had written to Babs and I also let several others who had known Billy for years read what had been written. They all said it was successful. Another hurdle had been leaped.

Now, it does not seem possible to me that the story of Billy's life could have been written without using his voice, and his voice *it is*. As used here and throughout the book the words in italics indicate how Billy, through intonation, loudness or softness of voice (usually loudness), emphasized what he meant. I have taken certain literary liberties with Billy's voice, but the facts remain as they were told to me.

It was not difficult to imitate Billy's speech because, of course, I had the transcriptions of our taped conversations. Also, I had lived next door to Billy for years and we saw each other several times a day. We were close friends, and I had come to know him as well as I knew myself.

Each day Billy would answer the questions that would arise out of my work the day before. If he did not have the answer, he would call or write to someone who did. He was so exact I came to view my job as one in which I should not interpret or analyze. Because of this I think his words must stand as they are and the reader can read between the lines and form his own judgments.

As I have stated, the original title was to have been "Billy Baldwin Celebrates," and though this was changed, the thought expressed is the thrust of this book. It is a celebration of what he thought and remembered as worthy of comment. It is true that there are people, events, and facts which have been omitted. He refused to have anything written about his health, his problem with the IRS, or those people who he had decided no longer existed.

However, most of his personal thoughts and feelings are recorded in this book, and he did not spare himself, although I do think he spared others. In a sense, Billy felt that he had created his life, and therefore what he chose to say or not to say about his private life was solely up to him. It must be stated that I agreed with him. Consequently, it will have to be up to another writer to resurrect, dissect, or exhume that which Billy did not want written. It was not the ambition or intent of this writer.

By the late summer of 1983 I had written almost the first half of the book. Until then, Billy had not read one word of what I had written nor had he even asked! It was hard to believe that he had that much control over his curiosity; especially since not a day passed that I did not discuss the book with him or ask more questions. I had been warned by several of Billy's best friends not to let him read the manuscript because he would want to change it, and even though he had agreed that he would not interfere after the manuscript was written, I, too, thought that it was very probable he would want to make changes.

I did not have the control over my curiosity that he had over his, and I told Babs that I was going to give Billy the manuscript. She, too, warned me, but I had to know what he thought. The next day I gave it to Billy after lunch.

The following morning my phone rang and it was he. "Michael," he said, "can you see me after lunch? I've finished reading what you've written." He did not sound happy.

When I got to his house he was in the bedroom on his bed with the manuscript beside him. "Well," he said, "as careful as you've been, I'm frankly a little surprised at the number of mistakes."

I thought, That's that. He doesn't like it, but better to know it now. "Here," he said, handing me the manuscript, "I've marked the mistakes, and I think we should go over them."

The manuscript was hardly marked! It took about thirty minutes to make the corrections: spelling errors of people's names, several wrong dates, some awkward sentences, and four or five sentences he thought implied something that was not correct. Of course, he was absolutely right.

He loved it! "I can see that it's going to be splendid," he said, "but can't you write faster?"

I promised him that I'd try, but it didn't seem possible that I could spend any more time working on the book than I was or write faster. I finished writing his life in December of 1984. Billy did not read any more of the book. He continued to be always helpful and encouraging; however, it seemed to me that after Billy had read the first half of the manuscript, he thereafter conceived of the book as having been completed. His absolute happiness with the concept was wonderful to see, and he knew that it was only a matter of time before his celebration would appear in the bookstores.

Michael Gardine
Nantucket, New York, and Key West
December 1984

Billy Baldwin

. . . of course if you should ever be a star . . .

*M*y life, as far as living memory concerns, really begins when I was three and a half years old, the date of my sister's birth. I have a slightly vague memory before that, but I assume most of it is what I was told.

I honestly don't remember the house in which I was born, in Baltimore, Maryland, on the outskirts of a fashionable brand-new thing called the suburb. My grandparents on my mother's side, who were called Bartlett, gave my mother and father, as a wedding present, a little house on Woodlawn Road in Roland Park. I remember not one thing about this house, not a thing, but I have seen photographs that show it was red shingled, small, and perfectly respectable.

In that house I was born on the thirtieth day of May, 1903, after what my mother told me later in my life was an agony of a struggle lasting more than twenty-four hours. She had the most horrible, difficult time because I was an enormous baby. I weighed 8¼ pounds at birth. All of that was borne out by photographs taken of me which show a colossal baby who looks like the mayor of Baltimore or some other politician. After my first birthday, I was stricken with a wild attack of yellow jaundice, and I really never recovered from it. In fact, I damn near died from the jaundice, and that was what stunted my growth.

Looking like the mayor of Baltimore.

My baby presents, as recorded by my mother in my baby book, were:

a brass crib from Grandma
a baby carriage from Grandpa
pink enamel pins from Aunt Kate and Uncle Lew
two caps from Aunt Lela
pink and white socks from Aunt Winnie and Uncle John
two gold pins from Aunt Mabel and Uncle Ed
a pink silk comfort from Mrs. Parmly
a pink and white afghan from Mrs. John Frick
a white flannel wrapper from Cousin Rita
a blue hood from Mrs. Dunan
six worsted socks from Mrs. Conklin
blue enamel buttons from Mrs. Ingram
a piqué cover from Mrs. Whiteley and Juliette
a white with pink border blanket from Mrs. McCormick
a pink and white afghan from Miss Allice Archibald
a gold pin from Mr. John Frick
a silver cup from Mr. Walter King
a rattle from Aunt Mazie
a silver spoon from Judith Whiteley
a red enameled spoon brought from Europe from my
    step great-grandmother Bartlett

The first letter I ever received in my life was from Allice Archibald, dated June 7, 1903. She wrote:

To his Babyship, William Williar Baldwin, Jr.

His courtesy Aunt sends most loving and hearty greetings and begs to inquire if the world, including relations and friends, are proving satisfactory. I wonder if you realize, little one, what an excitement and joy such a tiny mite can make among us all. Fairy God-mothers are not out of date but I hardly think you will ever have need of one, certainly not if you are half as smart as that lady mother of yours. You know or rather sometime will, that all mothers are nice but of course some are much nicer than others and you have been particularly fortunate. Allow me to congratulate you upon your happy selection of parents. Now your aunt of course does not know what career you or "they" have chosen for you yet—but my best wishes for you are health and wisdom (of course if you should ever be a star, a half-back in your college even, my admiration would be increased ten fold although I might have to be "rooting" for you in paradise at the time). And it would amuse you to think of an "old lady" floating around somewhere, urging you on. And now, William, may you have a long life and a happy one.

> God bless you little one,
> from Your Aunt Allice

My love to your most honorable parents in which my family join with congratulations.

I was christened on Monday, October 12, 1903, at Grace Church by Reverend A. C. Powell. My grandmother Bartlett was my godmother and Lew Bartlett and Harry Ford were my godfathers. Those present were Aunt Lela, Aunt Kate, Great-grandmother Bartlett, and my father and mother.

My first Christmas presents were:

> twenty dollars in gold from Grandpa
> a lace parasol cover and several toys from Grandma
> a music box doll from Aunt Lela
> a red rubber dog from Aunt Mazie
> a clothesbasket from Aunt Kate
> a red rubber rattle from Aunt Winnie
> a rabbit from Aunt Mabel
> a worsted dog from Cousin Rita
> a big Santa Claus from Mr. Harry Ford
> pink bedroom slippers from Mrs. Parmly
> a rubber baby doll and toys from Mother
> a boy doll and horn from Daddy
> a white wooly dog from Mary

Mary Gearty was my first nurse and I called her Maa. She was my nurse and my goddess and my love, more than my mother, more than my father, more than anybody for many, many years. Maa was an extremely handsome woman. There were several photographs taken of us together at my parents' first house which show Maa all dressed up in a great lovely black hat.

When I was about three and a half years old, we moved to a larger house at 204 Goodwood Gardens in the smartest part of Roland Park, and Maa was told at noontime one cold October day, the twenty-eighth was the date, in fact, that we might have to take a rather longer walk than usual. That, I suppose, was my first really vivid memory, that walk with Maa. I know that we went out and that I grew very cross and bored, and I didn't see why I had to stay out for so long. It was chilly and, as a revenge, although to my great discomfort, I wet my pants. Honest to God, I think I can still remember that cold chapped feeling.

My nurse, my beloved Maa, was very Irish, very Irish Catholic, very religious indeed, and she used to take me to Mass with her before my parents got up. When they were just waking, I would go to the kitchen to see another beloved servant who was called Rose Martin, a perfectly charming Irish old maid, who was the cook. Everything that she cooked was fattening, and she loved me and I loved her. Rose had a sister who had a very distinguished position in life. She was the personal maid to Dr. Claribel Cone who, with her sister, Etta, owned the famous Matisse collection and were cousins of Gertrude Stein. There was never any difficulty at all between me and Rose Martin, who was never called anything but Odie by me, and there was never any jealousy; we were always great friends.

Also quite early in my memory, there was a third most important part of the family, an extremely handsome Irish chauffeur named McLaughlin. He had a little house about three or four blocks away from ours, with a pretty Irish wife and two sons, almost my age. Everybody was young. My father and mother were very young. My mother was married when she was eighteen, and my father was nine years older, but they were all young. The chauffeur was young, the cook was young, the maid was young; they were all healthy young people.

The chauffeur, Mac, drove with the greatest possible scorn and pride in our Peerless Motor Car. It was a touring car, covered from head to foot with gleaming brass, solid fire-engine red in color, but you could hardly see the paint because there was so much brass, which he was constantly shining, polishing, and very proud of. He wore a beautiful black uniform and a very smart black cap, and I discovered quite early that when he wasn't busily doing the polishing of the brass, he was polishing all of the neighborhood maids.

Now, I remember very well after wetting my pants being taken upstairs to the room that I shared with Maa. She dried and powdered me, and when I was made all pretty and nice I was told that my mother would like to see me in her bedroom. The doctor was still there and a nurse, because while I was out my sister was born.

In I went to my mother's room and I remember it so distinctly. I could just see over the top of the enormous double bed she was in. It was an old-fashioned four-poster, which was very high, and at that time it seemed higher than ever to me for I was so small.

I remember thinking how pale and tiny she looked. She was very small, anyway, about five feet two, I think, and she was very thin. There she was in this bed looking at me and smiling, very pale and very adorable, with her small face and enormous, almost black eyes.

My father had blue eyes, and my mother black. My sister inherited my mother's eyes, and she was called Beads. My father had named her that, Beads. He disliked her intensely. I think he even disliked her that day. He never liked her, and he never liked me. He hated children, number one, and he was tragically, intensely jealous of my mother and, therefore, of both of their children.

Right off the bat I hated that little thing lying on the bed beside my mother. My mother said to me, "Darling, I want you to know that the most marvelous thing has happened, something you couldn't believe that I was sent, and I'm so happy to tell you I have a real present for you. I know you're going to have the most wonderful time. I have a little sister for you."

I was simply furious, burst into tears of rage, and left the room. I just left her right there, and Maa hugged me and carried me off to the nursery. Maa hated my sister, too, poor thing.

However, what I remember so well from the very moment that I could remember anything was pretty extraordinary, even to this day. It was the memory of where I was, and by that I do not mean nature, I mean inside a room, the room where I first saw my sister in my mother's bed, a big room with this lovely old-fashioned four-poster bed. This was their bedroom, my mother and father's.

As I grew older I became more familiar with the room. There was a very deep and elaborate paper border of pink roses in full bloom. There was a matching cretonne — it was cretonne, believe me — as a slip-cover on an enormous chest-couch at the foot of the bed and also on a couple of chairs, one of which was a perfectly enormous rocking chair entirely upholstered and covered in this beautiful rose pattern, big, enormous full-bloom pink roses.

In this chest below my mother's bed there were glories that I was allowed to see only every now and then. I could see them only when my mother was going to a dinner party and was going to be especially dressed up. It was where she kept her fans, scarves, and the many kinds of artificial flowers that she often wore. From this chest there was always a wonderful smell of a perfume called "American Beauty" and another one called "Mary Garden." The artificial flowers were perfectly beautiful; most of them were made in Paris, and a great many of them came

Billy's beloved nurse, his sister, and Billy in the large white hat.

off of hats and were used again for other hats. There were also little bits of fur, because sometimes she wore little fur pieces in her hair. She always wore dark fur. She loved it, and I can remember her wearing dark furs like Persian lamb, but never sable. She wasn't that rich.

When I was allowed to go in there early in the afternoon if she was going to a party, I would nearly go insane. Once when I wasn't supposed to be there I dropped the top of this huge seat on my hands. My mother was out, and I was going to dress up. She found out because my hands were bloodied where the top of the lid had fallen on them.

There were some photographs on the walls, two of them oval, and may have been of an aunt or two. I had one beloved aunt who meant more to me than any of my other relatives. She was Aunt Lela Bartlett, my mother's sister, the beauty and scandal of the family, who married three times.

Oddly enough, I don't think my papa had any interest in decoration whatsoever. He really didn't, but my mother did have, and she did a great deal of the decorating of our house herself with the assistance of a wonderful man called Mr. C. J. Benson, who had the big chic shop. When I was older and able to really see all this, my mother used to take me in to see Mr. Benson when she wanted to get some new curtains and go over all these wonderful samples of material. Mr. Benson was a great friend of the family, a gentleman, and not one bit sissy, not at all. He lived in a very nice house on Woodlawn Road with a woman who was a big, horsy type and their perfectly beautiful daughter.

This was about 1910, and I was about seven. Mr. Benson was not at all social, but he knew people, and I will have to say that I remember now that his taste was quite conventional, but very, very good, and he had the whole town. Everybody went there. Much later on, someone called Oliver Carroll Zell became the rage. He used to go to Nantucket every summer, and would go up with a group of Baltimoreans and stay at the Gordon Folger Hotel; but that was much later when I was grown up.

But back to the glories of that chest at the end of the bed. It really wasn't a chest and was called, in those days, a box couch. It had no arms or back and was wonderful for lying down. My mother used to take a rest there every day, piling it with pillows covered in all kinds of taffetas and cretonne. The inside was lined with a pretty pink. Pink was her color, and many of those marvelously extravagant things she used to wear were pink. Her favorite color, though, by far, was cerise. She despised magenta, but loved cerise. She thought magenta was rotten, spoiled like a dead flower compared to the other.

Although she didn't really care about clothes, she was always dressed very nicely by a marvelous shop in Baltimore on Charles Street, called Schoen. It was a charming small shop, and the most divine woman, called Miss Katie, was my mother's vendeuse. All the ladies in Baltimore used to go to Schoen, and I used to go, too. My mother always wanted me to go, and Miss Katie used to say, "Oh, now, Master Billy has this wonderful taste, and what does he think?" They would make me parade around like a little prince among the half-dressed women who were trying on the fall clothes from Paris.

I would be there with my mama, saying "yes" and "no" just as I did about the house when she picked out the chintzes and that kind of thing. My mother, you see, would decide that she wanted to do a room over, so we would go to this wonderful man, and she would buy, first of all, probably fifty or a hundred yards of some lovely cretonne material and take it home. Then, maybe quite a while later, perhaps even a year later, she would call and have him come out, and they would decide where to put it, and he would have it made up into slipcovers or curtains by his own workmen. I remember them all, and I was crazy about most of them.

The cellar of 204 Goodwood Gardens in Roland Park was a very impressive place. First of all, it was pretty big because the house was not a small house, and this was the foundation for all that went above it. About a third of the entire basement was devoted to my father's wardrobe, where he kept summer and winter clothes in the most beautiful condition in great closets of cedar, all of them padded and full of indirect lighting. You could walk in and walk out, and you could spend a very nice time there. It had pleasant little sofas, very comfortable, and my father spent a great deal of time there.

Another fascinating area was known as the terrapin bin. Terrapins flourished in Maryland, especially on the Eastern Shore. I remember as a little boy seeing them in all shapes and sizes, and my life has been impressed very much by terrapin turtles, and still is. We used to go to the Eastern Shore to stay with my aunt and uncle and go down the Miles River where there were terrapins floating around. There also were plenty of oysters. Above, ducks were flying, the ground was sprouting corn, and you could hardly look in any direction without finding something to eat.

The terrapins were bought and brought up to Baltimore to spend the winter in the quiet cool of the terrapin bin, where they remained dormant. It was really rather a frightening performance, because I knew they were dormant and didn't think they were going to do any harm, and they were not, but I would go in and lean over the top of the bin, which was solid terrapin to the brim, one upon another, and it always made me feel they might just possibly wake up and have a rebellion.

What happened was that, whenever there was to be a dinner party, the chauffeur would take several terrapin, depending upon the number of guests, in to the Maryland Club in the city of Baltimore and have them prepared and cooked by the colored cooks of the club; then the terrapin was brought back in great jugs and heated for dinner. A very careful amount of sherry was added to the terrapin, and a glass of sherry was served at the table.

The rest of the cellar, which extended into an area that was not as deep and therefore much lighter, was the laundry, the domain of an enormous black laundress called Lena, whom I adored along with all the other black people around me.

I cannot emphasize too strongly my father's feeling about what he wore. Number one, let us say that he had absolutely beautiful taste. Number two, let us say that he knew about style and cut, and let us say that he was extremely independent in what he wore. He went to a wonderful tailor in Baltimore called Oldham, and then he became interested in an English tailor called Barnes, who came from London, and who had an absolute field day with my father in Baltimore. When my father died, there were twenty-four complete and almost new suits of different kinds. Luckily, I was able to wear the coats because, although my father was taller than I, he wasn't that much taller, and the topcoats and overcoats could be altered for me.

In addition to the clothes, there was the haberdashery where he bought hats, canes, umbrellas, and shoes galore. The shoes, of course, came from Peel of London. He really, honestly cared so much more about what he had on than my mother did that it was almost a joke. But it was not such a joke at the end, when he died. His will, which left everything to my mother, showed that there was nothing to leave her. He had spent every cent that he could get his hands on or make, which was considerable. There was practically nothing left because it was all spent on his own peacock joy.

My father was a very attractive man. He was good-looking, he was intelligent, he was bright, he was very witty, and he had a lovely sense of humor; but underneath he was a devil and a demon. He had a terrible side, consumed by jealousy, and it was really almost impossible for him to sustain much pleasure. He always wanted to leave every party early, and never wanted to go out in the first place. I think he was perfectly happy with the idea of putting on beautiful pajamas and a beautiful dressing gown, reading a book by himself, and going to bed.

One day when I was alone with plenty of time for prowling without danger I reached into the top of the great wardrobe in my father's dressing room. In the near right-hand corner of the drawer were piled the most beautiful white linen handkerchiefs with his monogram, W.W.B. As I was busily poking around, I found to my great delight something quite hard at the bottom of the pile. Lifting the handkerchiefs up, I discovered a cigarette case about four inches square and curved to fit the back pocket of a pair of trousers. It was silver, entirely covered in brilliant yellow enamel, and the front of the case was decorated with a peacock feather in full color. I never saw this case in any other place, and he never had it on his person. Another added mystery was that after his death it had simply disappeared.

One thing about him, which is sort of inconsistent, was that he played tennis very well and was also a marvelous dancer. He became a very popular and well-known dancer at the Paint and Powder Club in Baltimore, where all of the young bucks belonged and where they gave a wonderful show Easter week every year for charity. It was entirely amateur and entirely done by men. He had the distinction of being the partner of Harry Lehr in the most famous of all the dances, which was called the Dudes Dance. I was not born at that time, I'm sorry to say, but it became quite well known, and so did Harry Lehr who went on to become a prominent figure in New York society, Mrs. Stuyvesant Fish's best friend, and a social arbiter.

Because he loved to play tennis, he built a grass court in the back of our property in Goodwood Gardens, which brought about very attractive little tennis tournaments, very British tea, and not so British mint juleps. My father liked to drink, but it was only in the latter part of his life that he became a real menace with alcohol. I don't know to this day why my father was so unhappy or what the specific ailment was that killed him, but I *can* say that he was ill for quite a long time.

You see, when anybody talks to me about being shy or modest, I don't know what they mean.

T he Brighton Hotel at Atlantic City was the most elegant, unpretentious of all the marvelous hotels, and lots of very nice Baltimoreans and Philadelphians who liked it better than the bigger hotels went there. It was flanked by two monuments of vulgarity, really. One was the Traymore and the other the Marlborough Blenheim. The Brighton was only four stories high, very long and low, set way back from the boardwalk on a most perfectly beautiful English green carpet of grass, which was lined with borders of geraniums.

From the time I was a year old until I was eight I went to Atlantic City in the summer to be there with my grandmother Bartlett and my beloved Mat, who had been my mother's nurse and took the place of Maa, after she left. She had no connection at all with Maa, my beloved nurse as an infant.

Maa left in floods of tears one night after my mother and father went to dinner. They had told her she could go, and she went. She came in to say goodnight and goodbye to me. I knew she was leaving, but I didn't know why, then. She stood in the semidarkness in the opening of the door to the hall: weeping, weeping, weeping. I later learned it was on account of the fact that she had been knocked up by the iceman.

I never remember in all my life anything so spotless as the Brighton Hotel. It was run with perfect service by a smiling colored staff of big,

The Hotel Brighton.

but not fat, men in perfect uniforms. The hotel itself was very simple compared to the decoration of that day, although it did have magnificent woodwork, including columns everywhere which were of yellow maple. There were also marble floors and a long dining room, which had quite a long walk so that everybody could be seen from the door to the furthermost table. One table had three ultra-chic women I had made friends with, even at such an early age, which amused my grandmother, and we called them the Vogue girls.

Naturally, there was dressing every night, and I can remember when we were just about to go downstairs for dinner and my nurse would say, "It's time for you to go and see your grandmother now."

When we got to her room my grandmother would be standing in the middle of the floor in a very modest slip indeed, and she would say to me, "Now we will choose what I'm going to wear." There were two or three steamer trunks in parts of the sitting room, which were left unpacked, but standing like open closets, and she would say, "Now look ahead." Well, I would start because I could stand up inside of those trunks, poke around, and find something for my grandmother to wear. I invariably ended up in one of the trunks that was filled with black dresses overwhelmingly trimmed with tons of black jet. I know they

were very heavy to wear, because she said to me, "Why do you always want to kill me? I don't blame you, because they are so beautiful, but look out for your eyes and also your head, because you'll knock your brain out." She would get herself all dressed up and down we would go to the dining room.

There was also something called the Brighton Cafe where every single morning before lunch my family and all the snappy young married people met and sipped Brighton Punches. I think it was like a rum punch. I used to be allowed to come in and have a sip out of a straw, but not to have lunch, because I was taken away to lunch with my nurse. A little later on when I got a little older I was allowed to stay, especially when I was there alone with my grandmother before my parents came. Atlantic City was terribly gay for my parents' generation, and they all had a marvelous time, for almost everyone was their age.

This was at the time of the Wright brothers, and I remember lying back so comfortably in a roller chair looking at them high up in the sky,

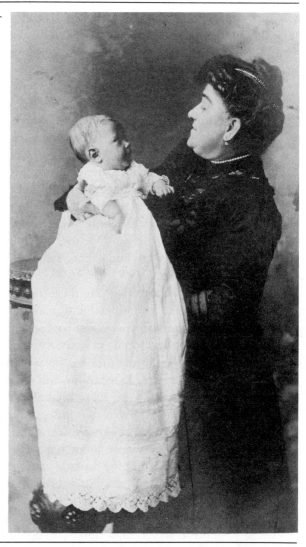

Billy's grandmother, wearing one of her jet-trimmed mourning dresses, holding Billy as a baby.

setting records in the air while I was being wheeled by a nice big black man, along with my grandmother.

The Vogue girls seemed to be terribly interested in the Wright brothers, too. They were, of course, the sensation of the whole country at that moment, and they did have dinner with the Vogue girls more than once at the Brighton Hotel, so the excitement was intense. I cannot imagine who those Vogue girls were. They could have been models or just very snappy New Yorkers, but to look at they were incredible, and they took a fancy to me.

The reason they took a fancy to me was because of the way I was dressed. Before we left Baltimore my father would see to the clothes I was to take. His extravagances were absolutely beyond belief. When out-of-town haberdasheries like Brooks Brothers or DePinna came to Baltimore, I was taken by my father to them, and he simply bought out the shop.

I was delighted and not at all shocked by accepting all those beautiful clothes. Furthermore, the Brighton Hotel had a whole room devoted to exhibitions of clothing, and from week to week all the New York stores and even some Italian ones would be there. The second my father got to Atlantic City the only thing that interested him at all was buying clothes for himself and for me, so my interest in clothes was very much encouraged as a young man, although I never, thank God, inherited it to that extent.

There was a small orchestra at the hotel, which played in the evenings, and I used to do little exhibition dances, which nobody asked me to do in the beginning. I was just past seven years old and wore a sailor suit, and I must have been perfectly awful.

Before dinner the orchestra played in a sort of palm court, and I did several numbers. I just got up and did them, and there were always two or three people who were mad about it, and some of them even got dressed a little early to see this performance. You see, when anybody talks to me about being shy or modest, I don't know what they mean.

Once, when I was about ten years old in Baltimore, a wild desire came over me to give a party one Sunday after church. I don't know why it didn't seem at all odd to me — that it wasn't something I should do. It was an autumn day and I had on a nice big beaver hat, a lovely dark blue coat, and a little cane. The moment church was over I went around to see about a hundred people, several children in each family, and invited them all for a tea party. They were all perfectly delighted and said they'd love to be there, and I went home.

When I got home I thought, We can't buy food because it's Sunday, but I didn't have to worry long because my mother came rushing up to me and said, "Where's your father?"

I said, "He's in the library."

She said, "Keep him there. I have to talk to you." We went into the living room and she said, "What is this about a party you're having this afternoon?"

Billy in his sailor suit.

I said, smiling like an angel, "Don't you think it's nice?"

She said, "Nice! You're just going to have to call every person that you invited and tell them there is no party. Right away!"

Well, it doesn't sound like much, but it was, and my mother always said it gave her an idea of what to expect of me in the future.

After I had been performing in the palm court for several weeks, my mother asked me to come in to see her one morning before I went to the beach. She wasn't even dressed, and she said, to my horror, "I have something very sad to tell you. You mustn't do any more dancing."

I said, "Why not?", tears gushing from my eyes.

"Because Mrs. Somebody from Philadelphia has complained. She doesn't like it, and you must stop," she said.

So she became known for years as Miss Complainer. I can hear it now. My mother hated her, of course. She was a very cross old bitch, and they all hated her, all of them. They were all on my side because Miss Complainer had to be listened to. That was a very exciting time for me.

Another thing that I looked forward to with excitement was the balloons. We used to go out on these roller chairs every day, and I was given a balloon, and every single day it would get away from me because it was filled with gas. It would float away, and I would scream and scream until I got another one.

My sister was in Baltimore at this time with her nurse, whom I detested and called openly to her face, in front of my mother, Mary Mutt. That's what I named her, you see. Even my mother called her Mary Mutt in a letter to me. Mary Mutt, poor soul, was a pitiful Irish girl with very red cheeks, a pompadour, and a huge fever blister, always. She hated me and I despised her. Well, we all hated each other, and there were two camps: my sister and her nurse, Mary Mutt, whose real name was Mary Murphy, against me and my beloved nurse.

Sometimes my mother would get cross at us, and she could be quite strict. She didn't spoil me, but when I was spoiled I was spoiled by her. She did discipline me, but I can't honestly remember now how she disciplined me if I did something wrong.

My father was the disciplinarian. He didn't do anything else. I hardly remember a nice, kind word that he ever said to me or my sister. I can't remember any nice words, and we never had any fun together. I remember once my mother said, "This is going to be a terrible day, I warn you. 'Your father,' " which is how she always referred to him, "is going to take you out in a rowboat and gather pond lilies, and it's going to be awful."

Well, pond lilies have these long attachments like rubber hoses and when gathering them you can be pulled overboard easily enough. So my father took my sister and me out in a rowboat, and we had a perfectly horrible time. I did fall overboard, and I could perfectly well have drowned. I think he wished that I had, but I didn't. That was one of the few times that my father indulged me in sport with him.

When I was nine my family began going to Sconset on the island of Nantucket. We went there because my mother's aunt lived there during the summer, and she decided that we should get out of the Maryland pollution. So up we went: my parents, my sister, my grandmother, two nurses, a cook, and a very ancient Pomeranian dog.

Getting to the island from Baltimore was an ordeal. We traveled by train to New York City, spent a night on a ferryboat going from New York City to New Bedford, and then took another ferry to Nantucket, where we then had to take carriages to the village of Sconset.

At that time, in 1912, there were no automobiles on the island. There was also no real indoor plumbing, and we had to go outside to the conveniences. My mother hated it right away because she did not like the cool weather and the rather rustic life-style.

On the other hand, I loved the island of Nantucket immediately and have continued to do so to this very day. The island has the best air, a clarity of light like none I've ever seen in the world, and wonderful flowers that bloom until the snow falls.

I also was charmed by the architecture of the little Sconset houses. There were some big Victorian houses along the North Bluff, but life in Sconset itself was very informal. Golf, tennis, and swimming were the sports.

The people who stayed in Siasconset, which is the Indian name, felt far superior to the people who stayed in the large town of Nantucket. Nantucket town is perhaps one of the architectural beauties of America. At one time it was very rich, and beautiful houses were built there. The three Starbuck houses on Main Street are probably unique in the world. There are also many classical Greek Revival buildings with porticos of wooden columns. All of the material to build these buildings had to be shipped from the mainland to this small island.

The fascinating thing about Sconset when I was a small boy was that it was a summer colony for a great many important European, English, and American actors. Isabel Irwin, a great Shakespearean actress, stayed there. Frank Gilmore, the first head of Actors Equity, did, as well, and Sconset really had first-class benefit performances by professionals of the first rank.

I remember eating cranberry jelly for the first time in my life, and I think at one time Nantucket was the largest grower of cranberries in America.

One thing that sticks in my mind about my first trip to Nantucket was that, as we were leaving New York City by boat for New Bedford, we passed a great German ship called the *Kaiser Wilhelm der Grosser,* which was steaming out of New York harbor. The First World War had

Billy's cousin, Rita Robinson.

not yet begun, but several years later when war was declared the *Kaiser Wilhelm der Grosser* was the first German boat to be sunk.

Celeste Marguerite Robinson was my mother's cousin and her maid of honor and only attendant at her wedding on April 23, 1901, and she spent her summers in Sconset for most of her entire life. She was the daughter of my great-aunt, Mrs. Charles Robinson of Brooklyn. This great-aunt Ella was a most pompous, conceited, difficult woman whom my darling grandmother Bartlett named the Mayor of Sconset because she tried to boss everybody, and she wasn't bad at it, either. Cousin Rita was an absolutely adorable little woman who just never had a chance at anything because of her mother.

My grandmother, who was really a very witty woman indeed, got along with her cousin Ella Robinson by using enormous tact. She called her "Put down Ella" because Aunt Ella wrote everything down. You couldn't speak without her taking a little reticule from her waist with a pad and pencil and writing things down as you talked. It was just to prove that she was going to be right in any future discussions as to who said what.

So this darling little cousin of mine, Rita, came along without an opinion in her head, but she grew flowers better than anybody I've ever known and had a little garden next to her house on the bluff where the prettiest flowers on the island grew. It was the talk of Sconset, and people used to stop and stare at it when it was in full bloom.

In spite of all these things that I have just said, Cousin Rita was very definite, very positive, very strong, and had good taste. If there was a yellow flower or a purple flower, she would practically call the police, but instead she would pounce on it and wring its neck, and if there were a cat in the offing, sprays of freezing water would practically drown the animal.

We became fast friends because she was an artist. She painted enchanting little landscapes of the island. I wish I owned one, but they escaped me somehow when she died.

One year she said to me, "Oh, you know how much I love Doone, your mother, but it is terribly difficult for me to give her any kind of a present, Billy, and I have decided that if you will take the time and patience and let me, I would like to do a watercolor portrait of you; and I would like to have it be a real secret. I can paint you in the barn where my studio is, and I don't think anybody will ever know."

So for many mornings, it seemed to me forever, I sat for her in a bright blue sweater and a Buster Brown collar. I remember thinking it was an attractive little picture, but it didn't look at all like me. My mother wept when she saw it in Baltimore on Christmas Day, but she was the essence of politeness. I think she didn't think it looked one bit like me, and she never liked it.

I have a newspaper clipping that was sent by an admirer from Detroit to the Nantucket paper about Cousin Rita's garden, after her death. It really is very nicely said and honestly expresses the point of view of

Billy's portrait by Rita Robinson.
(Andy Oates.)

everybody who came anywhere near the island and saw her garden on the bluff. It follows:

"MISS ROBINSON'S GARDEN"

Dear Editor:

I hope some one who writes well and feels deeply will write you about "Miss Robinson's Garden" (quotes really needed!).

It was a tiny spot of near perfection — a miniature English garden — or New England. She tended it with devotion and shared it most graciously with passers-by.

She was as much of 'Sconset as the fog and the sun.

Sincerely,
Joyce Daume, Detroit, Michigan

There were so many Julias in my family.

*M*y mother, born Julia Bartlett, was known from her infancy as Doone, a name given to her by the child closest to her, her sister Lela. She was the baby of six, doted upon by her mother and a pet of her sister Lela, who was very busy with affairs of her own and couldn't devote as much time as she thought she did to my mother.

My mother apparently fell in love with my father when she was very young, around the age of fifteen or sixteen, and never looked at anybody else; she never had any wish to become a debutante, and, in fact, married my father when she was eighteen years old, in a very glamorous and beautiful wedding at a church that the whole Bartlett family went to, called the Grace Protestant Episcopal Church. I learned about the wedding of my parents and their early life from reading newspaper accounts and from members of my family. A clipping from the *Baltimore Morning Herald,* dated Wednesday, April 24, 1901, described my parents' wedding thus:

On Tuesday the 23rd of April 1901 a large contingent of society attended the marriage at Grace Church last evening of Miss Julia Bartlett, daughter of Mr. and Mrs. Edward L. Bartlett, to Mr. William Williar Baldwin. The ceremony was performed by the Rev. Arthur Chilton Powell, rector of the parish.

25

Billy's mother and father in their wedding traveling clothes.

The bride entered the church with her father, by whom she was given away. She wore a French gown of renaissance lace over white satin, a tulle veil and orange blossoms, and held a bouquet of white lilies, tied with white ribbon.

Miss Rita Robinson of Brooklyn was maid of honor, and wore a gown of white accordion plaited tulle over pink taffeta and carried a cluster of pink sweet peas. There were no bridesmaids.

Mr. Harry M. Ford was best man, and the ushers were Mr. Clarence Holloway of New York; Mr. William Robins of Richmond, Virginia; Mr. Harry T. Poor, Mr. Wilson M. Carr, Mr. Talbot D. Smith, and Mr. John W. Frick. Following the ceremony a reception for the bridal party and intimate friends was held at the residence of the bride's father on Charles Street Avenue. Upon their return from a wedding journey Mr. and Mrs. Baldwin will live at Roland Park.

I was born two years after they were married, which was a decent interval, and, after another interval of decency, three and a half years, my sister arrived. It was a most conventional, regulated, proper performance where there was not a great deal of money, by any means, but, heaven knows, plenty. The house was always nicely run, and there was no thought of want in any way.

My mother was intensely domestic. She loved her house, adored her husband, was devoted to her children, especially to her son, and she really didn't care terribly about parties, although she played the piano very well and was in enormous demand because of it.

My friends were very, very fond of my mother who was sweet and kind and nice and great fun, especially when we had a little orchestra and she was at the piano. Colston Young, my oldest friend, played the saxophone, and Harry Parr, the best-looking member of a famously beautiful family, played the drums. She sat at the piano by the hour and played with them.

I danced. I really couldn't sing. I was the dancer and that's what I did. Needless to say, it always happened when my father was out of the house. He wasn't the slightest bit interested in one thing about my mother's piano playing or the music or the band or me or anything, not one bit. In fact, he was bored to death with our popular music. He liked music in a very sensible way. He went to the series of concerts given in Baltimore every season by the New York Philharmonic and the Philadelphia Orchestra.

Baltimore was a very musical town, and the Peabody Conservatory in Mount Vernon Place gave a concert by a ranking artist every Friday in the winter.

My mother was very small and had big soft dark eyes, full of warmth, kindness, and humor, unlike my sister's, which inherited only their color and were very piercing. As I have said, my father christened her "Beads" at an early age because her eyes were like black beads, and he also called her "The Secretary of War" because of her temper.

That was my sister, and that's what my father called her. He didn't like her very much, and she really despised him from the day that she was born. He did not help a child who was innately jealous of everything and everybody. She egged him on, and irritated him to a point I cannot tell. At more meals than not we would hear the words "Leave the table and go to your room," and upstairs she would go, screaming, but screaming with rage. She wasn't screaming with sorrow. She was furious, she was furious the whole time, including with me. My poor little sister. At those times I felt sorry for her. She could hardly be furious with my mother, but she managed to be not awfully nice to her. My mother was perfectly adorable with her, although it was a very hard job: because there was this constant battle between my father and my sister and my father and me. There was no battle between my father and mother, simply because she would not allow it.

I remember one chilling and terrifying experience in the night. Their room connected with mine, and the door was open so that anything that I might want or any danger that I might encounter could be attended to by my parents at once. I heard my father accusing my mother of the most absurd flirtations, which were absolutely not true. He had probably had too much to drink, but I know that my mother hadn't. She drank very slightly. She took a cocktail and drank some champagne, but she did not drink to excess. In fact, at that time, very few women did.

Although I remember seeing very few drunken women I certainly cannot say that about the men. Plenty of drunken men have been rolling around in my father and mother's house.

My mother was not at all athletic. Athletics did not come into my family life very much until my father got me interested in tennis, and they had a court built. But of course, the great game for Baltimore was lacrosse, played by Johns Hopkins University by a championship team, and a beautiful game it was. I can remember so many years later when Pauline Potter came to America as a child and didn't know much about anything in the way of athletics and sports. She adored lacrosse because the men's legs were so beautiful, and they wore nothing on them.

I can hardly say that my family had, in any sense of the word, an intellectual atmosphere. My mother and father read, and I know my mother liked popular novels. She was terribly musical, knew a great deal about it, and really played the piano well. She was able to go through and hum almost the entire scores of *Bohème* and *Butterfly,* and she knew what she was doing.

She was also something else; she was very religious. Very. My father was proper about it all, but I don't think he really cared. It didn't get in his way. He managed to get all dressed up and looked perfectly wonderful on Easter Sunday and maybe two or three other Sundays a year, but my mother went to church every single Sunday and was active in a great many church guilds.

We all went to St. David's Protestant Episcopal Church, and the clergyman to whom she was devoted was Dr. Foote. He was a nice, moderate man and not attractive, really, but very kind and sweet, and my mother adored him. He thought she was all right, too, and she certainly was from his point of view.

I remember one day when I was so proud of her. There was a theatre in Baltimore called Ford's Theatre, which was owned by the same family as the one in Washington where Lincoln was shot. Mr. Harry Ford was one of my godfathers, which meant that we were constantly being given marvelous seats at the theatre, very often boxes, so we had theatre parties in the way of entertainment. One year, I don't think it was for my birthday, but it might have been part of a Christmas present, I was given a box for a matinee of *The Silver Slipper,* which starred Elsie Janis, who was the great American leading lady. There was also a comedy team called Montgomery and Stone. Well, my mother decided to let me accept this present and have my own party. I think I was about twelve years old.

I had eight boys in the box, and my mother, and she just looked so wonderful that I never will forget it. She wore a dress with a long, very plain pencil-shaped black crepe skirt, and the most supershort cerise jacket with a sable collar and long sable-cuffed sleeves. The jacket was Directoire in style and embroidered with colored silk threads, and her brimmed hat matched the cerise color of the jacket. The brim was cerise silk velvet and the crown banded with sable and, tucked into it, were little cerise and pink apples and cherries from Paris. With her dark eyes and slender figure, she was the prettiest woman I have ever seen. I was crazy about her.

We lived at 204 Goodwood Gardens until my father's death, when I was twenty-four and my sister twenty-one and not married. The house was done by Charles Platt, a well-known New York architect. All the people in that one block of Goodwood Gardens had considerable fortunes, but my father did not, although his wife's family, the Bartletts, were quite well off.

I remember the house, even then, in the beginning, as being rather gloomy. When I was between nine and eleven, my mother decided the whole thing should be done over from the point of view of decoration.

Mr. Benson was immediately called in to help, and I saw every piece of material they were going to use. My father didn't care one thing about the decorative quality, but he cared very much indeed about comfort, and he was a lunatic on the subject of neatness. We were punished if we left a magazine in the wrong rack, or if we didn't plump up the pillows we were told to go upstairs to bed or to sit in a chair and not move. If *Town & Country* was in with the sports magazines, there was hell to be paid.

The main thing about this great change was the change from black oak to white paint. The dining room and living room had a very tall wainscot of hideously ugly dark black oak, which was scraped and painted white, with a very pretty scenic wallpaper about the wainscot. There were charming curtains of a rose color; the Jacobean furniture was thrown out, and very chaste Hepplewhite mahogany brought in.

I remember the music room as being pretty ugly, even when my mother did it over, because it was so cold. It was all medium blue and white, and medium blue is very medium indeed. That was where she spent a great deal of time at the piano, and where I was supposed to practice for my piano lessons, but never, ever did once in my life. I took piano lessons for seven years, and I couldn't, and can't, play anything now or ever. My sister was little better.

The hall was bright, handsome, and an immense waste of space. You went in, and it was an inverted T which spread out from both sides: to the left, the music room; to the right, the dining room; and it went back to a big window which looked out onto a garden, which later became the tennis court. A staircase bounded up to the second floor, with a bridge across the main part of the first floor and a quick turn to the level of its final height on the second floor. At the time that the house was built, the hall was dark, but during this change it, too, was painted white, and a very handsome bench was bought for it, and a quite beautiful Oriental rug, which was called a scatter rug.

As you went farther back toward the garden, the living room was on the left. It had not very good-looking bookcases; I suppose they were about a third the height of the room, and there again, there had been a very ugly dark brown wallpaper. My mother replaced it with a good-looking printed brown and beige linen that had clear, rather pale blue ducks on it. There was a great sofa in this same linen, several terribly good-looking upholstered leather chairs (upholstered furniture had already gotten to become much better looking), a perfectly decent big mahogany writing desk, long windows looking out over the garden, and a big opening onto a sunporch.

I remember distinctly that there was a slight battle, in fact maybe even a little more than slight battle, between my mother and father over the sunporch. He did say, "I will have to let you do what you want, but you cannot expect me to sit in that room if you do it as you're planning to." She was paying for it.

Well, it was very revolutionary, I can tell you that, and I remember that it was quite beautiful. The furniture was almost entirely wicker and had been painted a very soft green, glazed in blue, and the resulting color was a lovely bluey green rather like antique wood. The curtains were the same color, and around the room was a cornice of a printed linen of mauve rhododendrons. They were not mulberry colored, which was the chicest color of all at that moment. This was just before World War I.

In spite of my father's threat, he did spend quite a bit of time in it, and I know that we always spent Sundays and read the newspapers there. Outside there was a formal garden with a pergola, and at the end of the property down to the right was the garage, which was half-sunk in the ground and which you entered through the back. The top floor was where the chauffeur had his dressing room and a kind of sitting room, and there was room for two cars below.

In the house, upstairs, my father's dressing and bathroom were planned to make him more comfortable than ever. The dressing room was a very nice square that you went into from the hall, and it had a large closet for the clothes that he was wearing constantly, the rest being in the cellar. They had also built a very attractive arrangement for my mother's clothes, which incorporated a dressing table with a full-length mirror in the middle of it and was about one-tenth of the amount of room my father had. She didn't complain, though, because there was also another closet for her in their bedroom. I can't remember the color of that dressing room, but it was pink, if anything, because of the pink flowers and the roses in their bedroom. There was also a huge armoire for my father.

Off the master bedroom were two closets with a connection to the next room, which was first my baby room with a bath, and then my sister's. After her arrival I was sent down the hall to a room with a bath where I could be by myself without any danger.

The guest room was a dream. It was at the front of the house and had two beds, and sometimes, if I had guests, a man, you know, a boy, I would sleep in that room. Believe me, I would. It was connected with my room. Somehow I'd just go in there and do naughties all night long! That was an awfully pretty room because it had pale blue painted walls and a lovely chintz of blue and white lilacs. I think the bedspreads were lilac color, and it wasn't bad!

I don't remember the date when I was given by my parents the present of the wonderful experience of doing my room entirely over, including furniture.

The bed I chose was called a Windsor daybed. The head- and footboards were in the shape of a Windsor chair. The first antique in my life and the first antique in my family's life I purchased on Howard Street, which was the antique section of Baltimore. It was a very pretty simple American mahogany chest of drawers, and a very good one.

There was a gateleg table that I used as a writing desk. Bookcases were built in because I was crazy about books, and I continually ran up charge accounts, which were way beyond my means, for books. The chintz at the windows was beige with quite a wonderful tomato-colored flower, and there were two old ladderback chairs painted in lacquer red rather like the tomato color. Every room in the house had a fireplace, and mine had on it some very pretty blue luster and some Staffordshire figures, which I got from one of the antique shops, and the floor had a nice plain beige carpet.

A little later on, a decorator I have mentioned called Oliver Carroll Zell suddenly appeared in Baltimore. He had terrific taste, not at all like Mr. Benson's, and not at all like my mother's. It was really another thing, much better, in the manner of Elsie de Wolfe.

I had him make a lampshade for me for a simple white lamp that went on my desk. I used to haunt his shop; I'm sure I drove him crazy, and I know he didn't like me because he knew perfectly well I was growing up and I might even come along and be a competitor. He could see that I was destined to be a decorator. He made me a lampshade of mulberry and white striped taffeta, covered with gathered turquoise blue georgette. It was absolutely divine, and I don't know what I paid for it. He almost had to call my mother about the bill, but it was something I loved, and you can't believe with what passion.

I never knew a single Baldwin grandparent. They must have died when I was very young, and there were very few Baldwins in my life.

They all came from Baltimore County and lived in a place called Baldwin. My mother told me that my maternal grandfather was a charmer. He was a chiropractic doctor who drove around in a horse and buggy and had filthy dirty fingernails. She said she remembered with horror his reaching into a bottle that had pills and digging them out with his filthy fingernails.

My father's family consisted of one sister, Aunt Kate Brawner, who was a tragic creature because she was a victim of tuberculosis. Mr. Brawner was her second husband; her first husband was my uncle David Louis Bartlett, who died, and by whom she had two children. David Bartlett was also my mother's brother, therefore making Aunt Kate's two children my double first cousins.

Her surviving son, Cousin Ned, married a terrible woman, very beautiful, tough as nails, and they were soon divorced. He then married a charming girl named Marion Pease, from Hartford, Connecticut, and he went there to live. Like my father, he was in the insurance business, extremely good-looking, attractive, and very popular. My mother adored him but never adopted him, although he always stayed with us when he came home from Yale or that sort of thing.

On my mother's side there was an adorable grandmother, my perfectly wonderful grandfather, and a very distinguished great-grandfather. He and my great-grandmother both came from Connecticut quite early, established themselves, and soon became Baltimore millionaires. His name was David Bartlett, and he had a lovely wife called Abbie, who died. He promptly married again, to the horror of everybody, a woman called Julia Pettibone, and in the 1890s built a very famous house for her in the style of a Venetian palazzo, at number 16 West Mt. Vernon Place in Baltimore. She boasted of being a Huguenot and, being a great deal younger than he, she outlived him by years. She outlived quite a lot of people in my family and tied up all the money.

There were six children in my mother's family, three girls and three boys. One sister was called Aunt Mazie, and she disgraced the family by marrying a man from Jersey City, New Jersey. He was as common as dishwater. The other, a glorious girl called Lela, married three times. Her brothers were Uncle Lou, Uncle Ed, whose chief claim to fame was that he was one of the most brilliant of all the dancers at the Paint and Powder Club and wore the most marvelous costumes made by the greatest dressmaker of Baltimore, and Uncle John, who was an utter bum and had syphilis. Every single morning he walked three blocks from his house to a doctor to get a shot, and he was married to the most lovely woman, Aunt Winnie. I used to look at him with the most utter fear and loathing. Believe me, I did.

There were so many Julias in my family. My own grandmother was called Julia and, after her, my mother. Then along came this step-great-grandmother, and she was called Julia. My step-great-grandmother decided that all of them were named after her. They all despised her, but never mind. And then there was a cousin who was named Julia, another Bartlett girl, and my sister was christened Julia, and never called anything but Jule because my grandmother, whom they all adored, was called Jule.

Bartlett and Hayward was my great-grandfather David's foundry, and it was where all the dough came from, and from which I still get a little. The family did not like him, but they adored his son, my grandfather, who died of appendicitis while his father was still living.

My grandfather was the commodore of the Baltimore Yacht Club, and to my great sorrow I never saw his yacht, which was a side-wheeler called the *Comfort*. The family used to go on outings down Chesapeake Bay. The *Comfort* was supposed to have the best food of any in Maryland and the best mint juleps, and the deck was furnished with rocking chairs.

So there the family was, rocking away, and going down Chesapeake Bay on the *Comfort*. The only trouble about that was my Aunt Lela, who was her father's pet. She loathed the yacht and would say, "Papa, I'm going to be sick." Whereupon he would get the captain and they would turn around and go back to the Baltimore Yacht Club even if it was a beautiful day, because Lela hated it, and was going to be sick. Weekend after weekend they did this.

Lela Bartlett Mallory Lofland Hughes was my favorite aunt and the family beauty. She was a most tragic woman in many ways as she had no intellectual interests, but she was witty, bright, warm, and independent to a degree in her tastes and in her friends. She was a good reader of popular fiction, but she had no real interest in painting and only a pleasant social interest in music. She was interested in clothes, but only to the point that everything she wore looked wonderful, and everything she put on, she took off. It is only now that I fully understand her extraordinary career and sexy life.

It did not occur to me that she was devouring each one of those men in her life, for I knew she had a heart, a very warm one, and that she adored me. She had one daughter by her first beautiful great blond husband, a sportsman and man's man, but the child died soon after birth. Part of the sorrow of her life was there were no other children. Why, I do not know nor will I ever know. She wasn't at all interested in any of her other nieces or nephews, not in the least. My sister didn't exist. She did, however, love me.

One of her great friends was a very precious woman called Olive Reeder, who married very late in life and spent most of her time with horses and women. Only ten years ago, long afterward, when she was quite old, Miss Olive, which was what I called her, said to me, "You know, Billy dear, even in your crib you had charm." She never mentioned my aunt to me.

Miss Olive was madly affected, a pseudointellectual, and a wild social climber, which she did on horseback. She was an attractive woman, but a fool. I once even did some decorating for her when she married a most charming gentleman called Lurman Stewart. He was nothing but a horse, really. No mentality, but a great gentleman. There was a joke after they were married that she married him entirely for position, and he married her entirely for money, of which there was considerable in the Reeder family. Many people said that after they were married they were quite sure that he would approach the marriage bed and say, "May I, please, Miss Olive?"

Miss Olive and Lela, who lived next to each other, would sit at the country club, absolutely openly, every lovely afternoon of their lives, dressed in the prettiest clothes imaginable, and, of course, at that time, marvelous hats. They would walk up the hill from Boulder Lane, one block through to Club Road, and sit themselves in a most prominent position on the north porch of the Baltimore Country Club in a corner alone, have tea, and never stop talking. I do not think there was any more to their relationship than that. I don't. I think that my aunt might even have been innocent. I know that Miss Olive wasn't. But I really think my aunt was honestly not interested in her that way, because Aunt Lela was man crazy.

My mother was never fond of Olive Reeder. They had nothing in common because my mother did not like horses at all. In fact, if anything, she really disliked them, and therefore her country life did not exist. She was never part of the really great chic set known as the Green Spring Valley crowd, which had to do entirely with hunting, nor was my father. That was an entirely separate world in Baltimore to a degree that nobody could possibly imagine today. One can't explain it. It was just that the "Valley Set" was a separate thing. We went to school together, we went to dancing class together, we all knew each other, and there was some intermarrying, but mostly not. As time went on lots of the boys went to college where they met girls from other cities, and these girls realized that the boys were very attractive. They also realized that there was a wonderful life in Maryland for any young woman with money, especially if she was interested in horses. She could marry one of these beautiful young men, have a lovely house with her money, and a very good life in the "Valley Set." There were many, many such marriages, with the result that the district became known as "The Valley of Kept Men."

Today, they're all still very happily married. They all have children, and a number of the children are on the boards of the Bachelors' Cotillion and the Baltimore Assembly, and they represent a lot that is good in the town as well as in the country, but they're a country people. They are and they were. They're very provincial, but very attractive, and they have the best horses and very pretty houses, but they're kind of stingy in a funny sort of way. They will spend a fortune on a horse, but very little on a chair because they don't care.

Lela was first married to Dwight Mallory, and they lived quite near us. Goodwood Gardens was on a high hill that ran down to a street called Boulder Lane, which was very charming, and it had only two houses, and one was the house which had been given to her by the family when she was married to Dwight Mallory. The only trouble about Dwight Mallory was that he had no real domestic interest in his wife whatsoever. I don't mean he had a lot of other girls; he really just didn't care. He cared only about sports, and the thing that he loved more than anything in the world was ducking. He drowned one day when he was ducking along Chesapeake Bay. It took them something like a week to find his body, and I never will forget that. He was drowned the day I was giving a tea dance at the Women's Club in Baltimore. My aunt was there, and I remember that the next night he still hadn't called, and the following day they realized that he was lost.

Aunt Lela became the most dashing widow. My goodness, I remember her mourning clothes: beautiful crepe and great black veils falling from her hat to the floor. She had dozens of beaux, and she married a second time, a very unattractive man called Lofland. He was a not very recognized chiropractor, a perfect bum, and she divorced him. I was so jealous of him that I nearly hit him before they were married, for I adored her. My father refused to put him up for the Baltimore Country Club because he was not fit to join. He was a drunkard, and he used to come to dinner and fall flat on the floor, and my mother would say,

"Poor Bill," to me, "He's not feeling well again." He had simply passed out is what had happened.

One of the greatest scandals ever to happen in Baltimore occurred after they were divorced. Mr. and Mrs. Thomas Hughes, who lived next door to my Aunt Lela, were her intimate friends, and Lela fell in love with Mr. Hughes. His wife, Josephine Reeder Hughes, was Miss Olive's sister! The Hugheses got divorced, and Aunt Lela and Tom Hughes, who was a terribly attractive man, were ostracized. They married and moved right away to the Eastern Shore of Maryland, as a great many other people had done. They both became intensely popular, and eventually she died, but after my mother did. Aunt Lela died when I was living in Sutton Place in New York in 1936, and I was having dinner with my Aunt Mazie.

My Aunt Mazie was first married to a man called John Headen from Jersey City, who was very good-looking, believe me, but he was very common. They had three children. He died, and Aunt Mazie married a man called Joseph, who was, I think, twenty or thirty years younger than she. He was her sons' gym instructor in New York, and she idolized him; he had a most beautiful voice and everybody did their best to get him to join the Metropolitan Club, but Aunt Mazie wouldn't allow it because she was jealous of him. So this poor man who adored her just got fat and pitiful. Aunt Mazie used to tell my mother how great the muscles were in his back, and mother would tell her he was disgusting. However, he survived her and married a perfectly nice woman.

Those Bartlett girls were certainly something, except for my mother, who didn't do anything but spend her life married to this bastard whom I tried to persuade her to divorce. "I'll do nothing of the kind," she said, "You see, I married him."

My mother did have a terribly nice beau at the end of her life, but he couldn't marry her because his wife wouldn't divorce him. However, she had a lovely time. Alan Schwartz was good-looking and a perfect charmer. He had been a great friend of my father's, so that was all very nice, that part.

There were some terrible scandals among my relatives. Mason Bartlett, the son of Uncle Ed, had to disappear because he was almost convicted of murder in Baltimore. He had killed someone in a street fight and had to leave. He had a sister called Julia, of course, and another called Alice.

My sister really kept up with all the uncles and the different generations. She was very good about that. But I hated my sister Jule. I hated

A recently discovered photograph of Billy's sister, Jule.

her all of my life, and the tragic part is that I hated her from the moment I saw her in my mother's bed the day that she was born.

She was very strong, and all of my friends would say to me, "You just don't know how much better a person she is than you are." They thought she was splendid. She didn't do anything bad, not at all. No. No. No. She was just horrible to a lot of people, including my mother. We all hated my sister. My poor mother suffered agony with her. Jule was a terrible little woman, and I have not one snapshot of her. I tore them all up years ago.

"I would rather be an unsuccessful artist than a successful businessman."

M y first schooling was at a kindergarten in Roland Park conducted by Lelia Symington Goode. She was the niece of the
oldest Symington brother, Tom, and lived in a handsome
brick house on Ridgewood Road, a street in Roland Park just behind
my street. Her aunt, Mrs. Randolph, whose husband was the director
of the Peabody Conservatory of Music, lived next to her, and they were
the king and queen of music. I don't exactly know why Miss Goode
taught that kindergarten, because the Symingtons always had money
around them, but she did. I absolutely adored the ground she walked
on, and she was a friend until her death a few years ago, so you might
say she was a friend of mine all my life.

Miss Goode married a fascinating, marvelous man who was also my
friend all of my life. He was a brilliant architect named R. E. Lee Taylor,
whom his friends called Lee. Theirs was the first wedding I ever went
to. It was in St. David's Church, and I remember it vividly, standing on
an aisle pew and touching the bride as she went up the aisle.

Miss Goode was very small, very petite. Lee was much taller, and the
best dancer and the best ice skater when that became fashionable much
later. Her kindergarten was based upon what was then *the thing,* the
Montessori method. She was also, and I found this out increasingly as
we grew older, an immense bore. Lee Taylor was extremely popular

among the ladies, but there was never any suggestion of any kind of monkey business, there was not.

I went to Miss Goode's kindergarten for a couple of years. You'd be amazed to know how many of the children who were my friends then continued to be right straight through my entire life. Unlike a great many of my fellow students who later on went almost automatically to the Calvert School, I went to a country school for girls, exactly one block away from my house, where I was put into the youngest grade of the boys department where I was given the most elementary kind of children's education, like those who had gone on to the Calvert School, which was then the chic thing to do. I suppose it was quite natural for my mother to put me in school right across the street. There was nothing exactly sloppy about it. In fact, my favorite teacher there, called Miss Nolan, was the sister of the famous Miss Charlotte Nolan of Foxcroft.

As soon as possible, I was sent to the Gilman Country School for Boys, which every single half-civilized boy in Baltimore went to. There I was entered into the Open Air School, which was one of the first outdoor schools in the country. We were taught in buildings with only three walls because we were supposed to be getting fresh air.

Your fingers were frozen off, you had muffs, you had great bags that your feet were put in, and there were soapstones which were heated to keep your hands and feet warm. I was taught by an adorable woman called Miss Woolover.

There we were: reciting, studying, exercising, singing, all in the coldest Maryland weather, and, believe me, it's cold down there, and unless there was a typhoon blowing all of the papers off our desks and soaking us, we were never put inside. After being taught outdoors in the Open Air School, we graduated into the regular indoor school where we began with the first form and went through to the sixth.

I was at the Gilman Country School for Boys eight years altogether. I just honestly could not get beyond the fifth grade without a lot of trouble, mainly because of mathematics, which I considered unnecessary and boring. I was damn good at English and very good in history and French, because I thought that made sense and was attractive.

In the meantime, my father was wild with my low marks. I barely passed, just getting fifty. He decided that what I needed was to get out of Baltimore and to be put into a totally different environment. Therefore, I was sent to where my double first cousin, whose family had been a great deal in the North, had graduated from, a school called the Westminster School for Boys at Simsbury, Connecticut.

So at the age of fifteen and having never been away from home, without being with someone in my family, I was sent to boarding school. My mother and father took me up by train. They lunched at the headmaster's house the day that they got there, and after lunch said goodbye. My mother rushed, literally ran, to the car because she was in such tears. She didn't want me to see her, and my father was almost in tears of rage with her and me. He was delighted, of course, that I was getting sort of out of his life. So there I was. I knew two boys at the school; both of them were from Baltimore and had been there before. When I entered the school, of course I was "a new kid."

They had a system similar to the cruel fag system of the English schools. We had to line up, beautifully dressed as though we were going to dancing class, for dinner every night. There was a wonderful man called Dr. Cushing who was the headmaster. He and his enchanting wife had a lovely house that was attached to the school. One of their sons was Mr. Bill Cushing, a man with the most enormous charm, with a ravishing wife. Another, called Tom Cushing, was a playwright.

From the moment of my mother's drowning departure, I decided to kill myself. I hated everything about it. First of all, it was terribly cold, much colder than Baltimore, and secondly, I didn't like any of the boys. We slept in a long hall divided into cubicles, and all the walls were stained dark brown and there were dark red cotton curtains and no doors. We each had one bed in our room, and we were allowed to do anything we wanted with the walls because you couldn't hurt them. They were wooden, and stained each year. I thumbtacked mine with covers of *Vanity Fair*.

There was a committee of four seniors who literally ruled you. If you did something wrong you were sent to the locker room in the basement, which had windows that were left open at night and gave onto the windows of the corridor upstairs. In your cubicle you could hear the flogging and the screams of your fellow students being whipped. You can imagine what happened to me when they first came to see me, and they said, "What is the idea of these pictures?" These men came from perfectly nice families and were gentlemen, but there was a man, whose name was Bradford, who was cruel and who hated me so much that he really wanted to hurt me physically, but he couldn't. We had to say, Excuse me, and Thank you, and call them all Sir.

I remember the second visit that they paid to me. They arrived after study hall one night and Bradford said, "What's the real idea of these pictures? What do they mean?"

And I, shivering with the cold, in my pajamas, and my feet crossed underneath me on the bed under a red blanket, put my head up in the air and, clear voiced, said, "I would rather be an unsuccessful artist than a successful businessman." It enraged him because we were in a dormitory and everyone could hear what was said.

The school was very good-looking and the food was so good that it tasted as though it were from the Ritz. All the vegetables were grown there, and the service was perfectly wonderful. In the acres of woods quite a bit of distance from the school building, beyond the tennis court, a small golf course, and a baseball field, were charming little cottages that were occupied by seniors who had the use of them for a year, to sleep in if they wished, if they had a certain average in their marks.

They also had the privilege of selecting, among the new kids, two, literally, slaves. One freezing January night I remember the agony of having to carry a Victrola, which they wanted for their entertainment, from the students' room in the school building to a cottage. The snow was up above my knees and I had to wear snowshoes, which I'd never had on or even seen before, and after its delivery I was beaten and told to go to bed.

But there were a lot of very nice boys there, too, and some terribly attractive ones, and I even got to like some of the older ones. I learned more in that one year at school than I learned the whole time in the Gilman Country School for Boys where I learned absolutely nothing.

The most terrible thing that ever happened to me in my life occurred on my first New England Thanksgiving at the Westminster School.

We were told that we would stay at school, there would be no holiday at all excepting Thanksgiving Day and Friday, there would be no classes; but we would have to be on the grounds. They didn't want anybody to go away, mainly because on Saturday they had a big dinner for all the students, all the professors, any alumni who wanted to come with their wives and families, any ex-teachers, anybody connected with Westminster; that was the big day.

Also on that day, the entertainment was to be contributed by the new kids. This was a very small school, so I guess we were maybe about twelve new kids, and we were expected to make speeches after dinner on subjects which were going to be given to us at the time that we stood up. We had no idea what they were going to be. The only way I was in luck that day was because we would be called upon alphabetically, and Baldwin begins with a B. I believe maybe there was one A, and maybe one B even, and I know I wasn't the first, but I was very soon among the first to make my little speech. Well, up I stood in a nice little blue suit with my class, at my regular seat at the table; they were long tables in a perfectly lovely dining room. It was so good-looking because Mrs. Cushing's daughter-in-law had the best taste, and Mrs. Cushing was pretty darn good herself. The Cushings were all enormously attractive people.

Up stood the senior member of the senior class and said, "We will now have a little talk from William Baldwin, popularly known as Billy. His subject will be, Have you a little fairy in your home?"

I felt as though I suddenly had had every drop of blood taken out of me. It was as if my veins had been filled with ice water and fire, and I was absolutely furious.

I was facing some doors that opened onto a hall that ran through that floor and into the stair hall. And as I stood there, I saw Tom Cushing leaving by way of that hall, unseen by the people whose backs were to him at the table.

Well, I was fifteen and I wanted to cry with anger, cry because I was being insulted. Also because I was defenseless, and what in God's name was I supposed to do?

I felt like a child, really, and this is almost what I said: "I don't know who chose this, but it must be somebody who knows an awful lot more about these things that we don't know so much about, and I will therefore say that I don't know whether the little fairy is at my home or is standing here talking to you, or not. Thank you." And I sat down.

I couldn't deny it, and I couldn't do anything, and I know that, in my whole life, it is probably the moment when I was most embarrassed. It was so unfair.

The funny part was, when I sat down there was not one sound. Nobody said a damn thing. There was just silence.

I think I was pretty dignified, and I think *I behaved;* but even now, over sixty years later, I thought I was going to die. I really wished to die.

But, of course, I didn't die, and I had sat down and had to sit there in perfect agony through the whole long performance.

The ironic part, and perhaps a nice part, was that so many of the kids smiled, for I had slept with nearly half the room. That was my first New England Thanksgiving.

Another thing that happened frequently took place at night when all the new kids of early term were in bed. We were all about fifteen, and we called them the inquisitions. For reasons of health, windows were always to be kept open although it was below zero outside. Two floors below us was the locker room where the inquisitions took place, and they had the windows open there, too, because it was very hot inside, and because they wanted us to hear the tortures upstairs, which we did. We not only heard the whippings with belts, but all kinds of terrible, exaggerated language suggesting that the boys were being far more hurt than they actually were and making it sound all the more terrible.

You would very often be called upon to come down there to testify against another student. "Now," they would say, "isn't it true? Didn't you see him stealing that money?" They would say such things. It was absolutely primitive.

I really wasn't very happy there, but in many ways I certainly did have a good time; sometimes I would get up terribly early in the morning and go down to the river with the boy whose cubicle was on my left. He was trapping muskrats to make a coat of the pelts, which he skinned himself. He didn't make me do it because he couldn't as he was not old enough, but it was a pretty cruel thing for me to see. I was from the city of Baltimore and had never even seen a dead animal.

I did have a couple of wonderful trips from school to New York City, which really began my wild love for it. I was taken by my cousin Ned from New Haven to the theatre there because we had to stay overnight. I got my first taste of being in a hotel in New York City. Of course, I used to go with my family a couple of times a year, but this was not with the family, which was the whole point. Those trips were really my first exposure to New York City, and it was then that my passion for it was born, as well as my passion for hotels.

I love hotels because of the twenty-four-hour service, because they're clean, and have good food. Anyway, they all used to be that way. You could have what you wanted, and could come and go as you pleased.

The tragic part about the Westminster School was that Dr. Cushing was the most wonderful man, but he was also a very old one. He was beautiful-looking, and he waked you up by coming up and pulling your curtain aside and saying, "Time to get up" through a great beautiful white beard, so we gave him the name of Bush. He was really dying, though, that year, and as a matter of fact, during the summer he did.

Tom Cushing was the drama director, and he was an excessively good-looking man who never stopped for one minute from scratching his balls. He was a quite successful playwright, and he had a friend called Winthrop Ames who lived very near him in Simsbury and who placed his plays for him, one of which being *Blood and Sand,* which had been adapted from the Blasco-Ibáñez novel, and later became a movie with Tyrone Power.

Every year Tom either wrote an original play, adapted one, or used one that he had not sold for production. He immediately took a great liking to me, not sexually, but he knew what I was, even though I didn't know what I was. You know, one didn't know those things then.

Tom Cushing had told his mother and father and the faculty that the only way he could possibly get the boys, especially those with the leading parts, to have a lack of self-consciousness and get over any embarrassment, was to have them rehearse in the nude in his apartment, which was on top of the school.

After study hall up we would go to Tom's apartment with whomever we were to be with in the scene. It didn't happen to anyone except the stars; there were about six or seven of us, and some of the seniors who knew about it called us "The Bare Ass Club."

Tom's apartment was nice and toasty warm. It had an immense room with a great ceiling and marvelous things he had collected from all over the world. He was always dressed beautifully, and fully: tie, everything, and he always wore beautiful Glen Urquardt plaids.

In the corner was an enormous kind of double bed — Empire, I think — and you just walked over there and took off your clothes, and walked around or sat down or whatever in that lovely heated room with the fire roaring, you and whomever you were doing the scene with.

For one play the leading role was taken by a typical American boy, who bored me to death. He was big, he was blond, he was very muscular, he was the captain of the football team, and he was the son of the bishop of Philadelphia.

I can't remember the name of the play we were rehearsing, but he was the hero and I was the vamp. I really was the vamp, and I wore the most marvelous dress that my mother had bought the year before, which she had had sent up, with my father protesting wildly. It was from Paris and came from Schoen on Charles Street in Baltimore. Miss Katie considered it very daring. It was almost straight up and down, beige jersey, with long sleeves and a high neck, and was worn with an orange velvet turban. My mother and father came up for the play, and my father was not one bit amused. My mother was delighted, but my father didn't care for it at all.

Tom had written a very successful play called *Thank You,* and a couple of other plays that were quite popular. He was a great gentleman with great charm, and my mother said to my father, "Will, you must admit it's been worth the trip." The trip was quite difficult because they had to change in New York, and then again in New Haven. She said in front of me, "The fact that we met Tom Cushing made it worth it." Tom really did have great charm.

A boy called Henry Tate, the brother of Diane Tate, the decorator, who was Marian Hall's partner, suddenly appeared in our club. Tom was mad about him in every way. Henry Tate had the figure of an ideal young American man. He wasn't a football player, but he was a great athlete. He very often lay on the bed watching rehearsals, but he had his pajamas on. Well, before the play which my parents saw was performed, everything was going perfectly. I used to have to sit stark naked in the lap of the hero, the football player, he perfectly naked, too, and do these love scenes while there was Tom scratching his balls.

One day not too long before the play's performance, Tom, looking terribly upset and ill, said to me, "Billy, I've got something to tell you. You know I'm crazy about you, and you're the person that I really like to talk to most of any of the kids. Something unfortunate has happened; I have had to remove Harris from the play because he's a silly man and has told his father, the bishop, about our rehearsals. His father has been here and the whole thing came out, and, of course, I had to admit it and why, and that dirty old man thinks it has to do with sex." Tom said this to me. Imagine saying that *to me* and thinking that I didn't know, that nobody knew; but I suppose that was why he was so smart, you see, because he didn't hide it from anybody.

Anyway, the bishop came down, the boy was removed, and Tom said to me, "Billy, I think if you don't mind I'm going to try someone else for the part."

I said, "Do I still have to be undressed?"

And he said, "Yes. Why?"

I said, "Because, Tom, I really can't tell you what I'll do, but I'll try not to get excited." We did have rehearsals with him and behaved very well.

Years and years later, Woody Taulbee and I went to stay with Tom, who had a lovely house in Bermuda. And I said, "Woody, do you mind, but I've got to tell this man about something that happened about twenty years ago."

So Woody, Tom, and I had a lot of cocktails, and I said, "Now listen here, Tom Cushing, now I'm going to tell you. You are the dirtiest old man I have ever known, and how dared you have us all naked."

And he said, "Well, didn't you enjoy it?"

I said, "You're damn right I did."

Tom said, "You know, Billy, I have never gotten over the fact that Harris, who was the football player, didn't appeal to you at all, did he?"

"No," I said. "He had no more sex appeal for me than Madam Schumann-Heink."

"Well," he said, "I noticed that the other boy was quite different."

I said, "You should have seen us later."

When I got back to Baltimore from that school term, the first thing I did was to tell my father that I would not go back. I said that I hated it, and I said, besides, "You, by your neglect of me, have made my life hideous for having to learn about sex in a most unpleasant way." I said he had ruined my life and that I was not going back there to be the victim of those boys who were stronger than I was, and to be disgraced every night that I spent there. And I said, "It's your fault because I didn't know what they were doing." But I knew perfectly well what they were doing because I told them what to do most of the time.

The only result was his saying a little while later, "What are we going to do about you? I don't think that you should go back to the school if what you're telling me is true. Personally, I think you're just a little liar, and I don't believe one word of it."

I said, "Well, you can just call my best friend, because you and his father are friends. I dare you." I have to admit I was awful to my father. I have to say I was. I didn't help him.

Anyway, one day he said, "I think you'd better go back to Gilman; I really think you'd better. You too old to make a change now. I'm glad you hate it. I'm glad you hate the North."

I said, "Well, I don't know that I hate the North. I just don't like those dirty boys."

But really I couldn't get enough of them. So I was sent back to the Gilman School.

. . . I considered myself then, and do now,
superior and way above geometry and
algebra and any mathematics.

*M*y father had a brilliantly successful insurance business. He
represented a great many European companies, primarily
English and Swiss, as well as a lot of very important American ones.

He was quite an athlete, taller than I ever was but not tall, and he
had a beautiful figure, very muscular, for he had done a considerable
amount of tennis playing and had been to Cambridge, where he even
did rowing.

On Sunday mornings I used to spy on him. His dressing room, which
was large and had a window, also had two doors, one of which connected to my room. This door was always locked. No one ever entered
the room from that door excepting my father, and then very rarely.

So on Sundays, as the family slept later and did not have breakfast
until later, I would get up earlier than usual and get on my knees at the
keyhole to watch my father shaving, because he was stripped.

I suppose if I had been caught he would have killed me. I'm sure he
would have because he had a wild, violent temper. My sister got her
temper straight from him. I had one, too, and I still get flares of it, but
not like them.

Anyway, on Sundays there I was kneeling and having a fit, because
he was very handsome. I was very proud of him, indeed I was, there on

the floor looking at my father, and I guess it was kind of sad. Well, I did it for a couple of years.

He was wildly modest, and would really have been embarrassed if he ever thought that I had seen him. One thing I shall always wonder about: he had a tattoo on his right thigh. Had my father opened that door, I would have fallen right in.

He liked to drink and I never knew, in fact, until later in his life when he was so unhappy and so ill, that he had become a kind of drunk. I never knew why he was ill or why he died. He was young, though. My mother also died young.

When I'd gotten out of Princeton he astonished me by saying, "Well, you've made a mess of that and I'm not surprised, but we won't discuss it. Now we're going to try to see if you can do anything at all. And, naturally, what I think you should attempt to do is to inherit my business."

Pretty soon after that I went down to the Keyser Building in Baltimore, a very chic performance with a lot of very fashionable offices and quite a few handsome young men, especially in the real estate world, and I began to try to sell insurance. The idea, of course, I think, was that I would be dancing a lot with the ladies, and diamond necklaces would be hanging around their necks, which I should try to insure. Also, houses required fire insurance. My interest in houses was enormously keen, but I was in such a state of absolute boredom and unhappiness with the insurance business that I just knew I couldn't stay in it, and in fact, instead of going about trying to sell it to ladies or gentlemen in the social way, I found myself very comfortably curled up in a leather chair in the public reading room of the Emerson Hotel, spending the day reading the *New York Times*.

So, I told my mother, who realized I could not stand it, that I just absolutely could not sell insurance and that I would run away, and she said, "I don't think your father will be too unhappy to have you out of the office."

My great passion next to decoration and architecture was words. I loved them almost as much as I did chairs, so the next thought was a newspaper. My father had a great many friends on the Baltimore paper, which everyone called the Sun Paper, and he thought that I could perfectly well learn to become a brilliant reporter and hobnob with Henry Mencken, who was there at the time and at the height of his career. So at a little over the age of twenty-five, in preparation for this, I was sent to New York City where I was to learn about the insurance business and also get the experience of reporting in the world.

One of the insurance offices I was sent to was the Zurich Insurance Company, and I was taken from the office to the subway each day by one of the clerks to be sure that nothing happened to me. That whole business was a disaster, too.

When I was in New York City I stayed at the Wentworth Hotel on 46th Street, at that time a fascinating place because it was very fashionable for the snappiest actors and actresses of Europe to go there. Then I came back from New York and was on the newspaper for a brief time.

Now, I was just as unhappy there as I was in the insurance business. I was miserable. I did one or two reports of robberies, but I was bored stiff. I knew perfectly well that I simply had to be in the world of architecture or decoration. I didn't have a glimmer of hope in architecture because I never could get a degree at any university, because I considered myself then, and do now, superior and way above geometry and algebra and any mathematics. Even when I went to Princeton I felt highly above all that.

I said to my mother one day, "I can't bear this job."

She said, "I know. You look perfectly awful. What's the matter?"

I said, "I want to be a decorator and I want to work for Mr. Benson."

I can hear her words now as though they were being said today. My mother, in the nicest, sweetest, softest voice, with her great brown eyes brimming with tears, said to me, "This will kill your father, but you must do it."

In less than no time she'd seen Mr. Benson, who agreed to take me on in the most humble possible way. I was up in the room where the materials came in, measuring materials. I also was sent across the street where the workroom was. I saw chairs being covered and learned what was being done about furniture in the raw, and it was the greatest education I'd ever had.

In order to get from the main showroom of C. J. Benson & Company, which was the biggest and most spectacular in Baltimore, I had to cross the street to get to the workroom, which was in an alley. As you stepped out of Mr. Benson's establishment there was an inn called the Boxtree Inn where all the debutantes lunched every day, and where I walked back and forth in front of the girls, carrying huge bolts of material. Mr. Benson was terribly happy that I didn't seem ashamed to do this. I didn't feel ashamed because I felt simply thrilled. My career began there in the workroom on the seventh floor where the materials were.

There were three racks in the middle of the big room, and there was this very tragic young girl from Pittsburgh, whom I actually later made love to, who said to me, "You know, Mr. Benson likes to have different schemes of fabrics based upon the samples hung on the different racks. I want to put you in charge of that."

Well, it was an absolutely wonderful experience, of course, and the only thing I had to do was fold every single sample and put it back on its rack after the client had taken it out and straighten the room up every afternoon before I went home. However, one day Mr. Benson came up to me and said, "Billy, I want to know something about what's going on up here."

I was scared to death.

He said, "Who is responsible for the schemes that are being done on these racks?"

I said, "Well, Mr. Benson, Miss Hayworth has put me in charge of it."

He said, "I have to tell you, and I don't want to make you conceited, but I'm very impressed with what you're doing."

And I said, "Well, I'm so happy because it's the first thing I've ever done in my life that I've been paid for that I absolutely love."

He said, "You have it. There is something you have that nobody can learn and nobody can ever really teach you about. I'm very excited to have you here, and from now on I'm going to send for you occasionally when I have a client, because I think you can assist me."

I will say I didn't do too badly. I'll never forget the excitement when one of my friends, a charming girl, married and moved into a beautiful house done by John Russell Pope, the great architect, and they asked me to do the drawing room curtains. I got some material from Paris; the price was to be three thousand dollars a pair, and they were rosy pink taffeta embroidered in silver thread. It was a sensation that nobody in the shop ever got over. I wish I knew the date of those curtains, because three thousand dollars a pair would be thirty thousand dollars today.

I did a considerable amount of decorating in Baltimore, but when they really wanted to spend money, New York was where they went to have it done. I had a very boring time covering wing chairs, doing annual slipcovers, some paint jobs, but really very little of a whole house. They just didn't think I had the ability, and, as they really didn't care, they preferred to put themselves under the guidance even of Elsie de Wolfe, who did a few houses in the city and one or two in the country.

Baltimoreans are very dull usually, very conventional, but they live in a wildly comfortable manner: the women are always prettily dressed, the men wear extremely conservative clothes, and they all eat wonderful food and drink superb alcohol, but almost none of them care a fig for decoration.

My father was the kind of man that lots of women liked, but I can't say that I can really name an actually dangerous or foolish relationship that he ever had with another woman, and I don't think he ever did so. He was a very attractive man, and he worked very hard. He felt proud of his wife, and he liked the idea that people had, which by God they did have, that my mother and father were supposed to be an ideal couple. They had enough money, they both had looks, they both had charm, they had two children, and my mother's family had plenty of money.

I have to say about both of these people that they did have some fun together, and I know that in his strange strange way he was terribly proud of her, and I think he loved her in a way. The older I get, and I have to admit I don't like it, I can see his side more and more.

My mother and father had a funny life. He was so jealous that he made it impossible for her to have very much fun, so they didn't have a very active social life. He didn't want her to go out, and they entertained very little. They gave a couple of little dinners made up of maybe eight people during the season, or if there was a very big ball they would go to it, but they were very inactive, really.

Sometimes she had two or three dinners with twelve or more people during the winter, and nearly always there was the glorious terrapin, not everybody had it, I don't mean because of the price, but it was the trouble, getting the terrapin, getting them up from that bin, and getting the chauffeur to take them to the Maryland Club where they were cooked, and getting them back home was all very difficult.

Now at the time of the Baltimore Assembly, which was entirely run by various committees, there was one very important one called the Supper Committee. Each autumn, the ladies of the Supper Committee, which was composed of six women or maybe less, went around to three black caterers, sampling the terrapin, and chose one of them to cook the terrapin for the Assembly. They always had terrapin for supper in addition to the most beautiful champagne and every kind of food imaginable. I suppose that's one reason why I'm still interested in turtles today.

My parents' life was very quiet, but for many years they had three seats at the Lyric Theatre for the concerts that came to Baltimore, and were performed by the Philadelphia Orchestra and the Philharmonic. My mother and father and I, before my sister was old enough, went in to Baltimore from Roland Park six times a year.

Our seats were way down in front and on an aisle. If any one of the three of us could not go my family would leave a ticket at the box office, preferably for a student. Of course, we all knew each other very well and the man at the box office was an old friend. One winter night my father didn't feel up to going so my mother and I set forth in plenty of time and got there early. My mother went to the box office and said, "Here's a ticket which Mr. Baldwin's not going to use."

Down we went, down the long long aisle, and pretty soon I heard not a rumpus exactly but a little talk. The Cone sisters: Dr. Claribel, Miss Etta, and their brother Dr. Fred, who was as queer as he could be, were sitting across the aisle from us. They had occupied those seats for many many years. The slight confusion was about the fact that they had picked up that extra ticket for the friend who was with them, and as it was on the aisle no one had to change seats and a very tall man indeed who was wearing the most marvelous tweed suit which looked like orange marmalade sat down in it. His beard was also slightly the same color. I had a complete stroke and I whispered to my mother, "Matisse is sitting beside me." I was nearly crazy with excitement.

Well, the orchestra immediately began to play Richard Strauss's *Til Eulenspiegel*, which seemed so suitable with Matisse there, and finished it to great applause. Immediately after, Dr. Cone rose, which was quite an operation. She was an enormous woman, and always dressed in several shawls, marvelous paisley ones, and her hair was in huge loops around her ears with a large dagger knotted in the back. She was rising to introduce my mother and me to Mr. Matisse. It was a wonderful occasion. How I got through it, I don't know, but I did.

My father did like music, and my mother as I have mentioned played the piano very well. Aunt Lela would ask my mother to come to her house not because she wanted her, but because she played the piano, and she used to do it, sometimes until her hands were almost bleeding. My mother was a saint in a funny kind of way.

I do know that my mother and father both liked to dance, and they were both very good dancers. I'm sure of that. The whole family was. We were dancers. Jule was a marvelous dancer, she didn't really look so well when she danced, but she was a great dancer.

We had both been to Tuttle's Dancing Class, and it was really the most marvelous institution. It met every Friday in an ugly little dance hall in a tacky part of Baltimore. The boys and girls would go all dressed up, we in our little Buster Brown collars and dark suits, and we would carry bags in which we had our dancing pumps, which we put on when we got there. We had a great deal of fun and very often behaved very badly because we could not always keep our faces straight and look at Mrs. Tuttle at the same time. However, we got away with it and enjoyed ourselves enormously, and I wouldn't have missed it for anything.

It cannot be denied that the one thing in the world that I loved more than any other thing was dancing. I don't know if I danced in my cradle. I wish I had asked my mother, but I think I must have. I feel that as a child, an infant even, I was probably dancing in my cradle and waving around a yard of chintz, on the road to the decoration of houses.

It is too bad that I was a little short, but that didn't deter me for one minute. It seemed to me that there was something desperately appealing about large women because I always found myself dancing around tightly onto their waists. I distinctly remember in dancing class when Fulton Leser said to me, "Just stick your nose in their navel and pray."

My sister, fortunately for me, was a few inches shorter than I was, and I will certainly say she was a beautiful dancer. She was also the athlete of the family. It must be admitted that she had at the time of her debut several of the most attractive young men in the city of Baltimore as constant beaux. The outstanding ones were a group, all three at the same time, who had the latest motorcycles and the latest motorcycle clothes, including the noise, and my father was in a state of total desolation this whole time. My mother tried to tell him that this was all very normal, which it was, and that he should be happy that these young men were people who were sons of parents he knew. They were absolute knockouts and they apparently liked my sister because they were surrounding her. One of them was young Charlie Warfield, another was Horatio Whitridge, and the third was named Webb Cromwell. They later all married and had perfectly nice careers in Baltimore.

There came a summer when my mother sent me and my sister abroad. The whole point of this was to get my sister over a love affair. She wanted very much to marry and my mother knew it wasn't a good idea, and I was having a fit. I don't think my father even thought about it.

This young man was perfectly all right, but I just thought he was not awfully attractive, and Jule was mad about him. He was very sexy and sexy-looking. He hated me and I simply could not bear him. My mother said, "We'll fix it." So my poor sister was constantly being reminded by us that her young man wore such common shoes, or we said, "Isn't it too bad that he just doesn't have any manners," or "I know that boy will one day make good, but I can't imagine at what." Well, Jule couldn't take it. Nobody could, and finally Jule was in a state of nervous collapse.

My sister and I were not very congenial because we weren't interested in the same things, but my mother in her great wisdom said, "I think the only thing to do is to get her out of the country, and I'm going to send you both abroad." It was the year after Jule had come out and she had a lot of beautiful clothes, and off we went.

We went straight to Paris where we stayed and were chaperoned by a great friend of my family called Allice Archibald, who lived in a charming flat at No. 6 Avenue Matignon. Her father had been a senator in Washington, and Allice had gone to school in Baltimore where she had met my mother, and they became best friends. Allice never married, but she was a perfect knockout. She had a sort of job getting commissions on practically everything she touched for Americans. Elizabeth Arden was one, and Lucien Lelong, a great dressmaker at that time, was another.

In Paris I knew several boys who were going to Princeton that fall and we all really did go dancing all the time. In fact, Allice said, "I don't know where you're getting the money from, but after every night when you come in the next day, you've been to the most expensive restaurants and the most expensive dancing places in the city. How many times have you been to Les Ambassadeurs already, Billy?"

"Well," I said, "it is very expensive, but most of the time we've been invited." And I said, "The great thing about it is that I think that we look very attractive on the dance floor, and since we're young, the crowd loves us. Quite often they make us dance and make a circle around us and watch us. They call us the American dancers."

Les Ambassadeurs was where they had Florence Mills and her revue, and certainly it was one of the most exciting black performances in history. She was a beguiling, remarkable, extraordinary artiste. The whole performance was a delight, and watched over by an audience of the greatest style imaginable. Everybody who was chic from New York and London was in Paris at Les Ambassadeurs that summer.

At the time my parents were married and when I was growing up, most people were pretty nice to each other. There was no war, there was no income tax, there was no race problem. The relationship that we had with the blacks in Baltimore was one of the greatest harmony. There were dozens of blacks employed in the Brighton Hotel in Atlantic

City, all smiling and all perfectly pleasant. Don't forget that the blacks were the ones who cooked, and still do, a softshell crab like nobody else can, or ever will.

When my sister got married she got deep-freeze crazy and had some frozen crabs one time when I went down there, and I said, "What are these? I think they're terrible." She was furious with me. She once even presented me with some frozen terrapin. Well, it didn't taste like anything.

My mother planned our meals at home and we had Odie, our wonderful cook, and a series of very nice waitresses who were all youngish Irish women, and our food was wonderful.

I adored anything to do with crab, especially softshell and crab flakes, which were extremely difficult to get because they sent the best ones from Maryland to Philadelphia. I loved quail and some little tiny things called railbirds, which you even ate the heads of. They're tiny birds that hunters shoot at the same time they shoot quail. They're cooked in their entirety, and the heads become nothing but a little piece of something like fat, and the birds are eaten on toast. I adored hominy, which I think is called big hominy in the North. I loved all the things to do with cornmeal, like cornbread and corn pudding. I loved sausage, but what I really loved the best was Maryland fried chicken, not the terrible stuff that tastes like a wet blanket that you get all over the country including the South. Maryland fried chicken was a glorious thing to eat. Then, of course, the greatest delicacy supposedly in all of Maryland was the wild duck, which I didn't happen to like. I don't like game to that extent, and am not crazy about it. I think pheasant can be good, but I don't like wild duck and I used to have the most terrible time. My mother was ashamed of me and she said, "Now, don't let your father know or he'll die." Currant jelly was always served with it, and she would say, "Take a lot and smear it all over the rest of that bird and swallow it whole," which I used to do because the blood of the wild duck really made me sick. But canvasback duck was considered the greatest possible delicacy.

Now all of this really cost next to nothing. It may sound like wildly luxurious living, but it wasn't. My father had a very successful business, and I remember hearing that he made $25,000 a year. I suppose that was a lot of money then because that was about 1925. He had a dark navy blue Packard roadster, and my mother had a shiny dark dark blue Packard town car with a wicker back, which was driven by our chauffeur. They had a cook, two nurses, a waitress, a kitchen maid, and two chambermaids. They had eight servants, and that was on $25,000! Now, of course, my papa was helped out by my mother. She had her own dressing allowance from her father's estate, and dressed herself, and I know she helped out a great deal with the running of the house, but we were not considered rich people.

My father must have had a terrible time because I know that I was horrible to him, and I know that my sister was a devil to him. My mother was a saint, but almost too much so, and probably by his nature he felt left out.

After my father died, everything changed completely. My mother sold 204 Goodwood Gardens and we moved into a flat, my sister, my mother, and I, and that was when her beau began appearing, but her life didn't change, though. She wasn't any more social or any more anything, really. She remained the same all of her life.

*"Oh, you will have no fun in Switzerland:
all the women have goiters and carry little
baskets of sickle pears."*

The last two years of my education at Gilman finally brought
about my graduation and I was given a diploma, which my
father was very proud of. He went to the graduation, of course,
and so did my mother, and that fall in 1922 I was to go to Princeton at
the age of nineteen.

So that summer was the year that I was to go abroad with a man
called Boyd Morrow and his wife. Boyd Morrow was the senior master
of Gilman Upper School. He had a charming wife called Eleanor who
played a beautiful game of golf and was very good-looking. In a funny
way, I was devoted to Morrow, but I also was terrified of him because
he was my mathematics teacher for many years, and I absolutely intensely disliked mathematics. I thought it was considerably beneath me,
as I have said, and I paid very little attention to it, and not only that, I
just really couldn't get it through my head. But in order to graduate, I
had to pass geometry. Boyd Morrow was my geometry teacher, and he
had been given a handsome check to take me and four other boys to go
for the summer on a very nice extended, and very extensive, tour of
Europe.

Boyd gave me private tutoring and then presented me with an ex-
amination on plane geometry that I did just pass, so I was able to graduate. He could not possibly have taken me abroad, nor would I have

Billy, seated first on the right. Gilman, 1922.

been allowed by my father to go, if I had not passed, so I had my nice little diploma in my hand, and also we all had been given letters from our parents permitting us to drink wine and beer on the trip.

So off we went, the other boys and Jack Needles, my best friend of many years, a man with whom I had my first platonic love and friendship.

Jack was a boy from Roanoke, Virginia, whose mother had come from a very nice family in Baltimore. His father was the president of the Northern and Western Railroad, which meant a lot in those days, including a private railroad car. Jack's father was an enormous oaf of a man, but his extraordinary son was slender to a degree, had incredible honest blue eyes, marvelous charm, was a rabid cheerleader, a very good tennis player, an awfully good dancer, and all the girls loved him. During the last year at Gilman I sat myself beside him at lunch and dinner at the head table in the big dining room.

Next, there was an attractive boy, quite a little bit younger, called Lawrence, who had a remarkable career because his father and mother had been divorced. His father came back to the Gilman School in an attempt to kidnap his son from his mother. It was a failure, although they were paid kidnappers who had had the boy by the neck and rushed him from the classroom into a car.

Number three was a boy called Jack Bergland, who was awfully conceited, very unpleasant looking, and we didn't like him at all, really, but he had a nice mother and father and he was going to pay the bill, so he went.

Sad to say, the fourth boy was not really a friend of ours at all probably because he was younger than we.

We had the most glorious time because we went up to Montreal in Jack's private car by way of the St. Lawrence River to sail for Europe on the Canadian Pacific liner the S.S. *Montcalm* and stayed at the Ritz, which was a marvelously glamorous and wonderful hotel, for two nights and a day before embarking on our trip.

As we were ready to tear out of the St. Lawrence River into the ocean, there was this frightful sound and then all of the engines stopped. We were forced by an engine breakdown to stay there for four days.

The ship had a perfectly extraordinarily attractive crew of men and women, the nurses were perfectly beautiful, and the two doctors were the two best-looking men I have ever seen. So when the night of the masquerade ball came, they said, "There is a shortage of girls on the boat so two of you boys have got to dress as girls tonight." Well, I didn't say a word, but I was chosen as one, and I could wear Mrs. Morrow's sport clothes. So I got all dressed up for the ball, and one of the ship's doctors thought I was splendid except that he got very drunk and took me into one of the lifeboats and totally forgot himself.

We finally arrived in London where we had a perfectly marvelous time. It was late June and, of course, everything was going on. From London we went to Paris where my "courtesy aunt" lived. She just took us over, me and the boys. She put the headmaster and his wife up at her club so they were taken care of, and we went out on the town every single night. Often we went to a little nightclub called Les Acacias, where Elsa Maxwell sang risqué songs by Cole Porter and accompanied herself on the piano.

When I was a kid, I used to go with my father every year to Europe to see the insurance companies he represented, but now I was nineteen and the year was 1922. It was during this trip that I consider I first really went abroad, because I had plenty of freedom and fun.

We went to the races, the best restaurants, and saw lots of attractive people, but the most exciting thing was the Bois de Boulougne which was lined with restaurants, one of which was the Château de Madrid where they had thés dansants and the tango. In those restaurants in the Bois there were women with hats bigger than the rooms almost, so they had a hard time dancing. The men were the most beautiful things and the great ones were the Argentines with waxed hair like black glass, who were the best dancers to that wonderful music of the tango. It was the whole thing of the twenties excitement.

As a young boy I had been taken by my mother to the Louvre, and I loved pictures. I didn't entirely not go to the Louvre, but we had great freedom because of this aunt, and we could do anything we wanted by simply saying to Mr. and Mrs. Morrow, "Aunt Allice has arranged something for us." She was very cute because she was so nice to them, and we left Paris with all kinds of promises to meet again.

So off we went to see more of Europe and we went directly to Switzerland. The reason for going to Switzerland was to get a rest because we were having a very hectic summer and were to see seven countries in seven weeks. So we were to go to a quiet quiet place there called Vitznau, where there was one of those remarkable hotels called the Park something, I have forgotten its name. We were to do nothing but play tennis, swim, and go to bed early. There were no museums and nothing to do except climb a mountain called Mount Rigi. Our hotel was at its foot, and after we had gotten a certain amount of rest we were to climb the mountain and spend the night, then come down on the funicular the next day.

Well, the hotel turned out to be so comfortable. It was attractive and had wonderful food and the bar was divine. We were able to sneak away quite a lot of things besides just wine and beer, and the headmaster shut his eyes.

The bar was of dark oak with lots of stained glass and was very Swiss and Tyrolean. The people staying at the hotel were very rich, and very Swiss; there were practically no Americans, and I don't know how we ever got there.

It also had the great advantage of pouring with rain for two or three days, and so we spent the whole time in the bar where we never had more fun. When it finally stopped, it was announced that there was to be a special treat that night on the lake after dinner. It was to be a yodeling contest. Well, that first note convinced me that it was the ugliest sound I'd ever heard in my life. The yodeling was followed by what was popular at that time: ukuleles and Hawaiian music. I think that's a pretty hard combination to beat.

But anyway we had a small lovely dinner and I think we drank something very foamy called Pink Ladies, which were made with gin and grenadine, then we went out onto the terrace of this glamorous place. Now, it was glamorous in a funny way because the people really were not. They were highly respectable, mostly Swiss, and I know my mother told me before we left: "Oh, you will have no fun in Switzerland: all the women have goiters and carry little baskets of sickle pears." And, by golly, she was right.

So we sat around on the terrace in the dark, and great beautiful canoes filled with yodelers came across the lake. Well, they yodeled and yodeled, and everybody was fascinated and they had champagne for us in the hotel. Suddenly I noticed something walking slowly up and down in the darkness, and I thought: This is not the first time I've seen this apparition.

Well, what it was was a woman swathed in sort of gunmetal gray veils. You really couldn't see her body at all. It was wrapped in a series of these veils like Salome. Even part of her face from about her nose down was covered, so there were just these brilliant staring eyes peering at us in the night, and this apparition going back and forth, back and forth. And it was very funny, too, so we sat, because Mr. Morrow said, "Now, boys, look out! There's something dangerous on this lawn after one of us," and he laughed. Pretty soon Mr. and Mrs. Morrow went up to bed. They were very fond of each other and that was another reason why they were so divine because they were constantly disappearing. So in a sense we really didn't have any chaperones at all.

Well, Jack and I decided we would not sleep and so we sat up and had a wonderful time talking, as we always did. And I said, "Jack, I don't know what's going on, but I think that whatever that is — is after one of us."

Jack said, "Maybe. Maybe she's after both of us." And he said, "Are you sure it's a woman? It could be anything, because the disguise is complete as far as the sex is concerned."

I said, "I think it's a woman. There's no doubt about that."

"Oh, gee," he said, "this might be a wonderful place to lose your cherry."

"Well," I said, "yes, it certainly might be." We were both virgins. I was nineteen and I know Jack was a little older because he was a very dumb student. I think he had tried more than twice to get a diploma.

Not only did she keep walking back and forth, but she kept getting closer. She wasn't very far away and she was slowing it up, and I said, "Listen, Jack. Do you think you could?"

He said, "Oh, gee. I really don't know. I think I'm scared to death with the idea."

I said, "I think it would be such a wonderful way. I don't think you have to worry about the venereal point of view, because I'm sure she's okay, and I don't think you'll have to pay her. I just think that maybe she would like to get a nice young American boy and you might have a wonderful chance to get yourself robbed of your virginity, and in a very attractive way, 'cause I think she's staying in this hotel. And we're going to find that out."

So we found that out instantly by asking a perfectly charming young waiter about this lady who seemed to want to go to bed. He said, "Monsieur Baldwin, you're quite right; she wants to go to bed. She wants to go to bed with one of you two gentlemen. And that's why she's walking up and down."

I said, "That's lovely, but how can that be done?"

The waiter said, "Oh, she lives here. She has a beautiful room and a beautiful drawing room. If either of you wish to spend the night with her, you just stand up and walk over and say, 'Good evening, madam,' and that's all you have to do."

I said, "Thank you." Jack was getting scared to death and I knew I couldn't possibly do it. So I said, "Now listen, Jack baby, go ahead. It is true what this boy says. It's ideal. There can be no complication. I'm sure she's just a perfectly nice sexy woman with enough money to stay here. Maybe she's even kept by somebody and you would be extracurriculum; I think it's silly for you not to." So Jack left me.

When we had arrived at Vitznau, they had allotted rooms to us. Mr. and Mrs. Morrow had an attractive suite and each of the other boys except Jack and me had nice single rooms and baths overlooking the incredible Swiss Alps. Mountains always depress me. I really don't like them. I don't feel at all romantic.

Also we were forced to swim in the lake that was just at the foot of the lawn and fed by an ice cold mountain stream. We had to wear rented bathing suits of red and white striped cotton, which were buttoned from the neck to the crotch, and had little short sleeves and short legs. They had no jock, nothing. Those suits were the most immoral, indecent things I've ever seen.

The Morrows had decided that Jack and I should have a room together. We were the real, the best of friends. There was a tower and that was where we stayed. It had a room with four sides surrounded by balconies looking out into the world of mountains, with a perfectly wonderful view from sort of a mezzanine. The room had a bath, and we had breakfast on the terrace every morning, where I experienced for the first time incredible Swiss preserves. There were two feather beds and they had those wonderful, great, soft, mile-deep comforters. One bed was on one side of the room and the other on the other side. And that was where Jack and I shared our Swiss visit.

On returning to our room, I had to get off the elevator and walk up another flight, because it didn't go as high as our floor. That's how high up we were. It was a perfectly lovely night and I went out on the veranda to look at the view, and wondered what my friend was doing. Well, he didn't come, he didn't come, and I thought, This is wonderful because Jack must have had success, but I went to sleep finally.

I was awakened by a very soft sound of someone coming in, closing a door, and walking toward the other bed, and as I was awake, I said, "Jack?"

Speaking in a very quiet voice, he said, "Yes, Bill."

"Well," I said, "do you want to tell me anything?"

He said, "I think I do." So, not instantly but in a few moments after he had undressed and was in his pajamas and had turned out his light, he crossed the room to my bed, and collapsed on the floor on his hands and knees and put his head on the bed and burst into floods and floods and floods of tears.

I said, "What's the matter? Was it a disaster?"

"Oh, my God, no," he said. "I did it. I've lost my virginity."

I can say, I could understand perfectly his grief, but I feel that mine was probably even more so. It was the greatest ironic shock that I've ever had in my life. I loved Jack, and knew that he was not a homosexual, but we had had childish schoolboy sex during our Gilman School days and I also knew just as well that there was no possibility of his really caring about me that way, that it was just one of the things that happen at a certain age in most men's and boys' lives. And there he was, without even knowing it, making a denial of everything that had ever happened between us.

My mother adored Jack, and as a matter of fact, Jack really lived with us after his mother and father had both died and he was in Baltimore. He had his own apartment but he used to spend most of the time with us. There was a moment in my mother's life, poor darling, when she was sure he was going to ask my sister to marry him. He did the naughty thing of behaving as though he were in love with Jule. Well, somebody said to Jack, "You'd better cut out this thing about your friendship with Billy Baldwin because it's gotten so involved that you can't continue without taking on his sister."

Jack was anything but subtle, and he told me what had been said to him. "I have to do something," he said, "and I don't know how to explain it, but I won't be able to come and see you anymore." He never came again. He couldn't do anything halfway, so he just cut it out.

I was an usher at his wedding and a great friend of his wife. In fact, I introduced them and they got married and had three daughters. Jack died of cancer in New York Hospital, and his wife was wonderful and very noble. I asked her if I couldn't sit with Jack in the hospital some of the time to relieve her and I did sit with him twice, but I don't know whether he ever thought of that night in Switzerland over forty years earlier. Perhaps he had totally forgotten it.

After Switzerland we went to Italy and stopped in Genoa, which is something I don't think many people do. There we saw that extraordinary cemetery where all the death scenes are in sculpture. Of course we went to Rome and Venice, and stopped off in Monte Carlo and Cannes before returning to Paris.

We came back on a ship called *La Touraine,* which was the oldest ship afloat. It was owned by the French Line and one of the passengers was a young man called Alan Jackson whose father was one of its owners.

Alan said, "This is my boat and we can do anything we want to because it's the last time it's ever going to sail. It's going to be junked the moment we dock."

Harry Parish was on board with his sister. He was an absolutely weak charming knockout and his sister was very attractive and very, very bad. She fell for a marvelous-looking boy called Hawkins, and he thought she was going to marry him, but the minute she got off the gangplank she flung herself into the arms of her fiancé.

We spent twelve days on that boat and the dinners at night were absolutely wonderful. I never had such a good time. All of the deck chairs had been painted a lacquer red, and one terribly rough, really scary night, Alan Jackson said, "Let's have some fun. All of these chairs belong to me and let's throw them overboard." I shall never forget the excitement on that great ship of throwing a great number of those brilliant bright-red deck chairs over the rail and into those huge waves.

. . . in less than two minutes she made me promise that I would become her dancing partner . . .

In the spring of 1925 rehearsals were going on for the annual Junior League Cabaret in Baltimore. That year they were featuring dances of various nations, which meant Argentina and the tango. This was at a time when the tango was extremely popular, so it was not that foreign to everybody. Among the debutantes of the year was Mary Lawrason Riggs. Her father, Dudley, who had died, had been one of four or five brothers all of whom had married attractive women; the entire bunch were very much a part of the life in Baltimore. Dudley Riggs married a charming lady named Laura from out of town, who made herself very popular in Baltimore and who had by far the best taste of any of the Riggses. The result of their marriage was three children: Dudley Riggs, who grew to be nearly six feet six inches tall, his sister Betty, and the youngest, Mary Lawrason, who was a little shorter than I was. She was extremely pretty, had great charm, and dressed beautifully.

These qualities resulted in the fact that she was pursued in her debutante year by three musketeers, and that is what they were known as. These three young men were intimate friends: one of them was Jack Needles, the other Harry Parr, and the third, myself. It meant that practically every Sunday we lunched at her mother's apartment and then played bridge all afternoon.

Mary had been asked if she would do the tango in the South American feature of the Junior League Show, and she said she would if I would be her partner. I was the one who danced better than the other two, and so we started to rehearse. We had a lovely time; everything went beautifully, the moment of the performance came, and we had a great success with our tango. She was really so pretty that she couldn't help but be a success and we managed to pull it off very well because we were both small.

I had a beautiful costume of black leather with skintight bell bottom pants, a black bolero, and a very smart little black Spanish hat. All of this was relieved by a lovely embroidered ruffly white shirt. Mary wore a marvelous very pale pink embroidered flowered shawl. As soon as the dance was over and we went to the table where we had been seated, and as I was sitting down a friend came to me and said, "Billy, you are wanted at once at the table of Mrs. Garrett."

I said, "What's the matter?"

He said, "There's nothing the matter. She's madly in love with you."

So I went to the table and there was Alice Garrett with her husband, John, who had retired. His fortune was the Baltimore and Ohio Railroad. He had had a great many diplomatic posts, but at the moment was not involved. They had inherited an enormous house just outside of Baltimore which was called Evergreen and the address was 4545 Charles Street Avenue because it was an extension of Charles Street.

They had a wonderful life there together, as they were the most devoted couple that I've probably ever known in my life; he absolutely adored her. It is a shame that Alfred Lunt and Lynn Fontanne never portrayed them on the stage. They were that kind of ideal couple. Alice was extremely intellectual, extremely intelligent, and very rich through her mother, Mrs. Warder, and her father had been a senator from Massachusetts in Washington, where she was really brought up although she had been born in Springfield, Massachusetts.

Alice had not married until quite late because I don't think she was interested enough in most of the boys who asked her or maybe she just didn't fall in love until she met John. She was taller than most, and like a wonderful young racehorse in the fact that she was absolutely fit. She didn't know what being fat meant. She was firm as a young man, really; she had no hips at all, very broad shoulders, and was quite dark skinned. Her amazing black flashing eyes were always made up as though for the stage; she possessed a European style, and her mouth was very red and very big. When she smiled, it turned into a rectangle, absolutely square.

Alice Warder Garrett. (Evergreen House Foundation)

That showed in all her portraits and all the artists loved it. She had an extremely attractive, very deep voice, and she spoke all languages beautifully. She had been somewhat in the official world as the daughter of a senator, and had a perfectly good interest and knowledge of politics, but her passion was the arts; painting, particularly, and music. It cannot be said that she painted well, because she didn't. Nor can it be said that she really was talented musically. She did sincerely love English literature, but she never knew as much about it as she pretended.

Anyway, this meeting occurred and in less than two minutes she made me promise that I would become her dancing partner, which meant that we would give dancing performances in her theatre. All of this was very strange to me because the Garretts had no children. I had seen them but never met them, and had never been to their house because she never had anybody there under college age. She liked to have parties with beautiful debutantes and good-looking young men, but that was about it. So I was thrilled when she said, "Will you please come out and I will show you what I mean. I'll send for you." The time came and she sent a large, very old-fashioned-looking car with a very old-fashioned-looking chauffeur, and off I went to Evergreen.

Evergreen was surrounded by a twenty-six-acre park, and the lovely old house, which is pale yellow with white columns, was built in the Greek Revival style in the 1850s.

When I arrived I was taken immediately into the drawing room. I cannot say that it was a fascinating room. But there were those pictures! On the walls were hung a collection of Alice Garrett's pictures. This meant: a Bonnard, a Picasso, a Modigliani, Utrillo, Segonzac, Derain, and Forain. There was a portrait of Mrs. Garrett by Zuloaga, who was the leading painter of Spain at this time, and also a life-sized portrait of Mrs. Garrett by her friend Léon Bakst.

I never will forget my excitement that first time I entered Evergreen and walked up about five marble steps to be faced by an incredibly big red damask curtain that was hung on rings and that had to be pushed aside to enter the drawing room. It was to keep out drafts. The hall we passed through to get there had been covered with the same red damask.

So that you would not have a moment's chance to recover from anything, Alice had hung the walls of this hall with a great many contemporary paintings. Some of the artists represented were George Grosz, Diego Rivera, Henry Varnum Poor, Alfred Dufresne, Augustus John, and also a portrait of Alice's mother painted by Gari Melchers. I thought those paintings were marvelous because so many women of that time with taste and money, like Alice, turned their noses up at contemporary painters. It had to be French Impressionism for them or nothing at all.

The Garretts had lived all over the world because John had had diplomatic posts in The Hague, Venezuela, Argentina, Paris, Berlin, Luxembourg, Rome, and Washington, D.C. He was a brilliant man and quite fascinating really. He had been born a cripple, which was perhaps the reason he had never married before. I don't think Alice hesitated a minute when John asked her, because she was in love with him.

Well, there I was at Evergreen and Alice Garrett was so attractive and kind. Our conversation was conducted with John Garrett at the tea table with us. He seemed perfectly delighted with the idea that she would have a partner for the little exhibitions that she gave of her dancing and singing. This meant that I would dance in at least two of the four or five numbers in our programs. Alice took dancing seriously. She had Ned Wayburn, a famous dancing teacher, give us Black Bottom lessons, and we roared through the Charleston. At Evergreen I saw the rumba done

Mrs. Garrett performing one of her Spanish dances. (Evergreen House Foundation)

for the first time — by H. L. Mencken and Joseph Hergesheimer. We did any new dance that came along, and if anyone was staying at Evergreen as a guest, they were included.

There was a very nice woman called Carol Lynn who gave fancy dancing lessons in Baltimore; she came to Alice at least once a week to give her the choreography for the Spanish numbers, which was what Alice was wild about at the moment. So there I was, an answer to a prayer, really. I was thrilled and she was delighted. She said, "As far as I can see, the only thing you will have to do is to come out here in the late afternoon, several afternoons a week. We will have our rehearsals and learn the steps that Carol teaches us to do, and also I will get some pretty costumes for you."

That began our wonderful friendship, and also what it did for me was to open a door to many of the great people of the world, in the real sense of the word, because Alice had gathered every attractive person she had met from John's diplomatic posts, and when they were living at Evergreen all of these people came to see them.

Alice was one of the three women in my life who have meant more to me than I can ever say. She exposed me to the top men and women of their fields. Everyone who was anyone came out from Baltimore. From New York I met Mrs. Cole Porter, Mr. and Mrs. David K. E. Bruce, and Millicent Rogers with her husband, Arturo Ramos. From Washington I met Nicholas Longworth and his wife, Alice. I met Anthony Eden, Arthur James Balfour, and Dino Grandi, who were John's fellow diplomats, and I met Leopold Stokowski, Alma Gluck, Frank Lloyd Wright, Efrem Zimbalist, Marc Connelly, Walter Lippmann, Frank Crowninshield, Dorothy Draper, Lucrezia Bori, and countless others.

Every person who could possibly do it had either a meal, or a night, or a weekend at Evergreen. It was so much fun. People laughed all the time. There was always music and there were a lot of Baltimoreans at their house parties. A lot of them were hunting people. Alice did not hunt and she did not ride. I don't think she even knew what a horse looked like. She did play golf, supposedly for her health, and she picked Harry Parr as her golf instructor. Harry was a man of almost too much good looks and Alice was mad for him, but there was never any involvement with any other man but John in her life.

Alice made me realize that there's no reason in the world why you couldn't have a good time if you had a minimum of intelligence, a desire, and you applied yourself to it. I knew very early in my life that I wanted to be a decorator, and Alice made me know that Baltimore was not the place for me to do it. The Baltimoreans honestly didn't care about decoration, so the career of a decorator there was extremely limited.

After dinner John would go to bed because he was older and tired, and the rest of us would stay up. Most of the time the food was quite inedible. Alice didn't care one thing about food and saw no reason why anyone else should. Also she didn't have time, and she was terrified of getting fat, so you used to have this beautiful gold service which had been used at the embassy, and terribly bad food. She made me learn, among other things, how much more I valued a delicious piece of meat on a bad plate than a lousily cooked chop on a beautiful Sèvres one.

Alice was exceedingly kind, but not generous because she was stingy. I think she was stingy about everything including herself. However, her generosity was not even considered when it came to the Musical Art Quartet, which was at the time one of the great quartets in this country.

The Musical Art Quartet is now disbanded but then they came to Evergreen twice a year, each time for six weeks, in the autumn and in the spring. There were a number of very nice small cottages on the property, and she gave the quartet one of them where they lived absolutely free and they rehearsed privately. During their stay the Quartet performed alternating afternoons and evenings in the ravishing theatre, which had been personally stenciled by her great friend, Léon Bakst. Even though she had no limits to her generosity when it came to the quartet, I also know that she got quite a lot of pleasure from it as well. She never gave many presents, but she did give these wonderful concerts, and she did give these divine parties with bad food.

I used to go out after work and sit in that wonderful theatre with comfortable wicker chairs, a breeze coming in through the windows, and hear this divine music. It was the most luxurious thing I've ever experienced and quite remarkable. Alice, however, did the introducing and gave a little description of the quartets that were going to be played, and she invariably did it wrong. She would say, "We will now hear a charming piece done in the late years of Beethoven."

And the violinist would say, "Brahms! Mrs. Garrett, Brahms!"

The most unusual and unexpected quality about Alice was that she had a great sense of humor, including one about herself. In a previous book, I described an incident that concerned her and Proust, and it exemplifies her ability to laugh at herself. The story is nice because she told it to me one day in a rather offhand way. She said, "Of course, you know I am written about in Proust."

"Oh," I said, "I didn't know."

"Oh, yes," she said, "I'm the one in the pink ball dress in the ball scene."

"Oh," I said, "you knew him."

"Not exactly," she said. "What I did was to pursue him until finally I couldn't stand it any longer and I sent him an invitation to dine with me at the Ritz on the first Sunday in September. I sent him that note in June, and I received his response at once. He thanked me, and said that unfortunately he was unable to accept my invitation because that was the night he would be dining at the Ritz alone." Alice roared with laughter.

Well, she was very funny, and not at all domestic, and gave all these parties because of her enjoyment of the people who came to them. She cared not one thing for what people called society, and was totally bohemian. She was only interested in people who had done something or who had given the world something from their work. She certainly was what we would call big time. There was nothing puny about Alice in any possible way.

The only trouble about her was that she did something that many rich people are guilty of. There was absolutely no reason why she should perform herself. She should have left that to the artists, but not at all. She got to be a violent painter, which she did better than anything else because she imitated great paintings, some of which she owned herself. She got the paint on the canvas pretty darn well, and did get away with a show in New York.

Lucrezia Bori was at the Garretts' constantly because they had befriended her. At the height of her career, Bori's voice stopped like a clock because she had a frightful throat infection and the Garretts paid for getting her well and back to the Metropolitan Opera. Alice was almost wild, because she adored Lucrezia. Anyway, I guess the first weekend after Bori returned to the Metropolitan, she came down to Evergreen. She was there all of the time anyway, flying around wearing plenty of beautiful sables, and she said to me, "Billy, we have to do something about our little Alice."

I said, "What do you mean?"

Bori said, "Billy, we have got to make a bargain, you and me. If you promise that you won't dance with her, I promise that I won't let her sing."

Alice was totally unselfconscious. She had this raft of John's nieces and nephews who lived across the street, and the kids thought their Aunt Alice was crazy, and I have to say that she was kind of mad, every now and then. She always gave a birthday party for each of her nieces and nephews. To their perfect horror they had to go to these parties that she had for them, and they hated it.

One year for one of these birthday parties she decided to give a performance in her theatre based upon a beautiful picture painted by Fragonard called *The Lady in the Swing,* which is in the Frick Museum. So she had a painter do a nice stage set based on the Fragonard painting and she loved it. The stage settings by Miguel Covarrubias and Léon Bakst might just as well not have existed. The setting was completed and the swing copied. I was employed behind the scenery to pull the swing, which swung her out over the heads of the audience as she sang, every note off key. She was in full costume and had on a perfectly enormous Louis Quinze wig. Her nieces and nephews were in the audience watching this, roaring with hysterics of laughter, as were all their friends and all the mothers of the children. They didn't even know her because she didn't have any time for those nice mothers. It was terribly embarrassing, but she did it.

At one point Alice got very interested in Portuguese folk songs. Among her greatest pets was Marc Connelly, whom she adored, and he came for the weekend. She always had somebody who announced the program for her performances; they just picked up the program and introduced her when the time came. This time it was Marc who introduced her and he read, "Now we will find Alice Garrett of the richer classa singing for the poorer classa."

I cannot stress too much the fact that Alice was totally unselfconscious about her own abilities. Lucrezia Bori's voice lessons only resulted in sounds coming from her throat that could only be described as froglike. Alice couldn't even hear.

Harry Parr usually nearly died when he had to play golf with her. She played so badly and she cheated. She'd pick that ball up if she didn't like where it was, and she'd put it someplace else.

Alice was the worst dancer that I ever danced with. She was a big woman, not fat at all, lean as a horse really, but she had her own idea of dancing and you were wrong. She led you! So very often when I was doing these dances with her I had quite a hard time.

One day she said to me, "You've got to treat me differently. When you're dancing with me, I want you to treat me as though I was just some little Spanish girl you picked up."

So then I began to yank her around, but the only trouble about the yanking around was that at that time we were rehearsing a very theatrical variation of the tango. We used to have rehearsals and nearly always before the night of a performance, John would come over to the theatre after dinner and watch the rehearsals, and I do mean watch! Alice had one toreador number where she fell to the floor as if dead. John rushed up to the footlights and said, "You're really not dead, darling, are you?" He idolized her.

Alice gave a dinner for Ellen Wilson and Jack Needles one week before their wedding party, which was to be one of the great weddings of Baltimore and in which I was to be an usher. Alice had become a great friend of the entire wedding party despite the fact she was years older. Anyway, we were practicing dancing, Alice and I, and I said, "Now you've got to be my little Spanish girl," and I gave her a jerk and she landed on my knee, which bent the wrong way. Well, I couldn't get the knee back, so we decided — now imagine how pleasure-bent we were — to wait until the day after the wedding, a week later, to have it operated on. So I went through one week of boiling hot weather with a cane and crutches, and went up the aisle on crutches with a big white bow. The next day I was operated on, and a semilunar cartilage was removed from my knee, and that is why I have a beautiful scar on my knee.

Alice didn't really care about my operation, and she was a little bit mad because I couldn't dance with her at the wedding reception.

A great quality Alice possessed was that she never gossiped. She wasn't interested in gossip. She was interested in achievement. She was interested in people being happy, but scandal never entered her mind. In that way she was almost childlike. And she gave everybody kind of a wonderful break, always. I've seen Alice's face fall like a thud to the ground when somebody let her down intellectually or artistically. That upset her, but she didn't discuss it and she didn't criticize. I think she was, first of all, interested in herself, truthfully.

At one time she decided to take Evergreen in hand and rearrange it. One thing she wanted to do was have a new library. It had been pointed out to me that Evergreen held over thirty-six thousand books. So in 1928, Alice and John decided to have a brilliant Baltimore architect called Laurence Hall Fowler design a great huge square library, which could become a room where you could be happy with two people or twenty. So it was commissioned, built, and turned out to be perfectly beautiful. In it was a portrait of John Garrett painted by Zuloaga. Oddly enough John had been painted wearing a blue smock and this was not popular at all in Baltimore because the Baltimoreans did not think an ambassador should be painted in a smock. They really wanted him to be painted in full dress and medals.

I saw Alice arrange the furniture in the manner of an Italian palazzo. It was done with no regard to walls, which was the whole point. There were fascinating small groups of furniture — I don't think anybody ever had to get up and move a chair — and four big comfortable sofas grouped around like beds in a garden, also a lot of big ugly upholstered furniture because of Alice's stinginess, as there was so much furniture in the house already from her husband's family that they didn't have to buy anything. On the big table in the middle of the library there was the most beautiful Tang horse that I've ever seen, which had come with the house.

Well, about this furniture. One day she said, "I want you to see what I have done." She had placed the most beautiful pieces of silk, mostly in shades of brown, on all the chairs. The curtains in the room were made of brown velveteen and did not interrupt the walls when drawn because there were four windows in two of the walls. She had simply taken these lengths of material she had purchased in Italy where she bought six yards in one place, and six or seven yards in another, and laid them on the tops of the chairs, and tucked them in under the cushions, and as far as Alice was concerned, they were done. She said, "Now, Billy, don't think this is odd because this is done in Italy, and this is the way it is going to stay." And it looked perfectly fine: soft, not tight anywhere, everything had these instant slipcovers on and it looked wonderful! She absolutely taught me about slipcovers!

The big drawing room was an extraordinary room done in the 1890s. It had a very elaborate off-white plaster work, and was filled with a lot of small-scale drawing room furniture, a huge collection of blue and white porcelain, and those wonderful pictures! Of course, she had a garden and also greenhouses, so that all of the rooms were filled with flowers.

The dining room was smaller; she could seat twenty people there at the most, but when she had a big dinner party she had little tables all over the house and they were everywhere — in the drawing rooms, in the library, any place that was comfortable — and the meals were served on beautiful plates and looked perfectly wonderful, but as I have said, if you were hungry, the food was inedible.

Suddenly we were all electrified by the news that John Garrett was going to be sent as our ambassador to Rome under Hoover. Of course, we who knew them thought it was the most wonderful choice. Alice was thrilled, but upon arrival in Rome she immediately began doing little things that were not the most tactful, just as she had done in Baltimore, and one of them was that within the first week after she got there she had the Musical Arts Quartet come to Rome and play, which was a great mistake because the Italians were not too pleased.

But the next thing she did was not a mistake. She arranged for a small symphony orchestra, gathered together by the leading composers of Rome, to play in the embassy every other Monday night.

The Garretts took part of a baroque palace as their embassy, and the first thing she did was to cover all the walls with folds of gray monk's cloth, which hung on rods, and upon the gray monk's cloth she hung contemporary American and French paintings. Well, there she was, having these symphony concerts every other Monday in her palace, which were wonderful and pleasing the Italians because she was patronizing them.

Alice could not be universally popular because she wasn't a get-together girl, but I have heard people say, grown men really, that they were so thrilled to meet her that they would die when she came into a room.

One of the first things that happened to her when she got to Italy — she told me this when she came back — was that on the second or third day, without any warning, she heard the roar of motorcycles outside the embassy. The butler came in and said to her that Mussolini had come to see her. He came barging right in with his boots on and everything else, and sat down. He said, "Signora, I've come to ask you why you and Signor Garrett don't have any children." That is what Mussolini said to her! Alice said to me, "What could I say? But I said something like, 'We regret that, but we don't seem to be able to.' " Mussolini left at that, almost immediately, she said.

The next thing was that she got to be a great friend of Umberto, Prince of Piedmonte, heir to the throne of Italy. His father was still on the throne, and it was about the time when he, Umberto, was going to be married to Princess Marie-José of Belgium. Alice and Umberto got to be very friendly indeed. She told me that he was one of the most beautiful men she'd ever seen in her life.

Alice went to two of the leading dressmakers in Paris. One was called Augustabernard, and the other, Louiseboulanger, and they were both sensational; I saw the clothes when she came back to New York. She was delighted with them, and wore a different dress every night when she went to the evening concerts. She used to be dressed to the teeth in these divine beautiful clothes. She knew I loved them, of course, and that all the women were dying with envy. She looked wonderful.

What she found out after Umberto began calling on her frequently — by this time he was calling her Alice — was this. He said to her, "I don't know whether or not you have noticed it, but you and I are the same size and have exactly the same build. I think, too, that there isn't any reason why I couldn't wear your clothes. May I try some of your dresses on?" He said this to her in Alice's bedroom at the embassy in Rome.

Alice told me that she replied, "Of course you may." So Alice and the future king of Italy had a fashion show, parading around in clothes designed by Augustabernard and Louiseboulanger.

Alice had lunch with me a couple of times in New York the year before she died. She was adorable about me, but she also had a terrible failing which I am beginning to understand more and more. She could never get anybody's name correctly.

Alice Garrett, as she was dressed for the marriage of Crown Prince Umberto of Savoy and Princess Marie-José, only daughter of the King of the Belgians. (Evergreen House Foundation)

One day I said to Ruby Wood, "Mrs. Wood, will you come and have a drink with me in my new apartment?" I knew Ruby was dying to see it. I said, "I will probably have only one other woman."

"Who?" said Ruby.

"Alice Garrett," I said.

"That fool!" said Ruby, jealous to such a point!

So they both came and what do you think Alice did? She had no idea who Mrs. Wood was, not the remotest, she had never had a decorator, and she and Ruby did not have many mutual friends, she also had a thing that a lot of rich people have, terrible catarrh. She did it all the time, till she would look like a frog that was strangling. So that began and then Alice did it. Without even turning around, she said to Mrs. Wood, "Well, you know, Mrs. Ross, I am very happy indeed to have

Billy here with me." She had called Ruby Mrs. Ross, and that did it! Ruby never mentioned her name again.

After John died, Alice did not entertain as much. She had a very handsome apartment in the Sherry Netherland in New York, and the last time I saw her was for lunch one day at my apartment. I had also invited Jean Desses, a famous dressmaker at that time who was a very charming Greek. He and Alice had the time of their lives discussing clothes, because she knew all about the best dressmakers. She probably knew more about French dressmakers than anybody because she bought from them all the time. So for all those years, from the night of the Junior League Ball in Baltimore until my luncheon for her on that day, we were intimate friends and she died a perfectly normal death of old age at Evergreen.

". . . I have very little to say, except that I am staying in the most extraordinary house, one of the most attractive houses I have seen in years. If we ever recover from this goddamned Depression, I really think I would like to have you work for me."

Very soon after I took my job with Mr. Benson a most remarkable event occurred, which changed my whole career as a decorator. To my great surprise a most enchanting woman, Mrs. Thomas Symington, who was born Edith Reilly from Pittsburgh, came into my office. Edith had been married first to Granger Gaither and had left Pittsburgh to come to the fox-hunting and social world of Baltimore. It was only after her divorce from Granger Gaither and her marriage to Thomas Symington that the idea of Edith with a house came into anybody's mind. She had the greatest possible charm, all Irish, with the most extraordinary crystal blue eyes, slightly reddish hair, a ravishing figure, and enormous chic. I knew nothing at all about her taste.

I was sitting at my desk at Benson's when in came the glamorous Mrs. Thomas Symington, looking absolutely marvelous wearing beautiful clothes that she had bought during her honeymoon abroad. She sat right down and said to me, "Now, listen, young man." I can almost hear it. "I hope you have plenty of time to spend with me, because you are going to work for me whether you like it or not. I have finally found a house that I think can be made very attractive. It is in the country and I feel that the only possible way it can be made attractive is if you will help me with it."

March, 1974

Foxhunters of Yesteryea

Mrs. Thomas Symington.

I was overcome with excitement and I said, "Well, then tell me about your house."

She said, "At the moment it is perfectly ghastly, but it is on one of the most beautiful hills outside of the city on the edge of the Green Spring Valley. The post office is called Lutherville and I am sure you know it."

I did indeed know it and Edith had the wisdom to see that it had possibilities without spending too much money, and she had taken a long lease on it. We discussed it, and then she told me what she had done on her honeymoon. She had been to Paris, London, and Madrid where she had chosen the most imaginative, offbeat decorative furniture rather than serious museum examples. It was entirely for the personal, the unusual, and the unfamiliar that she had bought the great amount of furniture that she and I were to assemble in the house for her.

Mr. Symington had no say in it; in fact, he had no say in anything except to adore her. Indeed, he should have adored her because he had been away from Baltimore for quite a while and she was about to reinstate him there. He had had a very unsavory divorce in the state of New Jersey before he married her.

The moment came for us to go out to the country to see the house. It was indeed as she said, built on a lovely piece of land, high above the valley with a beautiful view. The house was late Victorian, and surrounded on the front and two sides by an enormous veranda. Inside, there was a large hall running from the front door and terminating in a big drawing room with large windows looking onto the garden. To the left of the hall was a very large dining room, and to the right there were two rooms separated by a hall going out to the front veranda. These were little rooms for cards or music and could be used as incidental sitting rooms. I could see we were going to have a wonderful time because so many of the rooms did not have to be entirely devoted to long sitting comfort. There was a big living room that took care of that, and the two little rooms could be after-dinner party rooms, or before-dinner cocktail rooms.

Edith, without knowing what she had been doing on her European buying trip, had picked out the most ravishing suite of Louis XVI furniture that I have ever seen in my life. It was small scale: painted off-white, had a settee, four armchairs, two side chairs, and was covered in cream-colored satin with strips of pink and cherry. This suite was to go into one of the two little rooms. She had also bought a big white Chinese screen with birds of brilliant plumage in magenta and blue. Her small collection of white Cappo de Monte horsemen I could see sitting on the mantel. There would be a good bare floor with a small rug to take care of the sound of the cardplaying or the cold. This house was to be lived in all year and could indeed adapt itself that way.

Across the little hall there was the other room. In it we put a wonderful group of Louis XV furniture that we promptly covered in orange satin, and we found the most wonderful lemon-yellow Chinese paper with orange and green bamboo for the walls. In that room were to be hung a pair of superb Chinese Chippendale gilt mirrors.

The living room was a big room, which we did in an extremely pretty pale absinthe green paint. Edith and I made a little trip to New York to buy materials, and we went straight to Macy's. They had wonderful stuff in their drapery department, and we quickly found, for the green room, a very pale yellow satin for slipcovers and upholstered furniture. We bought some black and gold Queen Anne lacquer tables and two remarkable Irish hunting pictures whose riders wore pink coats.

When it was all done, Edith had a party, and among the people who were there was Pauline Potter, and she was wild about the house. She told me, "I never expected to see anything like this in America, nor have I. I've seen lots of extremely attractive houses, but I've seen nothing with this much imagination. I have one criticism. Why do you have those two tomato-red cushions in the drawing room? I find when I go in that room I see them and nothing else. You have accented the most unimportant thing in the room. Just go out there and take them out of the room and see what happens."

I did, and I have to confess it made all the difference in the world. The note that I had thought a necessary accent had been totally destroying the room. Pauline taught me that at that early moment in our relationship.

In the dining room we painted the walls a shiny dark green, the color of a magnolia leaf. At that time there were very few dark green rooms. It is true that Elsie de Wolfe had done one, but it was years before, and I feel what I did was not to invent, but to revive and attribute to the great Elsie de Wolfe. The windows were hung with chintz, green with huge white magnolia blossoms. The chairs were Portuguese Chippendale, very offbeat, very carved, and the seats were upholstered in white leather, which for 1930 was a wild innovation.

At that time my great ideals were Syrie Maugham of London, who had taught us all the value of white as a color; Frances Elkins from California, the brilliant sister of the great architect David Adler; and Elsie de Wolfe.

Upstairs there were bedrooms for Edith and her husband. Hers contained a very pretty French bed, a lot of white muslin, and had great comfort. His was very chic, and painted a dark brown. There was a guest room papered in pale green paper with silver flowers, and a beautiful Venetian bed covered in brocade of the same coloring, and also a big double guest room with flowered curtains and flowered spreads on the bed. The walls were covered in a strong pink, blue, and yellow plaid wallpaper, and the last double guest room was all white with Nile green curtains.

When the house was completed, as I have said, Edith decided to have a party, a dinner dance for about fifty people, and believe me, those fifty people were picked for a few definite things: looks, charm, fun. Well, we all got there, including quite a number of racing people because it was the Maryland Hunt Club weekend, and the most marvelous thing happened, which was that Edith's horse won the race.

All of the guests had a tour of the house, and it must be confessed that they all looked absolutely overwhelmed. One of the most attractive girls said to me, "Billy, what is this supposed to be?" They literally had honestly not thought about the possibility of having anything but very good old mahogany furniture, perfectly nice chintz, and great comfort. They just didn't know what to make of it, and I don't think many of them liked it very much. It wasn't at all popular, but they all had a wonderful time at the party.

Ruby Ross Wood was staying with Edith that weekend for the Maryland Hunt Club Ball. She had been dragged down to it by her husband, Chalmers, because she despised every single thing about hunting and Maryland. She always referred to the Baltimoreans as "those peasants." Ruby loathed every minute of it and accused Chalmers of torturing her because she said, "Every minute of the day that you are hunting, I'm lying in agony thinking that your neck will be broken on one of those damned horses."

I had never met Mrs. Wood, but I had heard that she was going to be at the Hunt Club Ball, as I had met Chalmers, who was a most attractive agreeable person, in the hunting field, and he had said, "I'm so glad you will be at the Hunt Ball because Ruby, my wife, is coming down for it."

On the night of the ball, which was the night after Edith's dinner party, I was at a table across the ballroom, and I couldn't see Mrs. Wood in the crowd. There were the most glamorous girls you ever laid your eyes on, from all over the East, the best-looking men in pink coats, and as always, the club did the whole room in red and white tulips. To my great surprise, as soon as the main course was over, Chalmers came to me and said, "Billy, do you mind coming across the room to meet Ruby, my wife? She wants to meet you very much."

So I gulped, and as I approached the table I saw a woman with big dark glasses wearing a raincoat. Indeed, there were lots of drafts and it was chilly in the ballroom, but every woman was almost naked in her ball gown, and there was Ruby, shivering, in a rage, and in a raincoat! She said to me, "Will you please sit down, young man. I can hardly speak I am so cold in this wretched place, and I have very little to say, except that I am staying in the most extraordinary house, one of the most attractive houses I have seen in years. If we ever recover from this goddamned Depression, I really think I would like to have you work for me. The last thing that I ever thought was that I would have a man in my business. I have an extremely good staff at the moment, but truthfully, don't let me lose you."

Ruby loved the house that I had done for Edith, and you may be sure there was not much chance of her escaping me. Every time that I had to go to New York I went to see her, and in 1935, a telephone call came for me in Baltimore.

A voice said, "Hello, this is Ruby Wood. I would like you to lunch with me."

I said, "But, Mrs. Wood, where?"

"Well," she said, "at the Pierre Roof. Edith Symington will be there to make things easier for us."

When Tom Symington died, it was found that he didn't have a penny; he had spent every cent. He had died suddenly in Edith's arms in the train coming back from Fairfield, where there had been a horse show. It was thought, of course, that she was going to be a dashing rich widow, but she had not got a penny. Edith had become the great friend of the Woods through Chalmers and the hunting field in Maryland. When they came to New York, the Symingtons stayed with the Woods quite a lot, and Ruby adored her, but later Ruby didn't speak to her because she had become so jealous. However, after Tom's death Ruby said to Edith, "Now listen, my dear, Baltimore is no place for a poor widow. I am going to get you out of that goddamned place, and I will get you a job in New York and a good one."

She immediately spoke to Edna Chase, and in no time Edith had a job at *Vogue,* which payed enough to allow her a small apartment at the

Pierre Hotel. She became enormously popular in New York in every way. The only difficulty was that as a widow she became a plaything of the rich boys. In the summer, when all the wives were away, Edith was very much in demand.

The day came, and I went up on the morning train to New York. I arrived in pouring rain, and went at once to the Pierre Roof. There was Mrs. Wood, again in a raincoat, and there was Edith looking perfectly adorable. Mrs. Wood, I discovered at that moment, smoked without stopping, and said nothing. She didn't utter a word during lunch. Edith and I had to make conversation, which was not difficult, but it wasn't made easier by Mrs. Wood's not saying a word. So finally, when lunch was over, Mrs. Wood turned to me and said, "Young man, would you like to see me?"

"Oh," I said, "Mrs. Wood, that is really why I came."

"Well," she said, "come with me. Edith will have to leave us now. I'll take you to my office."

As we got in her car, I met Paul, her French chauffeur, who was to become a great friend. We rode down, from the Pierre to 57th Street and Madison Avenue. We walked into her office and she stationed herself in front of her desk, and removed from her wrists the most extraordinary gold bracelets, which had dozens of big gold seals attached. It was really quite noisy. Without turning around, she said, "I suppose what you want to know is how much I am going to pay you."

I said, "Well, Mrs. Wood, it would be very interesting, for I don't know whether I can afford to work for you."

"Well," she said, "that is going to be arranged somehow. I don't know really quite how, but it will be arranged. I have talked to my assistant, who is not too happy with your coming on. She is a top member of the firm and you can't possibly replace her, but you can add to her. I feel I need a gentleman with taste and I have found him in you, wasting away in Baltimore. We must get you away from there as fast as we can. There is obviously no work for you there. The house of Edith Symington stood out like a beacon light in the boredom of the houses around it. Will you take thirty-five dollars a week?"

I felt as though I had been shot, and I said, like a child, "I'll have to go home and ask my mother." I left almost immediately but I did have time in the station to telephone Edith and say to her, "I think I have a job. She wants to pay me thirty-five dollars a week."

Edith said, "Don't you worry about that. I'll see that you don't starve."

When I was at the door, Mrs. Wood had said, "Of course, I will give you my apartment to live in for the summer because Chalmers and I are in the country and you will have my maid. So you will have no rent to pay, your laundry and valeting will be taken care of, and I think we can even squeeze out enough gin so you will be able to have a nice martini when you come home every day."

So I got into a train that afternoon, crying with excitement and pleasure, and thinking, how would I ever get along with her, for Mrs. Wood hadn't really said much. I got to Baltimore and went home, and my mother said to me, "Where have you been? Have you been to town to see your old aunt?"

"No," I said. "I have to tell you that I have not been. I have been in New York."

My mother said to me, "Did you get the job?"

I said, "You know nothing about it."

She said, "I don't know anything about it, but I know that you went to New York about a job, and I hope you got it because you must go if you did."

So I told my mother, and bless her heart, she said, "I will give you fifteen dollars a week so you will have fifty dollars a week."

Mrs. Wood had told me, "After Labor Day when Chalmers and I come back to the apartment, you will have decided for me whether you are going to be a part of my life forever, or be out of it. On the afternoon of Labor Day, I will triple your salary, and see that you get a nice apartment which you will be able to pay for, or I will say, I'm terribly sorry, Billy, I made a mistake. The job is over."

On the second day I was at Mrs. Wood's office she said, "You are to sit in the office next to mine." It was the most striking thing I had ever seen. I had a secretary and was told that I was to do no work whatsoever, but I was given a list of shops to go to for a month. At the end of the four weeks I was to take Mrs. Wood to the shops and show her what I liked, and from my choices she would be able to determine my taste.

At the end of the probation she said, "Well, you passed." I got a lovely little flat, and something like $100 a week and from 1935 until her death in 1950 I worked for Ruby Ross Wood. Those years, no doubt, were some of the most happy and creative ones in my life.

Ruby was ill with a long agonizing cancer performance, and I wasn't allowed to see her the last six weeks before she died because she thought she looked too awful. It was absolute vanity, only. I could have talked to her and we could have had a perfectly good afternoon. She died in her lovely dressing room off her bedroom. Nobody saw her, not even her sister, because Ruby said, "I have become a spook."

I learned of Ruby's death from her husband; he said, "Billy, Mrs. Wood is dead," and he burst into tears. "Oh, damn it. I didn't think I would at the end. I've already cried for so long."

"As you know I have said, a young woman must be a debutante in Baltimore, a young married woman must be in New York City, and an old woman must marry a European, preferably in Paris, and live the rest of her life there."

O ne spring day, I had a telephone call from Mrs. Charles Morton Stewart, née Sophie McHenry, who was known devotedly by the vast clan of McHenrys and Stewarts, and by everyone who knew her, as Aunt Soph. She sounded rather faint on the telephone when she said to me, "I have to ask you to help me, Billy, and if necessary I shall hold a gun to your temple.

"Pauline Potter, a very young distant cousin of mine, is about to arrive from Paris. Her mother, Gwendolyn Cary, has just died tragically there, and her father has made it quite clear that he is going to have as little as possible to do with her.

"She will come here until we can find a suitable place for her. I am asking if you will come to tea next Sunday in the country. I've invited Natalie Wilson, who I think will be sympathetic toward Pauline, and Tom Roberts, who will be a wonderful friend for her. Tom will bring you out to the Green Spring Valley, and I am depending upon your friendship for me to come and meet her."

I was delighted, because one would go anyplace to see Mrs. Stewart because she was such an attractive woman. Tom had a rather famous automobile called a Jordan that was a very snappy battleship gray, the top was always down, and it had been turned into a personal racing car.

Sunday came, and Tom and I went out to the valley and drove up to the simple house where Mrs. Stewart lived among what would now be priceless Maryland antiques. She had very little money indeed because there were not very many rich Stewarts, but they all lived in lovely country houses, had the most fantastic looks, were wildly popular, and knew more about horses than anybody in Maryland.

When we arrived, we went into the drawing room. It was rather chilly that afternoon, and I saw the most extraordinary sight. Curled up and in a huddle of chill and fear was a young woman. She was dressed in a simple black cotton dress, heavy black stockings, and wore brogues. Her hair was braided into two pigtails tied with black ribbons. Although she was sitting down, it was possible even then to know that she was very tall. When, upon our arrival, she decided to unfold herself, which she did like a great gigantic yardstick, she ended up being very nearly six feet tall. I cannot be an accurate judge of weight, but she was pounds underweight. It looked as though she was starving. She had the palest possible skin, and hair that I can only describe as being hair-colored. She had on no makeup at all, and I realized that her face stopped at her lower lip. There was just no chin. But what there was, though, was a pair of the most enormous eyes, which were accented by the lack of chin and the paleness of her skin. She stood there looking frightened to death, and the saddest thing I've ever seen, but she spoke to us, and right away from her throat came one of the loveliest sounds I've ever heard, one that I was able to enjoy all of her life, which was her voice. It had a quality that is very difficult to describe because it was not throaty, it was just absolutely beautiful. There was not a trace of an accent, although she had learned French in Paris before she ever learned English.

Her mother had been born Gwendolyn Cary and was related to George Washington on one side of her family, and descended from Thomas Jefferson on the other. She was a woman of no beauty, but she had the most extraordinary style, and was what the French would call a *belle laide,* an ugly woman with enormous allure. She was tall and attractive, not a great mental heavyweight, but loaded with charm.

Her husband, Pauline's father, was Francis Potter — again, very tall and of great charm. He had been favored for a number of years by a lady who was a widow with a considerable income. During the time of his relationship with his lady friend, he married Gwendolyn Cary and was providing for her with the generosity from the lady. The lady provider met Gwendolyn Cary Potter, found her charming, and was perfectly happy about it, but when she died, Mr. Potter was left penniless.

The lady was unable to leave her money to him because it had been left to her in trust for her lifetime only.

So the Potters decided it would be cheaper to live abroad. Mrs. Potter's small income from the Safe Deposit and Trust Company in Baltimore made it possible for them to go to Paris. In those days as soon as they had no money many people in America went to Paris to the American colony. Their life there was a disaster and they were soon separated, with the result that Mr. Potter went his way, leaving only enough money to take care of Pauline.

Francis Potter had a very curious method of living. He had a small income from the Potter family, his base was New York, and he spent the whole of his income in about two months of the year. The other ten were paid for by the ladies whom he visited. Pauline hadn't seen her father for years at the time her mother died.

Her mother's death was a terribly grim one. When Pauline was about sixteen, Gwendolyn Potter abandoned her daughter, got on a train, and went to Biarritz. There, she went to a nightclub and, full of dope and alcohol, rushed onto the dance floor and flung her arms around the neck of a violinist whom she was in love with at that moment. In a rage of embarrassment and annoyance, he pushed her away. She ran off the dance floor into the night and shot herself.

There was Pauline, absolutely alone, in Paris; her mother was dead, and her father had disappeared. Nobody knew where he was, but after a great deal of effort, they found that he was floating around the Mediterranean with a lady on a yacht. He really denied Pauline, but gave her enough money to get a ticket to go to America. The head of the McHenry family was telephoned because there was a little more possibility of help there than from the Stewarts, and so off Pauline went. She was assigned to her aunt, Miss McHenry, who had the best school for girls in Baltimore, but before Pauline was able to come to America, Miss McHenry died, so she was sent to her nearest relative, who was Mrs. Charles Morton McHenry Stewart, Aunt Soph.

Many many years after I had met Pauline, Howard Sturges told me a story that shows how grim Pauline's early life had been like in France.

Howard lived in Paris in a very small flat. The glory of the flat was a bathroom, not quite so small, all done in gray marble and shades of gray by Elsie de Wolfe, in which there were, in addition to the bathtub, a chaise lounge and two priceless Louis XVI chairs, and he had tea there every day. Howard had a salon across the hall, which he used when the party was too big for the bathroom, and also an entrance hall done by

Jean-Michel Frank. It had been dark oak, and Frank had bleached it to the palest palest creamy white, and it had four wonderful tall Louis XIV chairs in cream-colored velum on a bare floor and that was all. Howard used to receive almost every day, and one met the most attractive Americans as well as Europeans at his tea table.

He was a great friend of Pauline's mother, and he told me that he was coming home very late from Montmartre one night, to quote him, "drunk as usual," and he said that this night, among his many drunken ones, he was alone, walking slowly down Montparnasse when he saw distinctly in the dark a form moving in the gutter. He went over to it and couldn't believe his eyes. The first thing he saw was a beautiful but outdated evening coat, then he bent down and touched the body of Gwendolyn Cary Potter. He said, "Poor Gwendolyn, what is this?" She couldn't answer, and he said, "I will take you home." Luckily, he was able to get a cab and take Gwendolyn to her house. They had to climb several flights of stairs; it was practically dawn, and when they got to the top, she fumbled but finally got the door open, and it opened against the body of Pauline, who was standing there waiting for her mother. Dawn was breaking and lighting the apartment, and caught in the light was a mass of white lilacs. They had nothing for breakfast but the room was full of flowers.

After Gwendolyn's death, Mr. Potter made it clear that he would see Pauline once. He had taken a house in Narragansett for the summer, and he had exactly enough money to live the way he thought he should for a month, with the house filled with servants and some of the ladies who'd been so kind to him in the winter months when he had no money. He had told Mrs. Stewart that he would have Pauline visit him for two weeks, and he would give her a sufficient amount of money to buy adequate clothes for her debut in Baltimore. There were dozens of people dying to take Pauline to the Bachelor's Cotillion where all the debutantes were presented. That went without saying because everyone was so fond of Mrs. Stewart and the Stewart family as well as the McHenrys.

That afternoon at Aunt Soph's, Pauline told us little jokes and stories which had us all spellbound, but she could have recited the alphabet with that voice and been bewitching, and we could hardly wait for the next time we could see her.

We soon realized that she had the problem of owning only her school clothes, and the problem of really everything. Pauline had never even heard a dance record on a Victrola. She had never done anything but go

Pauline Potter's debutante picture.

to school, and she had had no friends excepting the children at her school in Paris.

So, we left and we began seeing Pauline, who was still dressed in her pathetic clothes; however, she decided on her way to Narragansett she would go to New York and buy some simple cotton clothes to wear in the summer. On her return, she was to dress herself as a Baltimore debutante.

The Baltimore clan, which included the Keyser family, planned Pauline's debutante party. Mr. Brent Keyser, who was its head, was to give her a dinner dance in his house in Baltimore, and there were four or five other cousins who had met her and were ready to do anything they could for her although she had been in Baltimore only a very short while.

One day in October I was on Charles Street quite near the French Shop where all the ladies went, and standing outside were Peggy Stewart and a very tall young woman I didn't recognize at all until a voice said, "Bill Baldwin."

That, in itself, was remarkable because nobody called me Bill. Nobody. My mother, as a joke every now and then, did occasionally, but that was a name that I hardly answered to. The person who had called me Bill Baldwin seemed to me to be very nearly six feet tall, and was wearing a tiny cloth cap. She was wrapped like a cigar wrapper in a black, buttonless coat, and around her neck, from her throat to the bottom of her coat, which was about four inches below her knee, was a double silver fox fur. That was Pauline Potter as a result of her shopping in New York for a simple little coat. She wore that coat constantly.

That was the first time I realized that was the way Pauline was going to dress. She had bought a few expensive clothes and she wore them over and over and over, and she always looked perfectly marvelous. She had a way of doing things to what she wore; maybe she would add one flower or maybe carry an extraordinary bag, and the result was a very personal style added to great simplicity.

We three had lunch that day at what was a very chic restaurant called the Dutch Tea Room in the middle of Charles Street.

After that I began seeing Pauline quite a lot. It was true that she had never been in the arms of a man to dance. She knew about everything but not through personal contact. She had never had a beau. I don't think any man ever thought of kissing her, but she was a marvelous dancer and very popular, and Tom Roberts, one of my best friends, was wonderful to her. Pauline just knew how to dance and she was lucky because Tom was about the best dancer in the world, just about. He was a big man, and he really threw her around and they were marvelous together, and she looked wonderful dancing. There was a nightclub called Sherry's on top of a movie theatre, and we went there nearly every weekend. By we, I mean a little group of what was called a fast group of kids. The orchestra there was black, and they wore skintight white evening clothes, and it was conducted by a black man called Vernon who wore a tailcoat.

Luckily, Pauline was so attractive that all the girls were crazy about her, so her fellow debutantes did not resent her, excepting for a couple of real prunes who mentioned the fact that she had no chin, that she was not pretty, and that she couldn't talk about anything that they could talk about. They couldn't understand her wild popularity, which was so obvious because of her charm and because she was very sweet.

It was very evident, soon after you knew Pauline, that you were in for a unique experience. She was little more than a child, but she understood everything. She was sympathetic, and her willpower took the place of character. She was never bitchy. She was never catty. She was always kind. She was always bubbling with laughter, and she had the word *charm* absolutely cornered. My own mother, when she saw Pauline, practically dropped dead because she was so remarkable looking, especially for Baltimore. She could have been called a freak, really. But one "How do you do," and they were all lost. Pauline just had it more than anybody.

Life went along very well for her, as she had met a couple of very snappy New York debutantes in Narragansett and she had them down for a couple of parties, and the Baltimore males were in a dither about her and her friends.

Buck Stewart took Pauline to the deb ball, and she did a very naughty thing to him when she left Baltimore. She had borrowed two or three hundred dollars from him to pay for a party, which for Buck was a hell of a lot of money, and she never repaid him, not even when she became a Rothschild.

The time came when Pauline had to think about where she was going to live. She did not want to spend her debutante days in the Green Spring Valley because she couldn't drive a car, and she wanted to go to the nightclubs every night and dance her legs off. If she found something sufficiently inexpensive in town, she could have Mrs. Stewart live with her. Nobody wanted her to live alone. In those days girls didn't do that, so Mrs. Stewart was to be her chaperone, and share the house with her.

Pauline found a tiny house that had been converted from a stable. It consisted of a drawing room on the first floor, a dining room at the back, a kitchen, and a small sort of garden. Upstairs there were two very nice bedrooms and a bath, and on the third floor was another bedroom and a bath. Pauline said to me, "Isn't this divine? I have a little money, and I'm going to fix it up, and I want you to know what I want to do. I want to have it so that if I want to I can give a little dinner every night, and when I say little, I mean four people. Aunt Soph will not want to come downstairs and she can perfectly well have dinner in her room, which is a big room. After dinner and bridge, we will go out dancing."

Pauline created all this for herself at her very young age. She selected one or two of the girls who came out the same year to come to her parties. All of these girls were later to become Pauline's bridesmaids. It was a perfectly lovely, charming life.

Pauline was swimming around with the nicest people in the world and everyone, including Pauline, had the most beautiful manners. There was nothing but an atmosphere of great wealth around her, although she didn't have much money at all except for the tiny income left to her by her mother. God knows how little her rent was, I can't imagine. There were two or three other houses across Preston Street which had been taken over by other maiden ladies, or maybe a bachelor. It really was a very inexpensive life. Flowers in the big flower market were almost free. Occasionally there was the expense of some very good play that would open at a theatre on its way to New York. All the Noël Coward reviews opened in Baltimore, and *This Year of Grace!* came there first, so in the winter we had a lot of fun. At that time, we would all extend ourselves and how we met the stars, I do not know, but we did, including Mr. John Barrymore, who got stuck on Pauline briefly.

One of the most attractive things in the social life of Baltimore was the Supper Club, which was an organization headed by about six ladies who were the best dressed, the best looking, and had the best ideas for entertaining. In the autumn they would choose three very good plays for the winter season; they engaged the whole theatre for those Friday nights. Invitations were then sent out for the play and, afterwards, supper at the Belvedere Hotel Ballroom. There were always many stags and only those young girls who had come out the year before were invited. It was Pauline's second year and she went to the Supper Club, very much in demand indeed. It was very snooty; they didn't have everybody. They only had attractive girls who were going to have a very good time. Edith Symington was one of the originators of the club and was greatly responsible for the decoration of the ballroom, which was a beautiful oval Louis XVI room, done in gold and white.

So, that was part of Pauline's life. I don't think there was a serious beau because she was really a little bit too exotic for the Baltimore boys to think of her in quite that way, but that never became a problem because of the extraordinary thing that happened.

In the spring, the year after she arrived, there were some late parties around Easter season. My father's business partner, John Frick, had a wife called May. May was a cousin of the Duchess de Richelieu, knew it, and was mighty stuck up, but a nice old bag is what May really was. She decided to give a dinner party for a debutante whose name I can't remember in her house on Biddle Street, exactly across from where Wallis Warfield lived. We were all invited to her dinner, which was before a dance being given by some debutante's mother.

I said, "Pauline, of course I'll pick you up as usual. We'll walk around to Mrs. Frick's," which you could do in Baltimore then in the late evening. It was a small party, and at the table I whispered to Pauline, "Do you really want to go to this dance, or would you rather go to hear some very good music by one of the quartets from the Peabody in the house of a terribly attractive man who I know you'll adore, called Fulton Leser."

"Oh, darling," she said, "I would much rather do that. I really think for the moment that I have heard quite a lot of jazz, don't you? Maybe a little Mozart would be good." So that was that.

The Lesers were an extraordinary family. Mrs. Leser had been born an Agnes, the daughter of General Agnes who owned the *Baltimore Sun* and also owned a house in the Green Stream Valley named "Nacirema," which is American spelled backwards. She had three children: two sons, and a daughter. The daughter was called Frederica and was marvelous-looking, big, but beautifully proportioned and not fat at all, with red hair like Queen Elizabeth I. Frederica couldn't have been brighter, more attractive, or have a more evil tongue. She was very popular where she was liked, and she did pretty much what she wanted; she was quite a girl. There were two sons who were over six feet tall: one, Felix, the other called Fulton because his grandmother had been a Miss Fulton. Felix had red hair like his sister, and he was a great skier and lacrosse player. Fulton had more style to look at than almost any man I've ever seen. He wasn't good-looking, but he had an enchanting face, always laughing, bright blue eyes, bright red hair, and wore the most marvelous clothes I've ever laid my eyes on. It seems to me he once wore an orange tweed tailcoat. He was so funny that we used to call him all the time, and we used phrases that were entirely due to him.

The Leser house, on a corner on Calvert Street, was a big house with lovely furniture, beautifully decorated, and very comfortable. Mrs. Leser was very big indeed, with snow-white hair, and had the greatest, rather forward charm. Judge Leser, her husband, an appallingly tall man with snow-white hair, was mostly sat upon by his family.

We got to the Lesers', the quartet went on, Pauline went off with other people, and I went to join another group. When it got to be midnight, I noticed Pauline sitting in the corner with Fulton. I thought, Now it's time to go home, so I went over and said, "Pauline, darling, we must go."

"Oh," she said. "Do we have to go? I can't bear to leave Fultoni."

I said, "Well, I don't wonder."

Fulton gave me a great big smile and a great big laugh and said, "Isn't she divine. Now you know, Billy, weren't you smart to bring her!"

I said, "Well, then, we must have some fun. Will you be here long?" Fulton was living in New York at that moment, and was doing restoration work on the Frick Collection in New York with a group from the Fogg Museum.

We said goodnight, and left and got in a taxi. On the way home Pauline turned to me and said, "Bill, I'm very happy tonight." I'd never known her voice to be quite so beautiful.

I said, "Well, I'm so glad. Wasn't it fun?"

"Oh, wasn't it marvelous. Of course, I've had the best time, but after all there is something wonderful about a lovely house, really attractive people, and beautiful music, and besides, I've found the man I'm going to marry."

And I said, "You've done what!"

"I've found the man I'm going to marry," she said.

I said, "Who are you talking about?"

"Well," she said, "I'm talking about Fulton."

I was young. I was full of idolatry about Pauline and I behaved like a skunk. I said, "Pauline, just get that out of your head. You are not going to marry Fulton."

She said, "Oh, yes I am. When I decide something, I do it." Here came the willpower and determination.

And I said, "Pauline, how much do you know about the world?"

"Oh," she said, "I don't know that much. I just know that I adore him, and I know he'll make enough money, and I have a little bit, and

Pauline.

we'll live in New York." Then she said, "As you know I have said, a young woman must be a debutante in Baltimore, a young married woman must be in New York City, and an old woman must marry a European, preferably in Paris, and live the rest of her life there. And that's what I'm going to do."

So I said, "Well now, Pauline, I don't want you to be hurt, and I also, thank you very much, don't want to be responsible for this marriage idea. Are you really talking about Fulton?"

"Darling, of course," she said.

I said, "Well, Pauline, what do you know about men who really only like men and not women?"

She said, "Do you mean fairies?"

I said, "Yes, I do," and I said, "I just have to tell you something right now. Be prepared to find out that maybe Fulton is not the kind of man who will want to marry."

Billy wearing Madras bathing trunks — perhaps the first ones designed in that material in this country.

She said, "Do you think that's going to interfere with me? Because it's not."

Quite some time passed, I was sent to New York to be taught the insurance business, and there came a weekend when Hugh O'Donnell asked me out to Long Island for a few days. Hugh said, "You'll be happy to know a great friend of yours is coming, Fulton Leser, that awful man whom we all adore."

So I went out on the train and got there at noon and right after lunch, his wife, Lottie O'Donnell, who was not very attractive, not a bit nice, and hated us all, said, "Oh, I'm sure you'll be happy to know that your friend, Fulton Leser, is coming out to spend the rest of the weekend."

"Well," I said, "you know we'll have a good time, that's for sure."

"Oh," she said, "I really don't know. He's bringing somebody. He says his fiancée."

We all roared and I said, "I don't think that's very likely."

"You know it's not," said Lottie, "and I'm not sure whether it's a man or a woman, but he named somebody that he's engaged to and said he couldn't come unless they came along."

So late in the afternoon, Fulton arrived, stinking, with Pauline. This was about a year after Pauline had seen Fulton that one time. Maybe she'd seen him a couple more times in New York, but she was still living in Baltimore.

John Crimsky, who was wildly popular because of his great looks, was staying in a guest bedroom next to mine. We had a marvelous dinner party, and everybody got dead drunk, and after dinner, Fulton came into my room and said, "Wish me luck, I'm going to go and get Johnny Crimsky."

I said, "Well, I think you'd better let me bind your head because he's going to kill you."

"He's not," said Fulton. "But if you hear anything bad, come in and help me."

So I did hear kind of a funny sound, and I went in, and Fulton was being mopped up by Johnny as though he were a doll. I said, "Johnny, stop! What are you doing?"

He said, "That sonofabitch. I won't have it!"

I said, "Then just send him to bed. He can't stand up. You're not being a gentleman or a man. He's dead drunk and he is that way, and it's too bad."

The next day, as Fulton had gotten in some blows as well, I said, "Now you've got to pull yourself together, and both must come down and behave," which they did pretty well.

Fulton said, "This is going to be a very tough weekend, but I'll behave."

We all went to Jones Beach, which was not anything at all then. We took a boat across from where we were on Long Island, and had quite a nice time swimming. All the while Pauline and Fulton were supposed to be engaged.

Pretty soon Fulton came up to me and said, "Listen, kid, I just love you dearly and I want to thank you for saving me last night."

In the meantime, I had told Pauline what the noise was about because she asked me, but Fulton said to her, "I would not believe one word that Billy Baldwin says, he's just a little liar. He wants you, and that's the trouble."

So I spoke to Pauline in the middle of the day. I said, "I'm very upset. It's true about Fulton. I didn't make anything up. And I think you just must behave yourself. You cannot marry him."

"Well," she said, "I would appreciate it very much if you see me in New York and tell me. I've got to call my father and tell him I'm engaged to Fulton and I don't know where he is."

The next day in New York we did meet at Tony's and we finally found her father, who was on a yacht, and he agreed to see her the next day. Pauline believed Fulton and not me. She just decided to get married and she did.

Pauline led Fulton to the altar at Emmanuel Church with the biggest wedding I've ever seen in my life. She was dressed in banana-colored satin from her head to yards behind her, and she carried one Easter lily and wore a golden diadem. There were eight bridesmaids in apricot-colored taffeta embroidered with little violets, and eight of the best-looking men on the American seaboard as ushers. I was an usher.

One of the ushers who I was standing beside caught on fire because there was a candle next to him and it got into his frock coat. I put it out by patting him. Pauline had refused to come up the aisle if there was a single electric light on. She had demanded there be only candles. So I had to go around to the minister and say, "Miss Potter will not come up the aisle until you turn the lights off." She was already a half an hour late.

Fulton was so drunk he could hardly stand up at the altar. Felix, his brother, was his best man, and he loathed Fulton because he was gay, but he held him up by the back of his morning coat and got him married, and put him down in the limousine to go to the country. In the car Fulton said to Pauline, "I don't know why the hell you married me because you're not going to get anything, Pauline."

They got out to Mrs. Clark's, Pauline's cousin's house. The bridesmaids went upstairs to freshen up and so did Pauline, and she went into a room with Natalie Wilson, one of her bridesmaids, and told her what Fulton had said. Natalie told me that Pauline wept and wept and wept. Finally, she fixed herself sufficiently to go downstairs and receive three hundred people as the happy bride. Afterward, off they went on a five-day honeymoon, which was spent at the Chatham Hotel in New York, and they took all their friends to Jack and Charlie's, which is now called "21."

They had a flat in New York, which I had decorated with taffeta that was made to order in Paris by Brunschwig to match the color of her sunburned legs that autumn. The walls were very pale skin color and the curtains were of chintz from Rose Cummings printed with big white lilies. They had marvelous furniture because everyone gave them the

Pauline and Fulton Leser off to Majorca, 1932.

most wonderful wedding presents. Before Pauline's wedding, Frederica had married Dick Sears of Boston, so the presents from Boston were enough to make a beautiful collection in itself.

They began to entertain and gave many small dinners, but the stock market crash took its toll and Fulton lost his job, so they decided that the only possible way they could survive was to live in Majorca, mostly on her money, but also on a small allowance from Mrs. Leser.

Fulton's mother hated Pauline. She hated her because Pauline was bored with her. She wasn't really very nice to her, and Mrs. Leser wasn't nice to Pauline. It was very funny because his sister, Rica, and his brother, Felix, and Mrs. Leser were all on one side. Judge Leser didn't have enough sense to be on any side. Pauline and Fulton had become separated in Majorca, and Pauline called Mrs. Leser in Baltimore and said, "I'm sorry. I just can't afford him another minute. I've got the chief of police watching him at night so he won't be murdered. He is contributing nothing and I have now got a shop."

I heard it was the most attractive shop where she had natives knitting sweaters and carving things. She was supporting Fulton, and every queer in the world was there. Fulton was drunk all the time and very often was brought home and thrown in the door at night. The police officer adored Pauline, so he took Fulton over and didn't let him get killed.

Fulton was sent back to America, and Mrs. Leser had to accept him. She said, "I'm sorry, darling. I would meet you anyplace. It could be the middle of the Atlantic, if you'd only stop drinking and behave."

Soon after Fulton's return, Mrs. Leser died and he lived in Baltimore with his father and Felix. Felix had by that time become a total alcoholic, and night after night he would pulverize his brother, Fulton, with blows. Fulton went to bed every night practically bleeding to death.

Pauline stayed in Majorca until the Spanish Civil War. One day when she was swimming in Isabel Kent's pool with her and her guests, the rebels bombed Majorca, including the property of Miss Kent. They got out safely, and retreated in Isabel's Rolls-Royce to Paris. Pauline had nothing, but Miss Kent then took over, and gave her a beautiful apartment and a lot of marvelous furniture, and she, in return, paid Isabel for her stay in Paris by decorating some rooms for her.

Isabel also had an aunt, another Miss Kent, called Auntie Kent, who was very much a Catholic, enormously rich, and had a huge house in Paris. Auntie Kent was devoted to Pauline as well as to her niece, Isabel, and they all had a mutual friend, a charming German who later became a very popular art dealer in New York City. I think he had more knowledge than anybody I have ever known, and surely more taste, and Pauline learned a great deal about art from him.

Pauline's style was really so conspicuous that she soon got a job with Schiaparelli, the famous dressmaker, and began traveling back and forth from Paris to London. In London, she had a great friend named Susan Stewart, from Philadelphia, with whom she stayed. I remember the great tall Regency rooms hung with marvelous paintings and filled with black and gold Regency furniture. There was a lot of white satin, and some dark green satin, all very becoming to Pauline.

She always wore Schiaparelli clothes in London. I remember very well taking her to a beautiful, but unfashionable, nightclub that had been decorated by Oliver Messel.

I begged her to let me take her there because I wanted to see the decoration and because I was a great friend of Oliver's. But it was not a good idea for Pauline, because she was dressed in the most marvelous Schiaparelli dress which she was supposed to show off in fashionable places, and I must confess that the clientele at that nightclub was very "county." Her dress was designed like a full-flowered Spanish dancer's long skirt. It was many tiered and of bright green cotton printed with white tennis racquets in very small scale.

Then, about that time, the world broke apart and Paris was being besieged by World War Two. There were, of course, many Americans in Paris, and the idea was to get out. This was not an easy thing to do. Isabel had a great deal of influence in the diplomatic service, and she included Pauline in all her plans. However, Pauline had other ideas, much to the annoyance of her friends. The way out of Europe, at that time, was to go to Spain and get on a boat out of Portugal to America. Everything seemed to be planned, happily, for Miss Kent, and Pauline motored with her to Spain, but when she got there, she met a charming Spaniard who had a very important position in the Prado, and as she had never seen the Prado, she therefore decided it was a ridiculous thing for her to leave Spain without seeing it.

So she stayed and saw the Prado, including the heinous scene in the Prado Plaza when the rebels tied people to the merry-go-round and shot them.

She then left Spain and came to New York to the little flat that I had found for her on Sutton Place about two doors down from my own in a charming row of houses between 54th and 55th streets. The apartments had very low rentals, and were called railroad apartments.

The apartment I had found for Pauline seemed to me to fill her requirements, but I supposed we would have to make provisions for more closets, although I wasn't sure. She arrived, finally, by a very slow boat, and she had a perfectly comfortable bed to sleep in, an adequate dressing table in the bedroom, and a decent sitting room with some pieces of furniture of no importance which I had found for her.

The very next day after her arrival, she telephoned me and said, "See here, Bill, darling, I'm so happy. When are you coming to do this apartment? We must get at it right away because I have been given the most wonderful chance to have my own dress house by Louise Macy who is on *Harper's Bazaar*."

Pauline, over the years, had become a great friend of Louise Macy, who actually had a Baltimore connection because her mother was born there. She was one of three sisters by a Macy father from California and a mother whose name was Gill. These three girls quite often came to

Louise Macy and Billy reflected in a mirror in Ruby Ross Wood's office. (Louise
Dahl-Wolfe)

visit their grandmother, who lived in great majesty next to the Maryland Club. She was a huge and terrible woman known as Almighty Lou, still dressed in mourning for General Gill who had died forty years before, and she was always bitching and bossing everybody.

When Pauline's collection was ready to be shown, I didn't go to the opening because I wasn't invited, but that night she telephoned me and said, "Well, darling, I have to tell you something very interesting. It was a total failure. One dress was ordered, and that by Hattie Carnegie. One."

Pauline was flabbergasted and horrified because she didn't know how she was going to pay her rent, which was low enough, but a week or so later, she had a call from Hattie, who said, "I ordered that dress, and I want to talk to you." So she went to see Hattie and Hattie told her that there were a few pieces in her collection that she might like to have with certain alterations. She said, "If you want to be bothered with me, I am terribly interested in you and your taste," and this resulted in her becoming one of Hattie's designers.

Pauline was very sweet to me. She always invited three gentlemen to her openings. One was me, one was Glenway Westcott, and one was Monroe Wheeler. We sat in the background and watched every chic woman in New York sit there and order all these marvelous clothes at colossal prices, and there was Pauline looking very simple indeed, and very chic indeed, and just really having quite a success. After working for Hattie for half a year, she had turned her little flat into an absolute jewel.

There were two rooms: a long thin living room with a very simple mantel over the fireplace, and a long corridor going back to a bedroom with three windows on the river.

There was also sufficient width for closet space in the long hall, a kitchen was concealed behind a screen, and there was a fairly adequate bath. She painted the whole apartment white, but there were quite a few perfectly harmless little moldings in the drawing room about which she said to me, as though she were talking about chewing gum, "Of course, they must be done in real gold leaf, naturally."

I said, "Pauline, I'll see what I can do about it, but I've never done it before."

Well, we got together, and got the estimate, and it was a very expensive proposition because she wanted the real eighteenth-century manner of gold leaf on the moldings, which was done.

There were very simple white silk curtains, and a few pieces of Louis XVI furniture in the living room. The bedroom had unlined taffeta curtains of the palest cerulean blue, and she had a daybed especially made, and lived in luxury with a wonderful maid whom we found for her. And always, do not ask me how, Pauline had fantastic flowers. She also managed to give very attractive, very small dinners indeed. By that I mean only six at the most, and usually four, and she had marvelous food.

When Pauline escaped Paris in Miss Kent's Rolls-Royce, she took with her two small Vuillards, and some white Mennecy china which she used on her dressing table. These things appeared in her apartment and in later photographs of places where she lived.

Later on, when she got her great success with Hattie Carnegie, she was always dressed in her own clothes in Paris and always by Schiaparelli in New York, and she never considered herself exactly in trade when she was working for those designers. But she had one dress that had been part of her trousseau in Baltimore that she wore in Harlem, where we all went when Pauline and Fulton were first married. It was cloth of gold, banded with a huge swath of sable. I have been told since that it was never paid for.

Pauline moved quite soon from her apartment because it was not big enough. She didn't want more rooms, but bigger rooms. So she moved to the second floor of a house in the East 60s. It was quite a wonderful apartment with enormous style in a funny way. It had two beautiful big rooms, a large entrance hall downstairs, and she gave charming parties.

Success upon success crowned Pauline, and she was soon to buy a lovely townhouse on 70th Street. Her great friend, Anne Kinsolving, helped her find the house. Anne was a little bit older than Pauline and they had become friends in Baltimore and had a beautiful friendship that continued until Pauline's death. In fact, Anne married John Nicholas Brown one week after Pauline's wedding so her wedding would not conflict with Pauline's. Anne had all her bridesmaids dressed like Russian czarinas wearing crowns, and she was married in St. Paul's Church. Anne, who was Alice Garrett's best friend, first brought Pauline to Evergreen and Alice became as crazy about Pauline as we all were.

In this period of her great success, my favorite picture of Pauline was taken for *Vogue* in 1950, and during this time she spent the summers in Paris where she lived in a flat owned by a Polish countess. It was on the

Pauline with her white Mennecy china and one of the Vuillards. (Louise Dahl-Wolfe)

Billy's favorite photograph of Pauline. (Condé Nast and Horst)

bow of the Île Saint Louis and from the third-floor window of this flat the view looked down upon the Seine and the Vert Galant.

What Pauline did when she moved there was to have a Louis XV mantel installed, which was taken out at her departure. The room was sparsely furnished, the three windows giving onto the Seine were hung with pale blue and white striped unlined taffeta curtains, and I remember one day going there in the late afternoon while the sun was still shining. Dappled light from the river shone in through the windows past great six-foot-tall branches of white lilacs, which stood before the simple windows.

She had a few pieces of French furniture, and a black and silver table that she had had made, which could be rolled in from the kitchen and could seat eight; the chairs were an odd group of Louis XVI chairs upholstered in pale-colored silk. It was also a fantastic room because at any given moment one could see something outside.

One year when she came back from France, I had dinner with her; she was getting into her routine in New York, which meant designing an enormous collection for Hattie and quite a lot of entertaining. She loved to give dinner parties and she made an amazing collection of friends, all very much on the intellectual side, but also very much made up of people who liked to dress in beautiful clothes. There was nothing bohemian about Pauline. She became a great friend of Gilbert Miller, and told me that she only allowed Kitty when Kitty would get off her gossip-tracked mind.

During dinner she told me that I'd seen her through a lot of desperate years in her life in many ways, and that ironically they had also been among the happiest, and those were the years with Fulton. Pauline had loved Fulton and had tried to save as much of his life as it was possible to save.

In the meantime, poor Fulton, who had been the joy of so many people, had died in the darkness in Baltimore, and even though Pauline had been divorced, it meant that she was now free in a much greater sense.

Pauline had a lot of lovers. There was a most attractive Spanish nobleman, and several Americans. She was very sexy, very. But there was never much talk about marriage until one night at dinner in New York after she had just come back from one of those summer trips to Paris. She said to me, "Bill, I've got the most marvelous thing to tell you. I'm going to be married to one of the most eligible men in Europe."

And I said, "You are?"

"I am indeed," she said. "Philippe de Rothschild has begged me to marry him. He's the one who writes poetry."

The word got around because it couldn't be kept a secret, and it was amusing to many people because all of his life Philippe had been known to care for only three things: women, racing cars, and his vineyards. He had had a tragic first marriage. His wife, who was Jewish, was taken away to a concentration camp where she was killed.

He was mad about Pauline and wanted to marry her and she had promised that she would. Philippe had become extremely déclassé in Paris society. He had no position whatsoever in Paris, although his mistress at the time was a woman who was very much of a French lady. This was proven because one day Pauline and I went out to lunch at the Talleyrands'. Philippe drove us out to their beautiful house, but he was not invited to lunch. He went next door to lunch at a restaurant even though he had known the Talleyrands all of his life. When he came back after lunch to pick us up, he was admitted to the drawing room through the garden.

We drove back to Paris and went inside Philippe's house to have tea, and we had hardly finished it when he said, "Well, darling, goodbye. I'll see you in a week or so."

She said, "What are you talking about?"

He said, "I'm off now. Anyway, I'll be back, you know. I'm doing this movie for the state about the life of Mozart."

So off he went. Pauline turned to me, tears streaming down her face. She was devastated, and she said, "I'm just going to have to tell Philippe right now, in a very short time, it is to be marriage or nothing."

It was his way of getting her goat, of course. They were married in April of 1954, and Pauline did a very smart thing. She found out about French marriage laws. The bride has to have two men represent her, and she had David Bruce, her cousin, as one, and Elie de Talleyrand as the other.

So Pauline's marriage put Philippe back in Paris society. She was very much interested in the world of literature, the drama, and painting, she brought him back to the fold, and they began a life of extraordinary richness because they were both interested in literature, more than anything else, I think.

Philippe had a beautiful, very elaborate apartment that Pauline did not want to live in, so she found a little house nearby with a lovely garden, renovated it, and this turned out to be the most joyful possible kind of arrangement.

Pauline sent me a postcard several years after they were married in which she expressed an ideal relationship.

She recalled an article printed in *Vogue* entitled "How to live in one room," and she wrote to me that she had an idea for an article that would have a different slant. She described how she thought a drawing room should be decorated in one's husband's house so that the marriage would be happy.

She wrote that she would furnish the room with chairs and a sofa made for the brother of Louis XVI, place small tables with precious objects on them around the room, hang a few small oils by one of the masters, and, I recall with amusement, that the final decorative note was that she would have her husband's portrait done by Augustus John.

She said that the husband should meet his wife in that room every day at six o'clock, and that everything would then take care of itself.

And indeed, it was as she described because they would often have lunch together in her house or dinner together in his. Once I was having lunch at Pauline's house alone with her, and the butler came in with the telephone in his hand and said to her, "Madame, Monsieur Philippe would like to dine with you tonight. Is it convenient?"

"Yes, it is," she said.

She always believed, which she described in that wonderful card to me about how to be happy in your husband's house, that that was the way to do it. She believed you should never be entirely given up, or entirely surrender. That there should be constant interest and maybe a little doubt. She always had her own bedroom.

Not that after their marriage they either had any affairs, because they didn't. They had a long beautiful relationship, and in the summer months, they often took houses in the north. At this time Pauline was really not very strong, most of her life she was very frail because of her heart. I was in Paris one day and Philippe told me Pauline wanted to see me in town in his house, which didn't happen often. So I went there and she was in her bedroom which I had never seen before, and which I did not know connected with his. It was a room done mostly in pale gray. There were lovely white flowers, and lying in a beautiful pale oyster-gray-colored silk bed was Pauline, looking like something not alive, not dead. Her eyes were bigger than ever and she looked more emaciated than ever. She was going to go off to America with him. Philippe was not with us, we were talking very deeply with each other, and the connecting door opened and he came in and she said, "Hello, Philippe." Then

Pauline in her bedroom. (Horst)

she said, "Go away now, this is not your time. You can come back in about half an hour. I'm with Billy now."

So he backed away looking as if she had lashed him. When I left, he was outside in the hall to see me off, and trembling like a child for fear of her health.

Pauline's health did not improve, and she had to come quite often to America to see a heart specialist. She lived in perfect joy at the Ritz Hotel in Boston for several years because that was where she went to her doctor about her heart. She had a bypass and she did very well for several years.

I remember the last time that I had fun with her was one day in Boston when I went up to see her, and to my great surprise there in the Ritz dining room sat her old friend, John Butler, alone at the table and he told me to sit down, which I did. He said that Pauline was being late as usual. In fact, she was an hour late, which was very customary. It was the only thing that got Philippe's goat. He would be furious with her because very often at lunch, which Pauline would often have served in different rooms throughout the house, she would come in as we were about to get up. Time meant absolutely not one thing to her, nothing! It was very exasperating.

The day I had lunch with Pauline and John Butler was the last time I saw her, and she looked perfectly divine. She never apologized for being late. She just wandered across the dining-room floor, looking wonderful, dressed in a man's suit.

The waiter was so crazy about her that he could hardly wait on her. They spoke French and she just charmed the pants off him. We talked and she was in a silly mood. She quite often had the most absurd moods of laughing, and her laughter was so beautiful that you nearly died.

After lunch, she said to me, "Now, darling, I'll tell you something right now. If what we are going to do is too much for you, we'll cancel it. We're going to the museum." So we went to the museum. She had a letter to the man who was the Greek curator, a charmer. We were so late the museum was about to close, but they said, "Never mind, Baroness. You can stay. We'll keep it open."

Not really the whole museum but just the Greek wing.

We had the best time. The curator could not believe her wit, her humor, or her knowledge. At one point he said: "Baroness, you have to teach me. I've got to ask you the questions." She knew so much, that woman. She had so much knowledge about what she wanted to know. She was a wild student. She would sit up all night long reading, searching. If there was anything she was after, she wouldn't let it go. She was like a terrier with a rat.

I didn't get too tired, but I thought at one point, I don't know whether I can quite go on, and I said I thought it would be a good idea if I went outside and waited. She said it would be a good idea if we all left, and that we must thank this lovely man, the curator.

He was madly attractive and he thought she was too. Pauline was very naughty. By that, I mean she was always flirting. She couldn't help it. She had always been that way, with any age or any person. It made no difference. Several of her friends' fathers in Baltimore had been in a state about her, and those nice debutantes, well, you could just see them bristling.

I saw Pauline when she first moved into the Ritz and had only been there a day, and when I went back, two weeks later, she had moved all the furniture around and changed everything. She had people come to see her from New York and many from Boston, but she was bad about one thing. She just cut out most of the Baltimoreans because they were no longer in her life. Pauline forgot that she had ever done the Charleston.

Then came the time when I was called to the telephone and told that Pauline had died in Santa Barbara, California. She felt so wonderful there in the winter and her doctor was there. She stayed at the Biltmore where she had a marvelous suite on the ground floor, she had her dog, she had Philippe, and it was wildly comfortable.

She adored her Rajah, a golden retriever. Philippe was so jealous of that dog that he couldn't be decent to him. He was never jealous of John Butler, but he could well have been, because Pauline adored him. She simply adored him, and she financed several dance projects. Her adoration of John made Woody Taulbee so mad he could hardly speak about it. Woody thought Pauline was an affected ass and she thought Woody was going to meet a horrible end because his life was so self-centered and he was so conceited.

One summer after she had come back to America about some business of Hattie's, she lived in John's apartment, which was exactly across the street from Woody's. Woody and John were great friends, so Woody had to be nice to her. I went to dinner with them two or three times, and Pauline and Woody were horrid to each other.

Pauline said, "Listen, Bill, what is this all about?" She thought Woody was stupid, and from her point of view, I guess he was really. I mean he was not an intellectual nor was he wildly educated the way she was, and she let him know it. I had a very difficult time, being in the middle, but it was her fault.

Two weeks after Pauline's death, I went out to Santa Barbara to stay with Nancy Gray. Nancy said to me, "Billy Baldwin, I have had a fantastic experience with somebody that I know was Pauline Potter, and I've got to tell you because it was so terrible that you weren't here."

She said that every afternoon it was her custom to walk up and down the beach in front of the Biltmore. It's one of the few beaches there, and the sunset is perfectly lovely. "I used to go every afternoon. It's not far from my house and I would drive down about twice a day. On one of my walks I suddenly became aware of an extraordinary-looking human being who was walking along the beach at first with a dog, and then not with a dog."

And she said, "I didn't know whether the dog was permanently with her. Anyway, there was this woman, very tall, dressed like nothing I've ever seen in my whole life. She wasn't freakish, she wasn't fashionable, she was just wearing these enveloping capes and cloaks of eggplant color, very dark browns, the colors of Braque."

She said she didn't always take her dogs, in fact, very seldom, but "About two weeks ago, I went one afternoon and I had my two little dogs with me, and there was the woman with this beautiful dog. I was walking and suddenly the dogs came up and spoke to each other. Then I saw that the woman was leaning down talking to them," and Nancy said, "I got close enough to have her say 'How do you do' to me, and how nice it was that we had met," and Nancy said, "I have never heard such a beautiful sound come out of a human throat."

Of course, it was Pauline, and I could have died that they didn't introduce themselves. I often wonder what would have happened if she had told Pauline that she was my great friend — Nancy Gray.

My friend Pauline Fairfax Potter was born December 31, 1908, and died March 8, 1976.

Almost two years after Pauline's death I received a letter from Philippe Rothschild in which he thanked me for giving Gerry Dryansky any information I might have for the biography being written of Pauline.

Philippe asked me to visit him at Mouton because he thought I would be greatly interested in the continued developments there. I have to admit that I was emotionally overwhelmed as I read the concluding lines of his letter, in which he said that whatever he did at Mouton, he automatically thought of Pauline and how she would react. He added, almost as a postscript, that it seemed to him that Pauline would forever be a force that governed his thoughts. I, of course, knew exactly what he meant.

Farewell to Charms

J left Baltimore in July of 1935 after saying goodbye to my mother who was ill in bed with a bad throat from which she never recovered. She died soon after.

But before my departure for New York City, my friends, the Needles, had a celebration luncheon for me on June 23, 1935. There were about twenty of my best friends there, among whom were the Lee Taylors. It hardly need be said that there never were such wonderful things to eat and drink. I remember all that glorious rye whiskey in which floated sprigs of mint. I was to take the late afternoon train to New York. At the end of the luncheon, Lee Taylor arose to his charming full height and recited the following poem which he had written.

FAREWELL TO CHARMS

Oh, here we are at the mammoth luncheon
To celebrate the great ascension
of Billy Baldwin to the higher
Realms to which we all aspire.
Oh, see him show Fifth Avenue
Exactly what they ought to do.
Interiors that give them pause
And color schemes that confound the laws
And bring the smart set to his door
Not for a mouse trap — but decor.

The smartest women of New York
Postpone the coming of the stork
Consulting him who comes so late
To show them how to decorate
Even Mona Williams — you know — Mona
Thinks she really pulled a boner
Because the mansion at Palm Beach
Was done before our Bill could reach
The spot, and show the Miezener clerks
Exactly how to shoot the works.
The Russian Ballet will scarcely function
So sorely will they miss his unction
And thoughts of what things might have be-ee-en
Will come to crucify Massine.

But worst of all, this haggard bunch
I see before me at this lunch
Will have to fight the heart bowed-down
When Billy leaves this Goddam town.
When Ellen was a debutante
He took her on almost every jaunt.
Kathleen will have to buy reviews
To keep up with dramatic news.
They say that Sallie Jenkins fainted
When first this dreadful picture was painted.

God only knows when Dorothea
Has felt so psychic and so queer.
Whenever Lydia looks around
Her choking throat can't make a sound
And when she hears it, Alice Garrett
Will find she simply cannot bear it,
Not to mention my own wife
Who feels like giving up — for life.

The symphonies will sound satiric
When he's no longer in the Lyric
And even luncheon *chez Marconi*
Will seem inexplicably phoney
If Billy Baldwin is not seen
Ordering — eggs — Benedictine!
'Most any man will seem a dub
If seated at a Supper Club

Where near-by girls had hoped to see
Our peerless hero, Billy B!
When Meyer Davis starts to play
The Continental — lack-a-day
Who else will make the girls declare
"He's just as good as Fred Astaire"?

But what we lose in Baltimore
Is nerts to what he has in store.
Already thousands realize
That in New York he'll take the prize.
Eve Symington insists he shall
Redecorate the Place Pigalle.
Watch Rockefeller Center boom
When he repaints the Rainbow Room!

We hope he'll be like Ethel Merman
And hit the top with General Sherman.
Of course it's fine he's got this chance
But, oh my God, how he could dance!
The women cry, "All hope is gone
We feel we simply can't go on —
Not even death can now alarm us:
Morituri salutamus!
Oh, Death, where is thy sting if we
Must live without our Billy B?"

Lee Taylor to Billy Baldwin
June 23, 1935

"You are talking like a lunatic. I come from Maryland, and those little legs are like eating lacquer."

That summer of 1935, after I had been hired by Mrs. Wood, I used to walk home from her office, which was at 50 East 57th Street, near the corner of Park Avenue, straight down Park Avenue to 48th Street to her apartment at number 277, where I was staying until Labor Day. The apartment building took in the entire block from Park Avenue to Lexington, and in its center was a great open garden. Some very attractive ladies had been installed in many of the apartments, and as a result it had a quite famous, if not notorious reputation, and was popularly known as "The Acre of Love."

As I walked back down my path to go home after work in the late afternoon, I passed people who, almost without exception, were attractive-looking. Pride in personal appearance was very much an element then. Every doorman on Park Avenue, in fact, everywhere in Manhattan, looked immaculate. They wore clean gloves, were smiling, and had good manners. I don't think that any doorman would have thought of smoking a cigarette on duty.

The office girls who came out on the street to go to lunch looked marvelously well groomed, and as for the men, I can't even discuss it because they looked so well in their tailored suits and polished shoes. There can be no doubt about it, walking down that extraordinary avenue was a marvelous baptism to New York at that time. There was certainly a much more general atmosphere of friendship in the city then; in fact, this friendliness even extended to the doormen: we felt we knew them, and they in turn knew us.

Everything seemed fresh and clean and new. The taxis were much cleaner than they have become. It was safer then to put your foot inside of one in winter because they did not have great pools of filthy water in them, and there was pride on the part of the cabdriver that his cab be clean.

Park Avenue had a number of marvelous restaurants: Voisin, the Crillon, Sherry's, and the Marguery. At Sherry's and the Marguery there were often charming debutante parties, and lots of dinner dances that were beautifully done. In a funny way, a lot of those restaurants seemed to me to look more architectural than decorated. They had sound principles, and I think in general the food was as good if not better than now, and the people in them looked so wonderful. One thing must be realized and it can't be helped, but the people in New York then were much better dressed.

However, I hasten to tell a story about eating in one of those restaurants. In the early, early spring of 1936 I was invited for lunch at the Colony, which was one of the chicest places in New York, especially its little bar. The people whom I was with had had lunch with me in Maryland several years before, and we were thrilled because there were softshell crabs on the menu, and I had not had any since I left Baltimore. When I was served, I saw to my amazement three poor legless little things on my plate. I said to the waiter, "What is this!" He was French, and he said, "Softshell crabs." And, of course, I said to my host, "I think we'd better speak to the captain."

The captain, a very fancy little fat Frenchman, said, "Monsieur, what's the matter?" I said, "Why have you amputated the legs from these crabs?" and told him that I came from Baltimore where the crabs are born every minute, and that we ate them completely from head to toe, especially the little legs. He said, "Ah, monsieur, nobody can eat those legs." And I said, "You are talking like a lunatic. I come from Maryland, and those little legs are like eating lacquer."

They cut the legs off the softshell crabs in the Colony restaurant in 1936. They did! That was called elegance, I think.

But New York did have real elegance, which was seen especially at night when people dressed up to go out. If there was a big hit at the theatre, certainly fifty percent of the audience was in black tie, and all the women were dressed, and I do mean dressed!

I remember going to a party after the theatre at the brand-new Iridium Room in the St. Regis Hotel. To my astonishment, Mrs. Harrison Williams with those eyes, Mrs. William Woodward, and Mrs. Myron Taylor were all in the same ballroom. Men still wore white ties then, and there they all were in a public place filled with friends. White tie!

That was the first time I had seen Mona Williams. Of course, I had heard about her when I was in Baltimore, and I never knew anybody who had a more glamorous reputation. We in Baltimore were particularly pleased about Mona because she had come from Kentucky and was a southern belle. She had been born near Louisville, where she grew up the daughter of a man who was a groom and also a perfectly good gentleman.

Well, Mona was this: I was dancing and suddenly I looked up and saw, a little higher than eye level, a pair of eyes and a brow above the shoulder of the man with whom she was dancing. This man was Prince Serge Obolensky, who had been married to Vincent Astor's sister, Alice. I had never seen such eyes in the world and certainly never have since. They were enormous, an incredible blue color, and above her brow was the most startling short, very-premature-gray hair. It was a great cause of excitement, her gray hair, but a cause of extreme sorrow to her because she always thought it made her appear older, so one day she up and dyed it, really a golden brown; and I couldn't help feeling as a great many others did that the glamour had gone. Later she went to live in Paris and Capri and dyed it an almost golden color, which I think it has been ever since.

The Williamses had a fascinating country house on Long Island, and one of its remarkable features was an indoor tennis court that Mona had changed into an enormous aviary. There were trees growing inside, the most beautiful rosebushes, birds flying about, and it was absolutely as if it were out of doors. Mona adored flowers, and that mania turned into her whole life in Capri.

The brick Georgian house high up on Fifth Avenue, which was built for Whitney Straight and which later became the home of the Audubon Society, was one of the most beautiful houses ever built in New York City, and I remember going to dinner there when the Harrison Williamses lived there in the utmost grandeur.

The house had been done with triumphant success by Syrie Maugham. The floors in the living room, hall, and the dining room were entirely in white, and certainly there never were more beautiful curtains and pelmets. A great point and one of enormous interest was that almost all of the furniture was English. The majority of the upholstery was white damask, but there were a few chairs upholstered in pale pastel-colored brocade. This was before the great passion for the French style that appeared, a style christened by Virginia Sheppard and me: F.F.F., Fine French Furniture; just as the first families of Virginia were called: F.F.V. Unlike many of the rooms that were done in the style of the Louies, these beautiful rooms never looked vulgar or nouveau riche. I shall never forget my astonishment when I went to a Fifth Avenue apartment that contained the best of all French furniture. To my horror, the owners had blocked up the real fireplace in the drawing room and put in a fake one to make a better arrangement for their F.F.F. A fake mantel to me is a kind of hopeless vulgarity.

As the hostess at her dinner party in her own house, Mona looked more glorious than ever; however, I thought of Kitty Miller, who once cattily said that Mona didn't really dress well; she dressed expensively, and it must be stated that Niki de Gunzburg said that of all the Americans, Kitty should have been the fashion editor of *Vogue* and *Harper's* because she knew more about clothes than anybody.

We were at least twenty people seated in the dining room, which was long and slightly narrow. The walls were hung with the famous Sert panels that were later moved to Long Island and finally to Capri. The table was blooming with orchids from Mona's greenhouse on Long Island, and the drawing room was a mass of white flowers. Flowers were certainly the thing that Mona loved the most, and she dedicated her entire life to her garden on Capri, where her imagination and fantasy, not traditional tastes, determined her garden.

The evening was interesting because of who was there and who was not there. The dinner conversation was controlled by a remarkable collection of gentlemen of the arts including Jerry Robbins, Truman Capote, Tennessee Williams, and Lemuel Ayres, whose tragic untimely death deprived the world of a genius in design for the theatre. Harrison Williams was not there; in fact, he hardly ever was at one of Mona's dinner parties because he was not interested in the conversation.

There is certainly no doubt about the fact that she had the real thing called glamour. When she left America she sold her house on Fifth Avenue and gave a lovely goodbye party in the library room of the St. Regis for two hundred people, supposedly her best friends. I think I never saw so many good-looking people in one room in my life. I also think that Mona had a pretty strong idea about how we all looked. There was not any doubt about the way Harrison Williams looked because he

125

Mona Williams. (Condé Nast)

was one of the most distinguished men of all and would have been one of the richest if it had not been for the stock crash.

The St. Regis was quite a remarkable place at that time because everyone went there. Quite often sitting at a table would be the glamorous and notorious Morgan Sisters, Mrs. Reginald Vanderbilt and Lady Furness, with very attractive European studs, and later in the evening many of the actors and actresses appearing in great successes would come in to have supper, for it was at that time that actors were beginning to have an equal social status in society. One of the things that excited me more than anything in New York, aside from the feeling of absolute freedom, was that you knew that as long as you behaved yourself you were okay. People did not stare then. Today, most poor souls spend their whole lives staring.

The St. Regis Hotel was owned by Vincent Astor, and he thought of it as a pet, not as a profit-making concern. It had been completely redecorated by his cousin, Mrs. Cameron Tiffany, who had marvelous taste and was a great friend of Ruby Wood. From his house in Rhinebeck, Vincent sent in fresh cream, vegetables, and eggs to be used by the hotel, so when you had an egg, it had come from Rhinebeck, and it was fresh!

Restaurants became my greatest joy, and I have never gotten over it. I would indeed like to have a cook, because I think in many ways eating at home is one of the more attractive things you can do. However, for my own entertainment, nothing takes the place of the excitement of a restaurant, but when you go in, you're usually at the mercy of some arrogant, horrible man who is the maître d'hôtel. You cannot quite tell, really, how comfortable you're going to be, and you don't know about the food; but the risk is okay with me, and I love it, and I love people who are all dressed up, enjoying each other in an attractive place that is not home.

So I began my life in New York at some of the best restaurants in the city, mainly because throughout the week I lunched in them with Mrs. Wood. Mrs. Wood's famous cook, Minnie, a full-blooded Long Island Matinecoc Indian princess, was off every day when Ruby and Chalmers were in the city, so Ruby had to eat out. It was nearly always the same meal for Ruby: definitely the biggest martini in the city, and, hopefully, the smallest little lamb chop in town.

We went quite often to Voisin, which was convenient for Mrs. Wood because it was between her office on 57th Street and the apartment on

48th. There was also a restaurant she loved called Chateaubriand, where we would often see Van Day Truex with Count Lanfranco Rasponi, the well-known public relations man. Many glamorous people indeed ate there, presided over by a handsome headwaiter called Pierre, whom even Mrs. Wood admired.

It was at that time that many people began to do a lot of their entertaining in restaurants. The Gilbert Millers, who certainly entertained more than anybody, never had lunch at home. Their favorite place for lunch was the Colony, but they almost always had dinner at home, which meant being dressed to the teeth.

Once I remember a cozy little duo, Kitty Miller and Mrs. Byron Foy, who was born Thelma Chrysler, having lunch in the Colony bar. Thelma was not so very popular in New York. Hattie Carnegie refused to allow her into her establishment because she once threw the scissors at the fitter. The colony's sommelier, whom all the women were crazy about, bent to light Mrs. Foy's cigarette, but, instead, he missed and lit the end of her nose. And Kitty screamed! Kitty was always screaming. Of course, the entire city adored the incident.

Ballroom dancing was very fashionable then: the Biltmore Hotel had Florence Walton and Maurice. He was a superb dancer and she was marvelously well dressed. Leonora Hughes, who was equally famous, also danced there. I remember going to the Biltmore one night and finding, to my astonishment, my aunt Mazie two tables away with a very handsome young man whom she presented to me as her newest husband.

One of the great joys was that there never seemed to be any difficulty about going to the theatre. There was always something great to choose from, and getting seats was not the frustrating task it has become. I remember very well when Noël Coward was doing *Tonight at 8:30.* I was having dinner at "21," and it suddenly seemed it would be a good idea to see the play. I was able to get two good seats, while having dinner, for that very night's performance.

Now, as for "21," which had been the most wonderful speakeasy of all, it was and still is, in so many ways, absolutely first class. Even now, the food that is brought to the table is bought and prepared with nothing but the most colossal integrity. The beef is the best quality, and the chicken hash is like nothing else in New York. Everything about it was the top, and very amusing people from all over the country went there. It has become more of a business restaurant now than it was in the beginning, but in those days "21" was one of the really glamorous places in town. I used to simply love to go there, and they were very nice, even to young people like me. It is so funny; I go there so seldom, but when I arrive they always ask me where I have been. They make you feel extremely welcome.

One of the most welcoming features of the town was the great profusion of flowers that were everywhere. In private houses, in public places, everywhere — you were constantly surrounded by bouquets of fresh flowers. The florist shops were magnificent, and flowers were as much a part of daily life as air, but then flowers were not as expensive as they have become.

However, naturally the thing that interested me the most when I first arrived in New York was where I was going to live. I had kindly been given the use of Mrs. Wood's apartment until after Labor Day, when Ruby and Chalmers would come in from Syosset for the winter because it was easier for Ruby, and then they would only go to Long Island for the weekends. So I had to look around to see what I could find.

I really didn't want an apartment in a great big building and hoped I could find something that was a little more personal or attractive, and, as I have said, I lit upon a whole block of Victorian houses between 54th and 55th streets on the river side of Sutton Place that had just been done over by Dorothy Draper, for which she should be eternally thanked. Those brick houses were painted shiny black with white trim and had white shutters; each door was painted a different brilliant color, and my door was scarlet. There were two of the most remarkable doormen I've ever seen, a little bit old, but active enough, and they wore the most wonderful, extraordinary English guard uniforms with overcoats. That was my apartment and I remember very well that I paid sixty-five dollars a month for it.

Millicent Rogers lived in one of the apartments on the lowest corner, and it had a living room with three windows on the river side. Van Day Truex was one of her greatest friends, and when he came to decorate it he hung the whole room with folds of bright green taffeta. It was one of the most enchanting rooms and was filled with lots of Biedermeier furniture.

Millicent was, without question, one of the most glamorous of all the glamour ladies. She had the most fantastic looks, wore the most remarkable clothes, many of which were done by Charlie James, and everything that she had was uniquely her own. Later on, when she lived in New Mexico, she even got to making her own beautiful gold jewelry.

Every house she ever had was utterly personal. I remember Claremont, in Virginia, which she furnished entirely with Biedermeier furniture that she had acquired from her marriage to Count Salm in Austria. Millicent didn't do one thing to the outside of Claremont. She said, "I consider it a desecration in Virginia to change even one single architectural detail. Inside, you can do whatever you want because that is entirely up to you; you're going to see it, and you are responsible."

In New York she adored going to the art galleries. At every exhibition you went to, the one picture that you were drawn to, almost as if it had been specially lighted, was on loan from Mrs. Huddleston Rogers, the name Millicent took after her divorce. I never knew it to fail. Every time, the best picture or the prettiest portrait was loaned by Millicent.

I remember one day when, to my perfectly unabashed excitement, she called me and said in her beautiful soft voice, "I hope you're free on Saturday because there's a marvelous show of costumes at the Brooklyn Museum, and some of my clothes are there." She had given all of her old clothes to the Brooklyn Museum.

I said I certainly was free. Luckily for my romantic nature, we were to go out after lunch, as Millicent was very delicate, really, and couldn't do too much at a time. When she came by for me, I could hardly get into the car on account of the sables. There was a sable throw, a sable hat, she had her hands in a sable muff, and I was tucked away in the corner with a lot of sable around me. Off we rode to Brooklyn. It was a wonderful experience because she was so gentle and so kind and so perfectly adorable. Everybody at the museum worshipped her, so the reception we had was like a private preview, and we were taken around and shown everything.

I was an even greater friend of Millicent's mother who was known as Mary Benjamin Rogers, a woman of the most enormous taste and, of course, a great deal of money because of her marriage to Henry Rogers. They had, among other things, a house in Southampton called "The Port of Missing Men," quite a famous establishment.

Millicent and her mother were remarkably friendly, considering everything; she had three charming sons whom Mary adored, but her several marriages, her abandonment to romance, and her move to Santa Fe rather startled her mother. Millicent always claimed she moved to New Mexico for reasons of health, but I think it was also because she fell in love with everything Indian.

Poor Mary was slightly tired, to say the least, by the time Millicent died, and she said to Millicent's doctor, "I suppose it was her bad heart that killed her." The doctor said to Mary, "No. She didn't have a bad heart. She just had a romantic heart."

Perhaps that was what was so wonderful about New York City in the '30s. Its heart was romantic.

"Billy is small, but his sting is deep."

*M*rs. Wood and Chalmers were living in their country house in Syosset when I arrived from Baltimore in July of 1935. Ruby came to town to work during the week, and with her usual hospitality and kindness she asked me to spend my first weekend with her in the country.

The summer flew by, and I passed my test with Ruby. Everything about my new apartment had been settled by early September, and I was to occupy it in November, which was no problem in those days. My mother had died that summer and left me with a small amount of money, part of which I decided to use for the decoration of my apartment, which was called a railroad flat because the rooms were lined up back-to-back like boxcars. They went straight from the front of Sutton Place back to the garden that fronted the East River. It had a long narrow corridor going back from the living room toward the bedroom, and in it were a couple of closets, the kitchenette, which was hidden by a big white screen, and the bath. The bedroom was a small square room with two windows facing onto the river and garden. This meant that it had a very nice sunlight coming in during the morning, but would be dark in the late afternoon, and I was thrilled with the idea. I liked the idea of waking up in a very bright room, and then later in the day when I was back from work I knew it would be a wonderful contrast to look from

Ruby Ross Wood's country house in Syosset.

the whiteness of the living room back down the corridor to something dark at the end.

The bedroom walls, painted a very dark gray-brown, a bit like moleskin, but browner, were most successful, and the windows had yellow, dark brown, and cream-colored cotton print curtains which hung from the top of the room to the floor. The bed was covered in Scalamandre antique damask.

There had not been any problem with the cost of painting the apartment because it had been extremely simple, but I was determined not to let price enter into the choice of fabrics or furniture. The decoration of this apartment was terribly important to me not only because I was going to live with it, but because I knew it could be a point of criticism for Mrs. Wood and all the people who would come there to see me. I had always been hospitable, and I felt more than ever that at last I was going to have a place where I could entertain people who really meant a lot to me.

133

I did not let Mrs. Wood see anything until it was completely finished. I just did not want her to have a say in what I was going to do, and I thought it was only fair that since she had taken me on and given me considerable trust, I should do my best.

The living room, whose two windows faced onto Sutton Place, was a white room, and had a Knoll sofa in blue linen damask, two French chairs covered in the same material, and a little slipper chair in a tiny blue and white print.

My hideous extravagance was the necessity of plants in front of the mirror between the two windows. I remember a very funny thing I did when the room was photographed. I went out and bought half a dozen gardenias and pinned them on to the leaves.

The only picture that I had in the room, which I bought the moment I took the apartment in New York, was over the sofa; it was an oil in tones of black and white with a pale blue wintry sky painted by a Baltimore artist called Herman Maril who has since become extremely respected.

When I arrived on the morning of my move into my new paradise, I was somewhat stunned to find that a perfectly nice little building, exactly the same height as the one I was moving into, had been built about ten feet from my bedroom windows. There was no longer any river; instead there was just another little black building with entrances on 54th Street. One of the charming things, however, about the apartment was that there was a side window in the living room which looked onto the tennis courts on Sutton Place where so many attractive people played tennis, such as Helen Wills Moody and Horst of *Vogue*.

That day, when Mrs. Wood and Chalmers came, I trembled a little, of course. She sat down, opened her bag, took out a cigarette, and clicked her bag shut. She seemed to be very peaceful, peering over her glasses with cigarette smoke pouring up behind them and onto her bangs, making them look as though they had been tinted tobacco color.

"Well, young man," she said to me in her soft, lovely voice, "I see you're a damn good decorator."

A few other people came that day and we had a very nice time, but Mrs. Wood seemed to be lingering a little bit, although she and Chalmers were going to the country that night. She even walked to the door to say good-bye to everyone, and when they had gone she said to me, "I have one criticism." I said, "Please tell me what it is." She said, "I do not approve of the black borders on the valances at the windows. You see them too much."

Billy's first New York apartment, with the picture by Herman Maril. (Photograph by Samuel H. Gottscho)

Of course, the minute Mrs. Wood said that to me I couldn't see anything else. I had them taken down the next day and had the black border covered with the same fabric as the curtains.

It was the only criticism Mrs. Wood ever made about any of the apartments I lived in. She always seemed to be very proud of my work and encouraged my taste one hundred percent, with never one hint of jealousy.

When I had redone that apartment several years later, Ruby said in answer to a person who asked her if I was able to cope with the varied demands of being a decorator, "Billy is small, but his sting is deep." I believe her remark amused her, because as a present for that newly redecorated apartment she sent me a chest of drawers covered in white leather stamped with dozens of gold bees and, back-to-back, dozens of my own initials, BB, in black.

One of Ruby's great amusements was to change her apartment at 277 Park Avenue practically every other year. It was not difficult to do at that time because of the low rents. You could decide to move in August and get something pretty good to move into by October. I know of at least five different apartments that she had there.

Her last apartment was an extraordinary tour de force. The living room had a very nice fireplace and three neat windows facing Park Avenue with a view of Sherry's which was very attractive. The owners of the apartment building had planned for the dining room to be part of the living room, but Ruby decided against it; instead, she had a long dining room table placed down the middle of the entrance hall, which was quite big. More often than not, when you went there a ravishing buffet was set up on the table, with a bar with all the liquor at one end and flowers everywhere. The kitchen was right off the hall, so everything was easily taken care of by Ruby's cook Minnie, the Indian princess. No one entertained more beautifully than she.

During the summer I lived in "The Acre of Love," a most charming gentleman called John Stewart, whose apartment was beautifully done in a very English style, also lived there, and he had something which was to me a wild innovation, but was soon to become accepted everywhere.

The first time I entered John's apartment I immediately noticed, to the right of the door, a grog tray on a trestle table all set up and ready for a guest to go and help himself. But there were *bottles* open, not decanters! There were also various kinds of glasses, different kinds of mineral water, and a nice biscuit box filled with delicious English biscuits. When you went in, he would say, "Do have a drink, which I think you should make yourself, and I'm not going to ask you about a refill. It's there when you want it." I think he got the idea from London, and it soon became quite normal to display the liquor bottles without being shamefaced about it. The thing about having decanters all of a sudden seemed to be piss-elegant, and you really saw what you were getting in the bottle that the liquor came in.

It was at the time of my first apartment that I was to have the great fortune of meeting two people who were to become lifelong friends: Beatrice Simpson and Baron Nicholas de Gunzburg. Both of these remarkable people really cared about how they lived and by what they were surrounded.

One day Mrs. Wood said that she wanted to talk to me about a very interesting situation that had come up through the sister of Chalmer's

Beatrice Simpson. (Portrait by Vera Somoff)

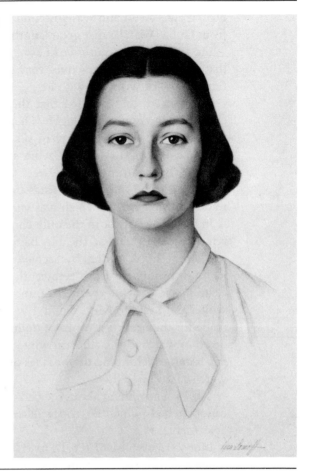

goddaughter, Esmee de Menocal. Beatrice, Esmee's sister, had recently married a Chicago man called Bill Simpson, and they had built a very elaborate house on Long Island. According to Ruby, the furnishing of the house had been almost completed, and she asked her husband for a present of the decoration of her bedroom, a small card room on the first floor, and a little breakfast room so she could be perfectly happy living there. Ruby wanted to entrust the job to me and, of course, I agreed.

The day came for Ruby and me to motor out to Locust Valley to see Beatrice Simpson and the house.

Beatrice greeted us with the utmost charm, something she has always had, beautiful manners, and great chic. She was dressed in a wonderful brown alpaca suit and was smoking a small, thin, matching-color cigar from Cuba. We talked at great length about what she wanted, not wanting to leave at all because we knew that here was going to be something that could be really attractive, very avant-garde possibly, and so much fun because of working with her.

We immediately decided that the little card room was to be done entirely in browns and beiges. There were to be two banquettes in a tobacco-colored silk, very plain silk taffeta curtains of the same color, and on the floor a couple of zebra skins, which at the time were very popular. Backgammon tables were to be set up for immediate use, and there were to be comfortable sofas and chairs. The tables and chairs were to be bleached wood, which was very new at the time.

In the breakfast room the only change was to be the addition of some remarkable curtains at the big bay window. Beatrice showed me an enchanting book written by Sacheverell Sitwell about plaster decoration in English houses of the eighteenth century. There was a picture of a ceiling that had intertwined, embossed plaster grapevines, white on white; and I said to Mrs. Wood, "What do you think of having curtains made for the breakfast room of unlined antique taffeta, heavily embroidered in white cord, white on white? The curtains would be like a wallpaper design, climbing up the sides of the window." I must say that they were sensational.

The principal thing about the bedroom was the purchase of a beautiful canopied bed, which Beatrice still sleeps in to this day in her New York apartment.

Not so many years later, Beatrice's brother, Dickie, married Angelica Weldon, who was the daughter of Julia Weldon, a cousin of Chalmers Wood. Mrs. Weldon entertained in the most enchanting way in her lovely house opposite the Morgan Library. She once gave a little ball the first year that Cecil Beaton, then totally unknown, was in America. Cecil decorated the entire first floor of her house in strips of pink and white paper ribbons.

I simply adored Mrs. Weldon, but she was a devil and one of the rudest women I've ever met. She had been born Julia Hoyt, and her brother, Lydig Hoyt, was one of the handsomest men in the world, although that cannot be said of her; in fact, she was very ugly. When Lydig married a great Philadelphia beauty who was later to become Julia Hoyt on the stage, Mrs. Weldon was not pleased at all because that was *her* birth name.

Julia Weldon's three daughters were known as the Three Graces because, luckily for all of them, they were just that, most remarkably attractive young women.

One knew when one was going there for a cup of tea or dinner that you were going to meet the most attractive people in New York in the world of art and literature. People wanted to go to her house because good parties were what she had. Like Alice Garrett, Julia collected attractive people, but the atmosphere was not at all the same. Julia was more intimate, in a funny way. She was a more intimate person than Alice.

I remember years later when Julia came to Ruby's exhibition called "Fantasy in Decoration," she looked like something not human. She wore a very chic hat beneath which peered those huge hideous eyes from which nothing escaped; she made some rather penetrating remark to Ruby about the exhibit. Ruby said to me later, "As much as I dislike her, I have to say that Julia Weldon is an intellectual, no phony, and extremely bright. I also have to say she is a very amusing guest." Ruby had to say that because occasionally, but not often, Julia spent the weekend with the Woods in the country.

In that year of 1935, a man of extreme elegance arrived in New York. His name was the Baron Nicholas de Gunzburg, and he had been exceedingly rich at one time. One of the reasons for his removal to New York was because he had spent most of his money. I met him very soon after he arrived, for which I give great thanks, because for all the time I knew him I had the greatest respect for him. I think that he had, in many ways, the best judgment about any kind of decoration, from a wastebasket to a palace, of anybody I've ever known. He was absolutely not capable of chichi, not of any kind of dishonesty. He had an immense knowledge, and until the time I met him plenty of money to execute his wishes, and, oddly enough, he was also a very hard worker. He got a job on *Harper's Bazaar* as one of the fashion editors, and a little while later was made editor-in-chief of *Town & Country*. That was a little bit too tough for Niki, and it lasted very briefly. Then came his move to *Vogue*, where he was indeed in the company of one of his best friends, Diana Vreeland.

Niki had taken an apartment in the Ritz Tower on the northwest corner of 57th and Park, exactly opposite Mrs. Wood's office. I do not know of anything that I have ever seen in my life that was more exciting. It had a very big, almost square drawing room painted white, and in it

Baron Nicholas de Gunzburg. (Horst)

one or two fantastic pieces of contemporary upholstered furniture, which were slightly Art Nouveau. One of the items which had been brought from Paris was a sofa of an enormous size, which had to be raised up to his high floor by cranes on the outside of the tower and taken in through a window.

Many years later, when he was to have a further reduction in money and was at the time working on *Vogue,* he decided he must sell some things, and one of them was the sofa; but there was just no apartment in New York that was big enough for it. However, one day to his great excitement, the miracle happened. Doris Duke had been there for cocktails and the subject of the sofa came up, and she said to him, "You can't move it, you don't want to store it, and if you really would like to sell it, I would like to buy it." It was agreed, and I remember it was the greatest excitement of the day when the sofa was hoisted down from the eighteenth floor to the street, as I looked with great amusement from my office window.

Another remarkable thing in Niki's Ritz Tower apartment was the decoration of his library. It was filled with beautiful French furniture, and the walls were covered in green baize and plastered with marvelous small prints in charming frames. The whole room was a mass of little pictures. It was the first time I had seen the contemporary use of hundreds of little pictures on the wall.

He was truly extraordinary, a wonderful combination of Russian, French, and South American blood, and he spoke Russian, French, and Spanish fluently. He read like a man starving. He read everything, and he read quickly, and he had without question the most brilliant sense of humor. He was a great athlete and skied like an angel, and he danced like no one else, and no woman ever looked better than when she was dancing in his arms.

"Brooke, have you done anything to this room?"

In the early 1930s when I lived in Baltimore, there was a woman, Mrs. Warrington Cottman, who had the most extraordinary taste, unsurpassed by anyone that I have ever met anyplace. She lived with her husband and one daughter, Mary Clare, who was my age, in a very unimportant house on the outskirts of Baltimore, and, completely on her own, she turned it into one of the most enchanting houses I've ever been in.

She had taken a dining room and a living room, which bordered on a hall, and converted them into one big room with six big windows, at either end of which was a beautiful Chippendale fireplace. When you entered the room, to the left of the fireplace were the dining table and chairs. This was the first time I ever saw a formal room with two uses — living room and dining room.

She had among her possessions a beautiful Aubusson rug that had seen its day, so she had it made into an enormous screen so that you didn't see the dining table instantly as you came into the room. The walls were covered with eighteenth-century French screens and the window curtains were a glorious crimson. The very English upholstered chairs were covered in chintz; there were lots of painted lacquer tables, and masses of flowers everywhere. It was one of the most extraordinary rooms I've ever seen.

Mrs. Charles Marshall. (Condé Nast)

One day, not long after I had been working for Mrs. Wood, she told me that she wanted me to go to Mrs. Charles Marshall's house as soon as I could. Mrs. Marshall was the niece of Mrs. Warrington Cottman, and, I admit, I could hardly wait to go there.

Mrs. Wood had just about completed a large, beautiful apartment for the Marshalls on East End Avenue, but I had never actually met them. A day later I had a charming telephone conversation with Mrs. Marshall, and she asked me to come to lunch the following Tuesday at one o'clock. I, of course, was perfectly delighted for several reasons, but, I have to confess, mainly because I wanted to see the apartment.

Off I went on that day, and there was no disappointment in the clarity and beauty that Ruby and Mrs. Marshall had created. Big rooms, high ceilings, and light colors made it a really glamorous, radiant place to live in, especially with the East River running along below. Mrs. Wood was pleased to death with the dining room because she had ordered the first of the glass and mirror mantels from Steuben Glass. The mantel was a heavy bolection molding backed with silver leaf and, although the design was entirely seventeenth century, it looked very modern. The rest of the dining-room furnishing was very simple: Biedermeier chairs, two cabinets, and four quite large panels of Chinese wallpaper with a white background and brilliantly colored flowers and birds.

There were eight of us that day at lunch. Mrs. Marshall had a wonderful square table that she had had especially made so that without any additional leaf two people could be comfortably seated on each opposite side. The eight of us who were there seemed to me to be a very glamorous group. There was an opera singer, an actor, and a very attractive journalist and his wife. It was all full of charm and also, in a way, very businesslike; the idea being that all of these people didn't have time to have lunch and just sit around; but they did have time to come and have a drink, lunch, and be off to work. That kind of lunch was unusual for me because it never happened in Baltimore, with one exception. Every now and then, Mrs. Spalding Lowe Jenkins, a marvelous woman, gave little luncheons like Mrs. Marshall's. Mrs. Jenkins was huge, and everyone called her "Porps," for porpoise.

I soon discovered that there was quite a special group of women whose time was valuable, and who did indeed love to give quiet, informal lunches in their houses. But I must say that it was quite a test for the New York decorators because not all of the rooms used for dining rooms were exactly brilliant by day. Controlled, businesslike lunches in contrast to long-drawn-out ones were one of the most noticeable differences between New York social life and that in other parts of the country.

Before I left the lunch party, Mrs. Marshall said she hoped I had a few minutes for her because she would like to show me through the apartment after the other guests had left. She also said she had a problem in the drawing room and wanted to talk to me about it.

The drawing room was a lovely white room with very simple Louis XVI furniture, and a considerable amount of other furniture upholstered in lovely soft colors; but there was one big gap in front of the wall to the right of the fireplace, and that was the problem. Mrs. Marshall felt that she needed more seating because this was really the only room that was big enough for a large party. Adjoining it was a much smaller library with beautiful pale eighteenth-century pine woodwork, and some small chairs upholstered in scarlet leather.

I immediately said that I thought there should be a French sofa for the room, and that it should not be a modern upholstered sofa. There was enough upholstery in the room. Mrs. Wood had not said one word to me about what she thought, but Mrs. Marshall said that she, herself, was very pleased by my suggestion. I told her that the only trouble about the sofa was that it would cost a fortune if she insisted upon an old one, but I explained that there were a number of firms in Paris that made beautiful copies of eighteenth-century sofas, and that is what I would do. It was also very obvious to me that it should be covered in the best possible medium blue velvet. This pleased her enormously and she said that she could hardly wait to tell Buddie, her husband, and she would let me know.

That meant that I had to get out and go to those firms that had representatives in New York and get photographs of the various types of sofas. It was one of the quickest little projects I ever had, because in a couple of days I had been to see them all and could go to her with photographs of the sofa and samples of velvet. She was perfectly willing not to see the actual sofa, and delighted to select it from the photographs because it was not a question of *the* comfortable sofa for the drawing room; instead, it was mainly to be beautiful and decorative and add to the glamour of the room. That little blue sofa was my first independent job, strictly on my own, when I first worked for Ruby Ross Wood.

As a result of this, I did work for Mrs. Marshall for quite a while, then tragedy came into her life and changed it enormously. Buddie Marshall died of a heart attack at their country place in Massachusetts. Brooke was left a widow in not the best of financial circumstances, and also she had the problem of being the poor relation of her husband's sister, Evelyn, Marshall Field's first wife. However, Brooke's enthusiasm for life, her charm, her niceness, and her intelligence saw her through, and she had a job on *House and Garden*.

I remember going to a lovely house for one of those lunches, not terribly long after Buddie Marshall had died, and Brooke was there, looking very attractive and very well, although it was known that the Marshalls had been an absolutely devoted couple. I was struck and somewhat flattered when Brooke took me aside after lunch and said, "I have something that I must tell you; I want you to know that I'm going to marry Vincent Astor. I'm sure you and the rest of the world know that his marriage with Minnie Cushing is no longer a success, and he has persuaded her to give him a divorce. This means that you will have to help me because we're not going to move from his apartment, as Minnie is going to move out."

Well, they were happily married, and Brooke moved into Vincent's apartment on Gracie Square. I interject a story here that happened in the apartment not long after Brooke and Vincent were married. They gave a very formal dinner party, and among the guests were Cole Porter and Clare Boothe Luce. After dinner Brooke announced that the ladies would retire and leave the gentlemen, who would join them later. Cole told me that Mrs. Luce got up from the table, and instead of leaving the room with the rest of the ladies, went over and sat down with Vincent Astor, where she remained. Brooke told me later that Clare did that all the time.

I had had quite a bit of experience in working for a husband or wife recently divorced who was staying in the same place, and changing the atmosphere for the new incumbent. Vincent Astor cared not one thing about decoration, although his apartment had been done very nicely. However, there was one big room, a library, which had been left alone, and in it were the contents of his yacht, the *Nourmahal*.

Brooke told me she said to him: "Vincent, we've got to fix this room up so it's decent. In the first place, the furniture is hideous, and secondly, it may be good, expensive furniture for a yacht, but it looks terrible on land. I'm going to do the room over. Do you want to discuss it?" He said, "Of course I don't want to discuss it. Go ahead."

They were going abroad and I had to have the room done while they were away, so I said to Brooke, "We must do one thing. I don't care what we do about color or anything else as long as he has a favorite chair in the place that he left it, or a favorite grog tray, so he does not have to learn the new geography of the room," and she agreed.

The day after they came back from abroad, Brooke called me and said, "Oh, we're so happy. Vincent loves the room, and I do want to see you and tell you an adorable story." So in a few days I saw her when I went to help her hang some pictures. She said, "I have to tell you something adorable about Vincent." Believe me, he was about as adorable as a tiger!

Brooke said, "When we got home from the ship, I took a lovely hot bath and Vincent put on his dressing gown and we went into the library. Vincent poured us a martini, and we spent a very nice evening in the new room."

From a room that had been almost all white, I had painted the walls a marvelous dark bottle green, and the furniture was covered in a fantastic Indian chintz in brilliant reds and all the different colors of the books.

"Well," said Brooke, smiling, "when we were just about ready to go to bed, Vincent said to me: 'Brooke, have you done anything to this room?' "

And that is not the only time that happened in my career. Some people just don't see!

Woody made it possible for me to materialize my dreams.

During the first days that I was in the offices of Ruby Ross Wood, which at that time were on 57th Street, Mrs. Wood had the top floor of the building, which was at best only several floors in height, and she had decorated her offices beautifully.

From the elevator you went into a nice square hall with some very nice pictures, and later on there were racks which contained samples of chintz. To the left there was a big room where her own desk was placed as it would have been in an ordinary sitting room. In fact, the whole room had that atmosphere and was not at all like a shop or store. She had painted the walls very, very pale blue and the sofas and chairs were slipcovered in navy blue cotton moire. This was the most lovely background for the profusion of flowers that were brought in from the country every morning and that lasted happily until Friday when she went back.

Mrs. Wood had initially sent me to various places where I was to make a list of appealing objects or materials that reflected my taste. One of them was a new wallpaper firm called Katzenbach and Warren. One of the owners, Bill Katzenbach, had been at Princeton when I was there, and was very active in the little theatre called "Theatre Intime." Consequently, the firm was one of the first places I went to. It had the atmosphere of success and the great thing of fresh strong color, quite different from any of the other wallpaper houses at the time. Even the salesmen looked different because they looked young and enthusiastic and proud of a product that was not banal.

When I arrived there I promptly sat down with my pad and pen to take the numbers of the outstanding ones to show Mrs. Wood when I took her on the rounds to see the samples of everything I had selected. That day I was waited upon by a young man whose enthusiasm was contagious, and he also had a great understanding of what was going on even though it was a new venture. I had such a pleasant time with this young man, whose name was Woodson Taulbee, and he told me that he, too, was just starting out at a new job.

Woodson had begun his life in the most dramatic way by being born of a woman from Kentucky who, when very young, had gone as an American teacher to Puerto Rico — not, mind you, San Juan, but into the remote mountains where it was very dangerous and very risky. His father, Colonel Miles Taulbee, was commander in chief of the American army in Puerto Rico. Mrs. Taulbee was extremely good-looking, very bold, and very strong. She had had several sons before Woody was born, and in the last months of her pregnancy she went back to Kentucky so that he could be born in America. Immediately after his birth, she took him back to Puerto Rico, so he really had a perfect right to say that he was born there. People would ask him where he was born, and he would always just automatically say San Juan. Mrs. Taulbee was a real American pioneer lady, and she worked very hard to give her boys the best possible advantages.

After a very modest education, mostly given him by his mother, Woody got a job at a newsstand in San Juan, which was practically on the docks where the cruise ships came in. One day, he was noticed by a passenger, who said that he thought it was a most dreadful waste of this young man, who was then about seventeen, and that he would certainly be glad to meet Woody's mother and discuss the possibility of taking Woody to America where he could have a proper education and grow up. So, very soon, off they went to California where he went to school.

Woody was one of those young men who was noticeably good-looking. He had olive skin, dark hair that was nearly black, and large violet-colored eyes. He could not help being conspicuous, although he really didn't want to be, but he had such extraordinary looks — the kind of looks that you couldn't hide under a bushel; they were just there. He also had a very engaging smile and made friends with people easily. He was a most successful salesman and was able to transfer his enthusiasm

149

Woody.

because of his knowledge and interest in what he was selling. It must be said at once, however, that he didn't like wallpaper at all. He thought that the only thing one should possibly have was whitewash. He loved the Spanish idea of a lovely whitewashed room with perhaps one great jar of different-colored flowers, but he certainly did not like pattern at all, and there he was in this blossoming, brand-new place selling the most vivid wallpaper which probably has ever been made in history.

A few weeks after I met him, I asked Mrs. Wood if I could have him to her apartment for a cocktail. She had been very attractive because she had told me when I went on my rounds that if I should meet anybody whom I thought that she should know, to please have them meet her.

I cannot say that their first encounter was the most successful one. I think that I have told the world that Ruby Wood was exceedingly frank, direct, not given to flattery, and very easily bored. Woody, who had very nice manners, could be quite brusque, and he always spoke the truth; there was not a possibility of any pretty talk with him because he didn't know how to do it. However, despite their differences in taste, their similarity in total honesty led to a mutual self-respect.

Woody was exactly the same with every single human being, cat or dog, boy or girl. He could not be anything but cruelly honest. He also had a splendid way of clamming up and not saying a word if he didn't want to. He was in many ways very antisocial and didn't like many people. He was mad about the theatre and the movies, where I think he spent as much time as he possibly could.

After we began seeing each other as very good friends, he realized that I had a pretty good time reading, so that diversion was added to his others and he became a great reader. He never minded being alone. In fact, I think he preferred his own company to that of almost anybody else. He dressed with beautiful style, rather conventionally, but there was always something about him that looked entirely different from anybody else, which was perhaps the simplicity of his remarkable physical being.

I, on the other hand, loved clothes, although I know I did not inherit the extreme passion for them that my father had had. It is true that he exposed me to the great luxury of beautiful tailoring, but he spoiled me for his own pleasure. My father decided what I should wear, and I didn't really care because he had this extraordinary taste.

My first tails were done for me by his tailor, Mr. Oldham. Later, a very distinguished English tailor, Mr. Barnes, whom my father practically kept in business, had the honor of making the most beautiful tails for me, and, I will say, the best I've ever seen. I wore them until they were almost in tatters due to my active life doing the Charleston and dancing every single night that I possibly could. I had them reproduced by the same firm years later, but the men who had made them were no longer there and the tails were just not the same.

When I was working, I had a natural interest in women's clothes only to the extent that they were going to be worn in the rooms that I was working on. Although I have not the remotest idea about the design of women's clothes, I know that I like them to be very simple, becoming, and lovely to the touch.

Billy's various garments made from Mr. Schantz's blue flannel.

Not long after Woody and I became friends, I went to get a couple of things from Wetzel's, which at that time had moved to Saks Fifth Avenue. It was soon after my mother had died, and I had been left a little money. Mr. Schantz, my man at Wetzel's and just about the nicest man who ever lived, always took a great interest in me. He was always smiling, and he couldn't get over my terrible extravagances, nor could he get over the fact that I really did know what I was talking about in regard to the design of a coat or a pair of pants.

Mr. Schantz said to me, "I want to show you something that will be the most wonderful thing for you. Just take a look at this navy blue flannel. It is very thin, completely washable, absolutely wrinkle-proof, and I'd like to have something made for you with it." I said, "Yes! How about some bathing trunks?" "Well," said he, "it hadn't occurred to me that that's what it would be, but I guess there isn't any reason why it couldn't be done." I said, "Well, I want the bathing trunks, a blazer, a couple of pullover shirts, and several pairs of trousers. I can mix them up with sweaters and other blazers, and I'll be set."

Mr. Schantz said, "There's not any question about that, but I think before we do this, you'd better let me find out what the cost is going to be." I said, "Never mind." I was determined to do it. The estimates were given, and I did it. I never had a moment when I felt quite so extravagant about clothes nor have I ever had a happier time. They lasted forever. None of them faded, not one bit of shrinkage occurred anywhere, and they just felt so marvelously comfortable. I wore them all the time in all the summer places I went.

Woody had one enormous asset that appealed to my sister when she met him, and it was the fact that he was an incredible dancer, one of the best, and all of the girls wanted to dance with him. My sister died over him. Among other things he did was a perfectly killing imitation of a wildly successful dancer of the time called Eleanor Powell, known as "Ding." It brought the house down every time.

Fortunately for me, my brother-in-law and sister liked him very much from the start, and they always wanted him to come and stay with them in Maryland when I was there.

Woody saw me as a faithful friend all through the war. I was stationed in Washington at the Walter Reed Hospital, my first post after basic training, and he did the heroic thing of traveling, which was then agony, every other weekend from New York to Washington. At that time I had the exalted rank of private first class. I really was literally nothing more than a hospital orderly. Walter Reed Hospital was a most fascinating place to be because it was a general hospital, and the head of everything to do with the Medical Corps in the army.

Woody was unable to go into the army because he had had a frightful automobile accident that totally incapacitated one of his lungs when he was a young man in Puerto Rico. He would come down from New York on the Friday afternoon of every other weekend when I was on leave until his war work sent him to Florida. You can imagine the nerve and excitement that I had when I would telephone the Mayflower Hotel desk and reserve a room and bath for myself for the following weekend, Private First Class William Baldwin. It was the most wonderful fun because I saw so many people I knew, one of whom was Horst, who was stationed at Camp Belvoir in the Camouflage Corps, where he belonged. Nobody will ever explain to me why I was in the Medical

Corps. I was not, nor have I ever been, neurotic; pills absolutely bored me to death, and I didn't know one thing about the Medical Corps.

Woody and I did not always meet in Washington. There were many weekends in Maryland where we stayed with my sister and her husband. It seemed to me to be a little fairer for Woody not to do all the traveling; however, I only went to New York for one weekend, and that was devoted to Ruby Ross Wood, even though I was visiting Woody. Mrs. Wood had a big cocktail party for me on that Saturday afternoon, and I saw many, many people that I hadn't seen, those who had been left behind in New York.

Woody stayed at Katzenbach and Warren for a number of years, doing very well, but he was not very happy because he didn't like what he was selling. He had wonderful taste, and that was evident in his tiny apartment, which we did at no cost because he had no money whatsoever.

I was living in my Sutton Place apartment with its two rooms which everybody seemed to like so much. Everyone wanted to live in that one row of houses on Sutton Place because they were amazingly inexpensive, beautifully run, and filled with charming people.

Woody had to find an apartment, and that meant nothing compared to what it would mean today. There really were plenty of choices. Luckily, he decided that he only wanted one room, not even a railroad two-room apartment like my own. I asked the manager of that block of houses what he had, and he showed me two one-room apartments, so I immediately took Woody around, and he was crazy about one, and signed a lease.

I remember writing an article for *Vogue* about trends in decoration which illustrated that apartment of Woodson Taulbee's. It was a square room with a bed alcove, a small fireplace, and two tall windows looking onto Sutton Place. I told him that I thought he simply had to have a wallpaper, and he said that was all right as long as there were no flowers on it, because he could not live in a room with flowered walls. We had the room papered in a pale gray and white striped wallpaper, and the curtains were in cotton of exactly the same gray and white stripe as the wallpaper design. The daybed was upholstered in it, and the floor was covered in wall-to-wall neutral carpet. I approve so much of smaller areas being done in wall-to-wall carpeting because I think it's not only good looking, but it's quieter as far as sound goes.

In my *Vogue* article I mentioned that his room had harlequin chairs. These were four pale wood ballroom chairs, which are seen at receptions and rented for the occasion. I had a different brilliant-colored pad made for each chair seat: red, yellow, blue, and green. The result was very attractive.

By that time I had redone my apartment. The walls were painted a light clean gray, and the curtains were cotton taffeta in the same matching pale gray. A big sofa and two comfortable chairs were covered in heavy, gray raw silk, and there were two little chairs, Louis XV, with cane seats and backs. The pads for the two French chairs I had covered in brown velveteen. I always said that the room looked like a man in a gray flannel suit who was wearing suede shoes.

Some years after I had met Woody, I resumed my interest in the Island of Nantucket. It had been so happy for me as a young boy, and there was another reason besides: my cousin, Miss Rita Robinson, was nearing eighty, and she liked to think of herself as my guardian, something for which I have always been thankful.

Every summer when I would stay with her, she would always say, "Now, I want you to ask somebody to come and visit you. At my age, I will not be able to go to the beach with you all day. I want you to go, but I'd be very sad if I thought you were there all alone."

Well, I was indeed fortunate because I didn't know whether Woody would like Nantucket or not, but he did. It must be clearly understood that he was a man of very definite tastes. I saw very little gray in Woody. He was all very black and all very white, all very loving and all very hating.

We had three or four marvelous holidays on Nantucket staying with my cousin Rita. We bicycled and beachcombed all over the island. That's what Woody really wanted to do — nothing. Poor Woody, all he could think of was retiring. He was a man who hated to work; his inclination would be to get up in the morning, maybe brush his teeth, walk out the door on the first floor, and sit down for the rest of the day, as you see so many people do in New Orleans. When I was working there I thought of Woody all the time. It was quite true that while in New Orleans, on my way to work I'd see some cadaver sitting down, and on the way back at five, he would still be there. That is exactly what Woody would have been perfectly happy doing. But in spite of that inclination, he worked as hard as anybody I've ever known in my life.

Woody and I were the best of friends in spite of the fact that our tastes varied enormously. He was really antisocial. I have always been the most gregarious person I have ever known, and I was delighted to go out

Billy on the beach in Nantucket.

every night, either to the theatre or to a dinner party. I cut out bridge almost as soon as I got to New York because I simply did not have time to play enough to become any good.

Woody would look at me in wonderment when he would ask, "What are you going to do tonight?" and I would say, "Oh, I'm going to the So-and-So's," and very often he would not even answer because he wasn't interested and he didn't care. He didn't go out, because he liked to stay at home, but we did have a few equally devoted friends.

There were two men who came into my life quite soon after I arrived in New York, and for which to this day I thank God. I had been invited to lunch at the Colony restaurant one spring day by Marian Hall, who, with her partner, Diane Tate, were among the tops in decorating. At that luncheon were two gentlemen whom I had never met: Stark Young, the drama critic, and William McKnight Bowman, a very successful and talented architect. Stark was delighted to seize upon me as a wonderful addition to the southern colony in New York, and Bowman looked so much like the Duke of Windsor that he was always called "Wales."

These two men shared connecting apartments filled with fascinating furniture, mostly Italian. In Stark's living room were bookcases filled with books bound in vellum. The books were charming because of what Stark did to them. He constantly acquired vellum-bound books with blank pages, i.e., the pages of the books were naked, blank pages and he would then affix to them whatever appealed to him. It could be Latin

Stark Young and Billy, the summer Mr. Young translated The Seagull.

poetry, photographs, printed material, or he might write in them. He really made his own books, a very personal library indeed.

For weekends they had quite an old house in Connecticut, which had plank board floors, and whitewashed walls upon which were hung very dark Italian paintings. It was furnished with simple country furniture, and all of the upholstered furniture was covered in monk's cloth. There was a marvelous garden taken care of by both of these remarkable men. Every room was filled with glorious flower arrangements that were entirely done by Wales.

I shall never forget the summer when Stark was translating *The Seagull,* which was to be produced late the following winter with Alfred Lunt and Lynn Fontanne. On many hot summer weekends he would read his translation, page by page, to Woody and me as we relaxed on a white fox rug under an apple tree.

Staying with Stark and Wales in their country house was certainly the most rewarding experience, and not least of it was the fact that nowhere have I ever had such good food. There was a perfectly good reason for this. Stark was a violent lover of everything Italian and also a violent lover of anything to eat. He managed to produce the most extraordinary southern food, all cooked by himself and combined with Italian recipes; you couldn't beat it. He was an incredible host, and during the summer many distinguished people visited him.

The grounds of the house fell sharply from a terrace, which had no railing, but the barrier was indicated by pots of blooming flowers. Among his annual visitors were Igor Stravinsky and his wife, and one of the things that enchanted Igor about going to Stark's for the weekend was that he could hardly wait until after every meal to go to the edge of the terrace and piss over the precipice.

Stark's friends were devoted to him, not because of the fashionable celebrity thing, but because of his wisdom, kindness, and wit. One of his great admirers was Mrs. William Adams Delano, the wife of the great architect Billy Delano; although I always thought she was even more fond of Wales. I used to go to Mrs. Delano's for lunch at her lovely house in Murray Hill. Mr. Delano was never there, she was always so vague, and the food was inedible, but when Stark and Wales were there the conversation was riveting.

One winter, my Aunt Lela died in her lovely house on the Eastern Shore of Maryland. Her estate, which she had no control over because of a will made by my grandfather to avoid inheritance taxes, was divided among many heirs, and I was left a small share. I wasn't sure what I was going to do with it, but I knew it was waiting for me in the bank when I wanted it.

Several weeks before the Easter holiday, I asked Woody if he would like to go to Bermuda. He said that he would adore to go because he loved islands and had never been there. I had decided that the weather would be just right at that time of year, so down we went.

We stayed in the town of Hamilton where we met a great many attractive people in a few pretty houses, and it was then that I discovered that two healthy men were fairly desirable in that kind of community. Woody's hair was beginning to get a little gray at this time, but that only made him look even more interesting; eventually he had prematurely white hair like his mother's.

At dinner one night, we met an extremely attractive woman called Jean Cookson, who was the best real estate lady on the island, and a

"*Little Bartlett.*"

couple of days later when we were cycling out to Southampton Parish (there were no automobiles allowed on the island and no traffic excepting bicycles and horses), as we turned a corner I said, "God! Look, Woody." There, sitting next to the road, was the most enchanting long sliver of a small house. When I got closer, I saw that the house was empty and it looked as if nothing had been done to it. It was not exactly a ruin, nor did it seem neglected; it looked rather as though it had been completely forgotten and ignored, and I was practically bowled over when I saw on one of the little gateposts a small board upon which was printed in faded, washed-out letters, "Little Bartlett." My mother had been born a Bartlett and I was absolutely insane with joy.

It seemed to take forever to bicycle to the Cambridge Beaches Hotel where we were to have lunch, and I immediately telephoned Mrs. Cookson's office and was told she was out, but that they thought they could find her. I couldn't wait and called back again in about fifteen minutes, and luckily she had just stepped in. When I described what I had seen, she roared with laughter and said, "Must you have a ruin?" But she knew the person who represented the estate and she said she could find him within twenty-four hours, but at the moment he was on the train between Hamilton and Cambridge Beaches.

The next day she called to tell me that the house was for sale. I was trembling that the price might be too high, but it was not. The price was exactly what I had thought and hoped it would be — one thousand pounds.

Well, we got the house and we began the great excitement of planning the restoration and decoration of it. It was nothing but a shell and there was no plumbing of any kind and no water tank. But it needed so little in a way because we didn't want any embellishment. The house was on the side of a bank where wild freesias grew and looked onto a bay across glorious water out to islands, and then behind it rose the high ascent to Gibb's Lighthouse.

From the level of the road, you walked through the front door into a little hall with a staircase going down one flight. To the right of the landing was quite a big square room where there was the possibility of cutting out one corner and making a nice square bathroom. The room was plenty big enough to have two beds in it, which were to be a pale pine wood like most of the furniture that I had planned for the house. The walls were to be whitewashed, and there would be no curtains because there were very pretty shutters. Opposite the beds I wanted a comfortable sofa and chairs like a sitting room.

Across the hall there was another room almost exactly the same size, which was to be the dining and living room. Off it was an extension, which we would use as the kitchen, and it had an exterior staircase going down directly to a terrace and the water.

The lowest floor consisted of a small room, which was possible to use as a double guest room with a very small bath, and another section, which could be used for the water tank that, as I remember, was going to hold thirty thousand gallons.

The colors were to be beige and white everywhere, because of the many, many curtainless windows that made the blue from the sea and sky become a color of the rooms inside. All of the material to be used for coverings was a heavy homespunny cotton and linen, and there were to be no carpets or rugs.

Much could have happened after we moved in, but alas, we never did move in because England went to war and everything that had to be shipped was subject to torpedoes. It was too impractical, so the furniture stayed on the dock in New York, and I sold the house.

I think it was the greatest blow that Woody had in his mature life. He had said, "We will never bore each other. You can read if you feel like reading, and I can run the house and do nothing." I certainly agreed that he could run the house. Also, my thumb is absolutely black, and Woody's was emerald green. If he touched a plant, he got the biggest gardenia or whatever it was, so he was to have done the development of the garden, and we would have been surrounded by more and more freesias.

I think we could have swung it, although you never can tell about something like that until you try it. However, I really did realize that I was not finished with my career and that a great deal of work with Mrs. Wood after the war was just about to begin.

But to Woody's career. As is the case with so many firms, success does not always improve the quality, and Katzenbach and Warren got enormous and very commercial. Woody had the opportunity to leave them and to be the head of the showroom of a firm called Pippin Papers. A large amount of the backing for this firm came from Pippin's friend, Lincoln Kirstein. Sad to relate, there was never a very happy understanding between Woodson and Kirstein, but fortunately the result of it was that Woody was able to start his own business, Woodson Wallpapers.

From then on Woody flowered like a beautiful rose. He was at last in complete charge, and the instant production of perfect matching wallpapers and fabrics came into being. It is quite true that in the nineteenth century, particularly in France, this was much in vogue, but it had not been done extensively in America. So here was the gate about to be opened, and Woody opened it.

It was a success, and the real reason was because of the trouble Woody took. There had been a firm or two that produced so-called matching wallpapers and fabrics that didn't match at all. They were just not the same color, and sometimes didn't even print the same way and were impossible to use. Having seen a few rooms that had been done with them, I can certainly say that nothing was more unattractive. But all of a sudden, the decorating world could see that Woody's things were really matched.

His firm made an immense success for Woody. In the beginning, he did produce some wallpapers he did not approve of, but later that was never the case. With only one lung, he himself carried bundles of wallpaper to the post office to be shipped out the day of the order. That was the kind of thing he did. His integrity wouldn't let him do anything else, and he knew a lot about integrity.

Woodson Taulbee's photograph, taken by Billy.

We had a fascinating mutual friend at this time, a man called Alan Porter, who was at the Museum of Modern Art. He had an extremely high reputation in the art world, and was the head of the Museum of Modern Art Film Library. He was color-blind, and he always used to say, "If you want to know what I see, go to the Metropolitan and look at the Ingres nude all in gray."

I had met him years before when I came to New York from Princeton on one of my many jaunts. He was very amusing, very eccentric, a marvelous dancer, and lived on West 54th Street in a huge apartment that looked into the garden of the Museum of Modern Art. His apartment was known as "Versailles," and was on the second floor of a pretty grand late Victorian house. There was a very big front drawing room, an enormous library, and a corridor going back to bedrooms. The ground floor consisted of a large entrance hall with a low ceiling, and a big kitchen and pantry.

Even though Alan rented rooms in his apartment, he was able to maintain a sort of hermitlike quality. He really only liked people who amounted to something and had gained fame. Since he lived very close to the museum, he got home from work earlier than any of us. I spent a few weeks there when I was getting ready to move into a new apartment after the war, and when I got back from work he would already be ensconced in the library in a very comfortable though slightly shabby upholstered chair under a very small lamp, doing needlepoint. One of the things he did was a design of two nude gentlemen by Paul Cadmus. It was entirely in gray except for a scarlet background, which was the only color that he could see.

It is not surprising that he knew Greta Garbo. There were times when they ran special showings of her movies for her, and the result was that she and Alan had become really great friends. Sometimes Alan would say, "This afternoon Miss 'G' is coming to see me," (she never allowed him to call her anything but that) "and I would be so happy if I could have the library to myself." This did not inconvenience his boarders because each had a very adequate sitting room of his own.

The front bedroom was occupied by Woody because he had come back from his war duties and had no place to stay until he found an apartment of his own. He had volunteered for defense work and been sent to the Ream Hospital in Palm Beach, where he worked in the supply department. I was waiting for my apartment in Amster Yard to be finished.

Miss G. (Cecil Beaton photograph courtesy of Sotheby's London)

One day Alan was very generous to all of us because before Miss "G" left, she was presented to us. We were absolutely limp, and I did notice that she seemed to be interested in Woody.

That Christmas, soon after our presentation, I had planned to have Alan and Woody for Christmas lunch in my new Amster Yard apartment. I had a servant at the time who was a Frenchman and who treated me like a prince. He took care of my clothes, polished silver like nobody in the world, arranged flowers, cooked the most marvelous food, and kept a glass jar always filled with madeleines. He was wildly temperamental, thoroughly crazy, and very prone to tears; however, he was a wonderful character and he was in charge of me.

Alan called me the day before Christmas and said, "I want to ask you something. Suppose Garbo decides to come; may she?" I said, "Of course she may. It's not going to be much. We're going to have some caviar and plenty of champagne because I know that's what you all love, and I'll have some cold vodka because I know Miss 'G' loves it."

After a heavy snowfall, Christmas Day turned out to be bright and sunny. Woody arrived first, and it has to be admitted that he and I were both very excited about having Miss Garbo all to ourselves for lunch. Mrs. Wood had made me promise that I would telephone her in Long Island the minute that Garbo arrived and let her know what she did.

What she did was to come in and shake some of the snow off her feet in the little hall. Off the hall was the bedroom, and opposite the open door was a very big mirror, which reached to the ceiling. She went into the bedroom and made a dive at the mirror, throwing her hair forward and then back. She then took off her coat, and she was set for the day.

We had vodka and caviar, and lots of it. She was in a gale of a good humor, very happy, devoted to Alan, and obviously struck by Woodson Taulbee. Woody thought that she was pretty attractive too, and, needless to say, so did I. I telephoned Ruby and told her that all was well, that Garbo was there, and that she had made a little entrance with great charm and enthusiasm. Ruby said, "Oh, my darling Billy, I'm so glad. I was afraid she wouldn't appear, and I didn't want you to be disappointed on Christmas Day. Tell me more tomorrow."

There was not really an awful lot to tell because she was just natural and funny, but she did say one remarkable thing to me. This was at the time that she had a really warm feeling for George Schlee, and they had been spending quite a lot of time together on the Riviera. She said after our little bite of lunch, "You know I have to leave you now. He knows where I am, and I'd rather not be seen with you or anybody here because he is a gentleman, and it wouldn't be a good idea." Those were her words. Well, we had a very nice time, and even Alan was in heaven. So, off she went. Possibly a year later, or maybe sooner, something occurred that was extraordinarily significant because it was so unheard of — she asked Woody and me to her apartment for a drink.

In the meanwhile, I'd better be truthful and say that she had been to Alan Porter's apartment quite frequently. John Butler, the ballet dancer and choreographer, was living there. John and Woody had become great friends, and I was living in my Amster Yard apartment.

So, Garbo, and Porter and company, nice intimate friends, spent a lot of time together. Garbo was crazy about her ballet lessons from John Butler. Woody told me he couldn't bear it sometimes because he was made to dance with her. I wish I could say why Woody could not bear it, but that I cannot do! But nothing really could ever surprise me about Garbo. She was so strange and complicated and, in a way, heartbreaking, because you wanted to be a warm friend, but she simply wouldn't let you. I never heard one word from her when Woody died, and she had been crazy about him.

It was quite suitable that Woody always managed to live in the most attractive surroundings. The harlequin apartment lasted very happily for several years, and although very small, it suited his needs and he loved living in it. He was not an extravagant person. He adored good food, went to the best restaurants, spent a good deal of money on the best theatre seats, and was fantastically generous to his mother, who by this time was living very comfortably in Florida in a house that he had provided for her; but he never saw any reason to live in a large apartment.

So he moved into what I consider one of the most attractive apartments I've ever seen, and one of my great pets. It was one of those marvelous one-room apartments in New York, and the decoration of it was based entirely upon a beautiful Matisse drawing that I had bought for nothing from Kurt Valentine in 1965. The drawing was of two women sitting in front of a table on which there was an open book, and behind them there was the most magical black ink tree. I said to Woody that I thought the tree would make the most marvelous wallpaper as well as fabric. He was terribly excited by the idea and got to work. The result was a tour de force, and we covered the furniture in his apartment with it. It was such a wild success that Woody manufactured it through the entire color spectrum, from black and white to pale pink.

Quite soon after that, I went to see a Matisse exhibition at the Rosenberg Gallery and had a brilliant idea. I took Woody back with me to see

One of Billy's favorite apartments, the decoration of which was based on the Matisse drawing seen in the background. (Horst)

it and, in particular, a still life of anemones and lemons, and said, "What do you think about producing a wallpaper on a clear white paper with groups of anemones in their glorious reds and purples and, every now and then, a lemon?" Well, pretty soon that paper appeared with a shiny white background and became another triumph.

One of the most revolutionary moments that we had was when I told Tom Hoving that I would be glad to contribute to the decoration of one of the ballrooms for the Metropolitan Museum Anniversary Ball. It was to be the discotheque, where the fountain restaurant is, and I had decided to cover the walls with fabric and slipcover the chandeliers.

With great generosity, Woody said to me, "You can have any material in any design you want, and I will charge you only the cost." and I needed twelve hundred yards! At that moment I was crazy about the extraordinary Art Nouveau paintings of the Austrian painter Klimt, so I said, "Why not make a print based upon the marvelous patterns that you see in his work?" He did it, and I must say that it was very beautiful.

Woody took such trouble about everything, much more than almost anybody I know in the wholesale world. He couldn't possibly do a thing too often in order to get it to be what he thought was perfect. He was a wild perfectionist, in fact, about almost everything.

I had such a wonderful time with him because I was an active decorator and he had the best of taste. Many of the ideas I had were possible to execute only because of his knowledge of wallpaper and his judgment. We produced an exciting line of materials and papers. It was practically like having your own establishment and could not possibly have been done with any ordinary wallpaper house. He would do anything for me. Woody made it possible for me to materialize my dreams.

One of the charming things about him was that as he grew successful, he was to become more and more interested in his birthplace, San Juan. He went there by himself a couple of times and was enchanted by revisiting a lot of the places that he'd known as a very young man. One day he said, "I'm dying to have you go to San Juan with me," and I said, "I'd love to." Down we went and stayed at that fantastic hotel called El Convento.

Woody had really gone to San Juan on this trip to buy a house. At the foot of the El Convento property was a charming little street, and on it were four or five very small houses, and one of them appealed to him. The house he liked looked very small from the street, and like so many Latin houses, the façade had only one small window and a not-too-tall door. However, when we opened the door and walked in, we realized that it went on for miles in back and also that there was a very attractive patio overlooking the harbor. On the opposite side of the patio, the house rose four floors in the style of a loggia. Well, he bought the house and we began the fun of restoring it.

I have seldom known envy, but really had that feeling about his house. Enclosed by the walls of that house, I've never been happier. We used to sit on the terrace in great peace and quiet and look out over the harbor.

However, it was very hard on one's patience because nobody kept his word about anything. You could wait for two weeks for a plumber to come and fix a leak, or you would sit at home a whole day to keep a morning appointment you had with a man to put a screen in. It was endless, and there seemed to be no kind of responsibility.

The exterior staircase, which climbed the side of the house looking onto the patio, was a disadvantage, but an element of great beauty. It

The room in which Billy's pet possession hung before he gave it to Woody. (Richard Jeffery)

was a terrific climb, and when you got to the fourth floor you stepped into an enclosed loggia through which were two guest rooms and two baths.

Woody's bedroom and sitting room were downstairs on the ground floor, and he had been terribly lucky in grabbing enough black and white square marble tiles, which had originally come from Cuba, to cover it entirely.

While the house was being restored, I happened to see in an antique shop in New York some of those marvelous lacelike chairs and tables that were made in India at the time of Queen Victoria. It seemed to me that they were eminently suitable for the San Juan house, and that they could probably well have been brought to Puerto Rico by some merchant at that time. I had them painted white, and they looked clean, fresh, and lovely. Everything was covered in white linen; in fact, the dominant color everywhere was white.

I got so excited about the house that I let Woody have my pet possession, which was a large, eighteenth-century portrait of an English hound. It was so perfect in scale for the room that I just let it go out of my life. Not long after the house was finished, Woody became fatally ill. After a long and tragic fight against lung cancer, he died in 1974, and he, too, went out of my life.

CHAPTER FIFTEEN

The bedpan was my gun.

J ust before the war, my favorite restaurant by far was a tiny little place called the Newport, and it was run by a charming, intelligent Frenchman called Fred. It was almost impossible to get a table there because it was so popular, as the food was extremely good, the menu was very wise, and the atmosphere was attractive; and they had been very lucky in having the restaurant designed architecturally by William McKnight Bowman. He and Stark Young went there quite often, and we all preferred it, really, to the Colony, because it was more personal and less show-off.

Ruby Ross Wood gave a most extraordinary dinner party there in my honor the night before I was to go into the army. Everything about it was charming, except that poor Ruby had a different re- action. That night she had her usual martinis, which ordinarily made her laugh; this time, however, she got into a colossal crying jag and couldn't get out of it. She said, through her tears, "He's the only one whom I will really miss. Nobody else will care, but I will miss him."

Thank the Lord, the party was not too big. There were the Woods, Stark Young, Wales Bowman, Marian Hall, Diane Tate, and Woody. I was particularly happy that Marian was present, because she had been a friend in Baltimore before I came to New York. Woody was awful. He said to Ruby, "For Christ's sake, stop crying!" I must say that neither of them behaved too well.

The next morning at an early hour I was in a building at the corner of 57th Street and Lexington Avenue, ready to become a soldier. We marched down Lexington Avenue in a very informal array to Grand Central Station, where we were assembled with several other groups to be sent off to our war. I had a terrible hangover and sat down in a corner and felt sorry for myself. It was still quite early, around eight o'clock; by noon, I could see there was, at last, something going on. We, of course, were to be sent off, but had not the slightest idea where we were going.

We got onto a train, and I discovered that my companions, who were to make up the company I was to be in, were very young men, mostly Greek, from undertaking establishments or restaurants in Elizabeth, New Jersey. One young man asked me what I did, and I told him I was a designer. He said, "You know, it's a funny thing, but I've heard of a couple of people who were designers, and they were sent into the Medical Corps." That made sense to me, because I thought maybe the army thought that a designer would have a sense of line, which might be connected with medical charts, et cetera.

Down we went into a pitch-dark car, which had a few electric lights on because the curtains were drawn, and soon we left the station. Well, in spite of everything, there was something about it that wasn't altogether too depressing. Most of those kids had decided to be in a good humor. The one point that was a shocker to me was the fact that I was almost twenty years older than anyone else who had been conscripted. They changed the age about two days after I had been inducted on October 15, 1942, in New York City, but it was too late for me.

The kids were from nineteen up to twenty-five, and I was thirty-nine. I didn't have one word in common with any of those boys, except that some of them were very agreeable, and some were very nice. There were also one or two demons. During my intimate moments on that train, the first of many, I realized that most of those boys had had no advantages. In fact, I recognized two boys who actually had been unloading bricks from the back of trucks at the Pierre Hotel, where I had been working on the decoration of the dining room. Almost right away, one of them said to me, "There's something different about you. I know those shoes were made to order. I can tell you that."

On the train I had a nice upper berth, perfectly comfortable and clean. There was not one soul to speak to, and I found that the two boys I was with could not read or write. I wrote two passionate love letters to their girlfriends for them. They mailed them the next day and said, "Jesus, Bill, we'll never forget what you've done for us."

It seemed to take hours and hours before we finally arrived at our destination, and it was getting dark. I had already had a strong warning about my future. We had had to fill out many pieces of paper, and I noticed on three of them the symbol of caduceus, which is the insignia of the Medical Corps.

I couldn't possibly believe that that's what had happened — to be drafted into the Medical Corps when I was the age I was. I had had very little illness in my life, except all the regular ones like chickenpox and measles. I had never had a knife anywhere inside of me, and I never had had any days of absence due to illness in school, college, or work. So I really was not terribly well versed in the subject of medicine.

We got out of the train about dusk and were divided into groups. It was then early winter, and it was extremely cold, and we had arrived at Camp Dix, New Jersey, which seemed to me to be the most terrible, frightening place that I'd ever been. Castrated by the memory of my dinner party the night before, I was faced with a charming item at Camp Dix that night. I was assigned to the duty of dishwashing, an experience that I cannot call particularly appetizing. Some of the participants were perfectly nice, but some of them were absolute beasts.

The following morning we left Camp Dix and went to Camp Pickett, Virginia, a bleakness that I can't describe. Its dreariness was caused by the fact that there was no grass. The camp had not been completed, and the buildings were standing in mud. One of the things that we were to do, almost the following day, was something called "sod duty," which meant we were to cover the ground of the camp with squares of sod in order to make it possible to walk.

When I had had my army clothes thrown at me the night before, at Camp Dix, an extraordinary miracle occurred. I wear a 5D shoe, and somehow I found a pair of shoes that were really very comfortable. I'm sure this made all the difference to my life, because the army shoes were not only comfortable, but a great protection against many of our as-signed duties, like scrubbing the floors in hospitals.

The next morning, we lined up for reveille in pitch-black, freezing cold, and howling wind. Added to the bleakness of it all, there was a slight snowfall, and visibility was almost impossible. We marched from reveille to the mess hall, where we had a very good black, black coffee. I have to say that I made an exception to my life by drinking two cups instead of one. During the brief time that we were there, the entire company decided to go to the bathroom. It was quite a performance, and a very difficult one because there weren't enough toilets.

The second job I had after putting down sod in the winter weather was latrine duty. This meant that every other morning, after being excused from our first class, a young man and I were in charge of turning the john into a place of immaculacy, after thirty boys had used it. It is impossible to describe what the latrines looked like before we cleaned them. There were a couple of boys who, before being inducted into the army, had never used toilet paper.

Well, various duties were assigned to various people, and a great many of us took general instructions and sat through lectures in the great assembly hall, where the emphasis was not at all on the war and the army, but on peace and the life of a hospital.

In the army there are classifications for hospitals, and one is a general hospital. As soon as I got my feet on the ground, I worked until I nearly died of exhaustion. I wanted to prove to myself that I could qualify to be sent to the greatest of all general hospitals, Walter Reed in Washington. I was determined to be sent there because of my vanity, a torment that none of those poor boys had.

The basic training we were given consisted of a course that had been reduced to six weeks, instead of twelve. This was before the African campaign, so they did not need as much in the way of hospital rooms in this country for the return of the wounded as they thought; but they were preparing for the worst.

I had furloughs every other weekend, many of which I spent in Washington. Camp Pickett was only one hour from Washington, which is pretty close to Baltimore, so I was lucky. I simply didn't attempt to go to New York and didn't want to, because it was too strange. At least in Maryland I was with my family and very old friends. I didn't allow any sympathy.

I remember so well the first weekend I spent in Baltimore dressed in my khaki uniform, which was certainly not made by Wetzel, but I rather liked the hat. I couldn't believe it when I sat down on an upholstered chair in my sister's house. The boards we sat on in the army were indecent, and when I sat down, my sister said, "What's the matter?" I said, "I can't believe it. This chair feels like it's going to go through me."

During my basic training I had lost pounds, and I was starving. I did my best to eat, but the food was terrible, and the manners on either side

Billy in his khaki uniform.

of me and across were so repulsive that any appetite you might have had could not possibly survive.

There was nothing really wicked or evil about any of those boys, excepting for one or two bullies who are everywhere in the world. I remember one night after we had gotten back to the barracks from a night march and we were to take hot steam showers. Everybody was in a strange mood, and there was a very tough little man from someplace in New Jersey who screamed at the top of his lungs, "Baldwin reminds me of a movie actress." I said in a cold voice, "If you say 'Shirley Temple,' I'll slug you."

However, most of the boys were okay, and I helped them with things that were perfectly simple to me, but impossible for them — like writing. Across from my bed was another bed with a footlocker at the bottom of it. Very often, seated on the footlocker, shining his army boots, there was almost the biggest man I remember ever having seen. He had been an officer guarding the Lindbergh family, and the Lindbergh horror was still fairly fresh in everybody's mind. We became friends, and he and I used to lead the parade.

My sergeant was an extremely good-looking young man from Massachusetts. He had been a truck driver for a medical firm, and as he was stationed permanently as an instructor at Camp Pickett, he was furious, because he wanted to be overseas. He thought he was being a kind of slacker, and he couldn't bear the idea.

Very soon after I got to Camp Pickett, in fact that night, he said that he wanted to talk to me. He said, "Baldwin, sit down. You've got to help me. I know that you and I are not the same sort. You've had every advantage and I've had practically none, and I think that with your advantages you have the understanding that I need. So do you mind if I consult you if I have any trouble with any of these kids?" I told him that of course I didn't, and I did see him a lot, and often there was a problem with which I could help.

He picked me to be the model for all of the hand-to-hand combat demonstrations, because, as he said, "you are quite short." I was supposed to be a prisoner, and I used to want to die because he'd put me down on the floor and spend most of the time lying on top of me demonstrating various holds, and I just nearly went crazy, that's all! He didn't know that, nobody knew that, but it was terrible. He had a girl, and they used to write wild letters to each other. He was a wonderful American boy, and I wonder, I wonder, I wonder where he is now. I certainly would like to know.

I was at Camp Pickett that Christmas, and I will never forget the colossal assembly hall where the local Pickett ladies represented the Virgin Mary and the Holy Family in the most elaborate possible tableau. There was also a magnificent choir with two organs, and when "Silent Night" was sung, I could hardly hold my head up, I was so wet with tears. There was no point in going home because we had only a twenty-four-hour leave, and I decided to save that for another time.

I have to state very strongly that I made some friends at Camp Pickett, and I consider without a single doubt that the army was the best experience of my life. It made me realize that I wasn't all that hot myself, and there was something quite remarkable about those boys who were either illiterate or very cruel. They soon learned that you just couldn't be that way. The Medical Corps taught them about the elimination of pain and giving comfort, and exposed them to knowledge.

Basic training was going very well, and they seemed to think that we were a fairly bright class. Suddenly we were told that we were going away and that we would be told where in a couple of weeks. Naturally there was no indication of our destination, but as I had graduated at the top of my class, they said that it was very likely that in my next place I might be given the rank of sergeant.

Our departure day came, and off we went on another dark day in a very dark railroad car, and I realized fairly soon that we were going into a city which I knew must be Washington because it was so close to Camp Pickett.

When we arrived in Washington, it was night and a beautiful big bus took us out to Walter Reed. You can't imagine what we felt like when we saw those beautiful brick barracks. Our urinals, the baths, the show-ers, and our rooms seemed to be the height of luxury. You could close curtains at the windows, and I had a room with two other boys at the end of the long barracks, rather like the room that my sergeant friend had in Camp Pickett.

We had time to go to dinner and although it had gotten dark, it was within walking distance. That night, we had what tasted like "Newport food" in comparison to what we had eaten at Camp Pickett. The Med-ical Corps had everything that was the best. Furthermore, all the distin-guished people from Washington, the army, or anyplace in the world were patients at Walter Reed Hospital.

It was a perfectly beautiful place, although it had that terrible, depress-ing atmosphere which I think is the atmosphere of all hospitals, and I felt that the only way I was ever going to get out of it was by dying. I felt that way more often in the winter months when I was outside freez-ing as I swept the garden or washed windows, and I got to be very good at washing windows with a newspaper.

I had a very difficult time at Walter Reed because, here again, there were these kids, and they really were kids. I knew that there was a funny kind of jealousy about me, and they knew that I had been educated in a different way, but most of them were nice to me, although many were not. I had to practically kill myself to be nice to them, and it wasn't an easy atmosphere at all. They were literally of another generation.

We got up in the early morning and walked across the road to where we had breakfast, and then reported to the different classrooms for lectures. I had to learn about everything connected with medicine and the male human body, something I never thought I was going to have to do in the army but, in regard to that, my age helped me because I was able to concentrate on my studies much better than my compatriots.

Very often in the dark of early morning, as we marched to our assignments, we had to pass different wards housed in various buildings. One building, which we passed nearly every morning, had enormously high windows from which a brilliant light was always shining, and from behind those bright lights came the most terrible sounds and shrieks of madness, for that was where our Red Cross nurses who had been captured and tortured in the Philippines had been brought, with the hope that the Walter Reed staff might be able to restore their sanity.

However, in regard to our course of study, we had to learn everything about the surgical end of medicine, and I was in a constant state of almost tearful depression the whole time. I also discovered that I was not much at ease with blood; I could not give a hypodermic syringe because I didn't trust myself and knew I would be hurting someone. I used to always beg off with anything having to do with a needle, because I just couldn't do it. There were many simple necessary phases of nursing work that had to do with incisions, etc., and I was absolutely not any good because I fainted quite often. Still, I worked so hard that I was thought of as a very bright young man, but I was neither young nor bright. I was much too old, and I despised the whole business too much.

Despite that, I was classed, with the greatest honor, as a surgical technician. One morning as we lined up to go to class, the sergeant picked me and two others, and told us to come with him. We went straight to the operating room. The sergeant said to us, "You are to do nothing but watch. I don't want you to have any ideas, and I don't want you to say anything. You are only to witness this operation."

We got unmercifully close to the victim, and I couldn't believe what I saw. I didn't know there was that much blood on the face of the earth. The surgeon had become scarlet with it, and he was working very busily and rather quickly. I was appalled and grabbed on to the uniform of the sergeant I was with and said to him, "I cannot believe this. I have been studying male anatomy for weeks, but I can't recognize a thing in that man on the operating table." He said, "You're telling me, you silly son of a bitch. It's a female."

It was a cesarean operation. I got two steps from the edge of the operating table, fainted dead away, and was carried out.

The sergeant was naturally very impatient with me, but he said, "I'm sorry, I know you can't help it, and you may never get over it. Some don't. If you can possibly manage it, I think you should tell the commanding officer, but it would be smarter to wait and see if it happens again." Well, it was almost duplicated.

I began losing weight, and I became so nervous I could hardly get through anything. One weekend when I went home, my sister said to me, "What has happened to you?" I weighed much less than I did when I went into the army. She said, "Well, something's got to be done." I said, "There can't be anything done, because I have already suggested to my company commander, who's a sympathetic, nice man, that I be transferred to the Quartermaster Corps."

When I returned from leave, the major, my commander, said to me, "You will find that it is almost impossible to change from one branch of the army to another. God can't do that; but what you can do is get out. I'm going to recommend that you be gotten out of the army, because I think what you're doing will be no good and a waste of everything."

He was right, because the next day I was to give a lecture demonstrating three important bandages. I stood up and demonstrated all three bandages inaccurately. The major, who was horrified everytime he looked at my chart and saw my age, sent for me and said, "I'm afraid this is bad. What happened to you?" I said, "I haven't the slightest idea." Consequently, I received my honorable discharge on March 6, 1943, with the condition that I do defense work.

There were, of course, some extraordinary episodes during my time at Walter Reed. For a brief period I was transferred to the cancer ward. There was a very old man who had been there for a great many years, who was just slowly dying away. He had no pain, and was hardly conscious of his horrible disease. A nurse, not in her first youth, said, "I want you to come and help me give this man his bath." So off we went and approached the bed with basins, soap, and sheets. You didn't know what you were looking at because he was so ancient, so ill, and so pitiful. We had to change the sheets with him in the bed, and I thought that whatever she did, I would do the same. So I was on one side of the bed and she was on the other side, and she was doing it very quickly, I suppose just to get it over with. That poor man, I don't think he was even able to utter a sound; but suddenly she screamed, "Stop that! Do you know what you're doing? You're not tucking in the sheets — that's that man's skin!" That was the kind of thing that made me throw up.

Another of my gaffes occurred in the ward for soldiers in traction. Side-by-side in two beds were two very nice looking young boys who could hardly speak, and the nurse said to me, "Here are almost my two favorites, and they both have the Purple Heart." I said in the clearest voice imaginable, "How terrible. Will they get over it soon?" I'd never heard of the Purple Heart, and how in hell could I have heard of the Purple Heart, since this was just the beginning of the war and that decoration was first being given.

After being honorably discharged, my life was saved by my splendid brother-in-law, Charles Miller. I called him one night to ask if I could stay with him and my sister in Maryland until I found out what I was going to do. He said, "Come as soon as you want, and we'll come and get you in Washington. You can stay with us indefinitely."

When I got to my sister's house, my brother-in-law said to me, "Billy, fortunately I am in a position to give you a defense job — ironically enough, in your great-grandfather's foundry. Bartlett and Hayward is now a wildly successful defense plant, and I help run things there."

So, very soon I was living with my sister and her husband in their charming old house outside of Baltimore, and I was working at Bartlett and Hayward. My gratitude to them is never, ever going to be repaid now, because they're both dead and it is impossible.

One evening, my brother-in-law told me with a mournful face that they were reducing the personnel at Bartlett and Hayward, and I was going to be dropped. I knew that I had to do something connected with defense work, and didn't want to ask my sister to help me again.

At this time, I was beginning to have trouble with my lungs. I knew it would be impossible to go through another winter somewhere in the cold. I had done a great deal of work in Florida, and I knew many people there, so I telephoned to find out if I could get any kind of defense work there. The answer was yes, and so in a very short time I went down. I stayed with Mrs. Taulbee until I could find my own apartment.

I got a perfectly ridiculous job in the medical supply department of what had been the Breaker's Hotel but was then called the Ream Hospital. This was one of many hotels on the Florida coast that had been partially converted to hospitals in order to take care of the wounded from the African campaign, which was due at any moment. I say partially converted, because the hotels were not really completely converted, and it was a great scandal in many ways. For instance, the maternity ward in the Ream still had thick red velvet carpets on the floor. They had not removed them when the Breaker's Hotel was converted, and you never felt there was any real sanitation.

The floor above the maternity ward was where all the female patients were. All the cousins, sisters, nieces, and wives of the men in the army were there, and it was considered by some to be the most desirable floor in Florida. If you wanted to have a little adventure, you would take a buddy with you to one of the rooms where you knew a charming girl who was a patient. Usually you stood at the door and made conversation to yourself to keep your friend from being interrupted in his pleasure inside the room. That was done all the time, and I guess there must have been more pregnant women in Palm Beach that year than anyplace in the country.

I, however, had absolutely nothing to do with the patients. I was seldom, if ever, in the wards, because I had no reason to be. I was in charge of packing, shipping, and receiving medical supplies. It was hellish work because of the time element. They would say on Thursday that by Friday we would have to have all the aspirin shipped to Valley Forge, and it was the devil to get it out on time to make a train or plane. God only knows how much money it cost.

I spent seventeen months in Palm Beach and it was an amazingly strange place to be. In the past, I had done quite a bit of work there as a decorator, so I knew a great many people; but it was very peculiar because there was actually no feeling of social life nor any real feeling of war. Palm Beach was a rather pitiful, nasty neutrality of all kinds.

I had a wonderful friend, Mrs. Barclay Warburton, who had been born Minnie Wanamaker. Her brothers were responsible for Wanamaker's Department Store in Philadelphia and in New York. Mrs. Wood got her real beginning as a decorator when she headed the first department of decoration in a department store, called "Au Quatrieme," on the fourth floor of Wanamaker's–New York; and it was because of my association with Mrs. Wood that I happened to know Mrs. Warburton so very well.

Each Sunday, the Warburtons had ten soldiers out to their house to have a little fun. One day, one of those marvelous spring Palm Beach Sundays, Mrs. Warburton invited ten convalescing young soldiers, to be selected by me, to come to have tea and even sneak a drink. They were all in Palm Beach because of some physical disability, and I, of course, knew them all because of being at the Ream Hospital.

There was a young man of colossal height and amazing looks who had lost his ear. It had been sliced off in the war, and he wore a remarkably well done fake ear that clamped very easily onto the side of his head. He was on the way to Valley Forge, where all of the plastic surgery was being done for the army at that time.

Off we went to Mrs. Warburton's house, which was on Lake Worth, opposite the Everglades Club. A beautiful tea table was laid out in the sunshine, and the boys all sat around it having a pretty good time, considering. You really didn't know what might happen because of these boys who had been cooped up for so long, and here they were sitting around with these beautiful girls. Terrifying!

What happened that day could not have been expected by anyone. I was sitting in a little circle with the tea table in front of me. Next to me was Mrs. Warburton and opposite was the man with no ear. I think he had been sneaking a little drink or two at the bar, for suddenly he said in a very clear, loud voice, "Mrs. Warburton, this is the best time I've had since I left home." With that he took his ear off and placed it on the table. Poor Mrs. Warburton let out a scream and fainted dead away.

"Stop. Somewhere on the floor there is quite a large emerald."

In 1935, the summer that I went to New York to work for Ruby Ross Wood, I heard a rumor that she might open a winter office in Palm Beach. There was also a rumor that I would go down to Florida to live there and manage it for the winter months. This was a terrible blow to me, because I was living with the thought of being in New York with Mrs. Wood. That was why I had left Baltimore. However, I had to be sensible and think that she had a good reason if she were to direct my life in that way.

This business was to be owned by Ruby, Bob Dalton, and Major Barclay and Mrs. Warburton. Bob Dalton had an antiques shop at the corner of Madison Avenue and 53rd Street, where he was the first in this country to show pale, bleached nineteenth-century English furniture. The more I heard about it, the more fascinated I became, and the more terrified. The Warburtons had a daughter called Mary Brown who was very attractive and lived in a ravishing wing of their house, which was certainly the most romantic of all the houses of that romantic era. My fear was that, through some unreasonable or unfair incident, the slightest little quarrel with her could lose me my job.

The proposed venture got more complex and more difficult, and two months before I was to go to Palm Beach the whole thing fell through with a big crash. So, although I never lived in Palm Beach then, I was lucky because Mrs. Wood was very busy doing several houses there, and I gained a great deal of experience, and never really had to stay any longer than I would have if I were supervising the installation of an interior that we had designed in New York.

There was no place on earth at that time that was more luxurious, more decadent, more extravagant, more beautiful, or more comfortable than Palm Beach. The shops that lined Worth Avenue were the choice of the world in the way of women's clothes, men's clothes, jewelry, decorating shops, art galleries, and splendid and wildly expensive restaurants.

One of the most attractive things to do was to walk up and down Worth Avenue in the late, late morning. Nobody was up too early, but by noon that street was like a flower garden. The men and women walking up and down it were just the most beautiful things that ever were. They were more beautiful than "the beautiful people," and also marvelously dressed. One of the sights not to be missed was Gary Cooper walking up and down Worth Avenue. It just seemed that everybody who was wonderful looking was there.

Everyone knew each other, and it was like a great big club under the leadership of the Warburtons. Major Barclay Warburton was a great charmer who took no active part in anything, but Mrs. Warburton was, without question, one of the most elegant women I've ever seen. I apologize at once for using this word in connection with her, except she really was; and most of the people who use that word today wouldn't even recognize it. They don't know what they're talking about.

I used to say that Mrs. Warburton could sit in a chair for an hour and say nothing and have more charm than somebody who was sitting there talking her head off. Her taste in decoration was simply brilliant. Of course she had the great advantage of first choice of all the merchandise that was purchased by their representatives in Europe. Nancy Mc-Clelland, the great wallpaper expert, and Ruby Wood went to Europe together to buy for Wanamaker's. That duo ended in a row of jealousy, but they did buy extraordinary things, one being a palace in France, which was listed in the catalogue of that year for one million dollars. It was sold immediately and transported to Cleveland.

Mrs. Warburton, "Aunt Minnie" as she was affectionately called, was a little bit short and had coiffured gray hair and very prominent features. Her clothes were of the most brilliant possible colors — magenta, purple, and lilac — and she wore a lot of wonderful knitted things. Aunt Minnie was a great walker, which she did principally for her health, and

Mr. and Mrs. Barclay Warburton and their granddaughter, Mrs. William Gaynor, and their great-grandson, Vere Gaynor. (Condé Nast)

you would see her with her walking stick prancing up and down Worth Avenue just before teatime in the afternoon. She said hello to everybody she knew, which meant that she never stopped saying hello because she knew everybody and everybody knew her.

I think that the Warburton family represented more style and chic than any other family in America at that time. They were also amazing because they were blessed with looks, and one or two of them were even beauties, especially Mary Louise who married Gurney Munn. They made the most wonderful looking couple and had built a marvelous house in the Spanish style, designed by Addison Mizner, who was the great architect of Palm Beach at its best. I, myself, still think that on the totally artificial, manmade island of Palm Beach, the Spanish architecture of Mizner is eminently more suitable than the prissy little English Regency houses that have followed.

I'm sure that there's never been a Spanish-style house more beautiful than that of Harrison Williams. It was originally done as a very simple house surrounded by wonderful gardens and built smack on the ocean. Very near it was another Spanish house done for the Joshua Cosdens. He was an ex-carpenter from Baltimore who had struck it rich. Mrs. Cosden had beautiful taste and a remarkable house. Her house and the Williams house, both decorated by Syrie Maugham, were among the outstanding houses in Palm Beach until 1936.

Then the Wolcott Blairs built a Regency-style house that, to me, is just about the best house that was ever done in America. It was H-shaped, and the drawing room formed the crossbar of the H. From inside this arched glass room you looked to the west across the patio, pool, and lawn to Lake Worth; east, across the lawn and beach to the ocean. It was quite large, with very big spaces, highly practical, and Mrs. Wood's staff had the great distinction and pleasure of working with them on its decoration. The architect was an enchanting Swiss fellow called Maurice Fatio, and I remember so well that my beloved friend Cole Porter wrote a little song called "I Want to Live on Maurice Fatio's Patio." The house was a triumph, and even after all these years the brilliance of its architecture and decoration make it seem as though it were done today. Let there be no doubt about it: that house has a classic timelessness.

People entertained a great deal at home in Palm Beach. It was irresistible, if you had a beautifully lit patio and very good servants, not to have dinner parties with dancing afterwards in your own house. An equally popular way of entertaining, if you didn't have a staff, was to go to the Patio, which was really a nightclub. There were also two extraordinary clubs: the Everglades Club, which was devoted primarily to golf, and the Bath and Tennis Club, which was devoted to swimming. They were run in the most luxurious tradition; dining at either was under the best conditions and the food was marvelous. Everybody was smiling all the time. There seemed to be no possible idea of any limit to the amount of money that was in Palm Beach, and everyone was having a pretty good time, I must say that. It was a very superficial life indeed. But when you had the Gurney Munns, the Barclay Warburtons, and the entire Wanamaker clan, who were second to none in manners, the Harrison Williamses, and the young Francis Kellogs, you got a good start for charm and beauty.

At that time, in the Mizner era, there was a sort of king and queen of the resort, and they were the Edward Stotesburys of Philadelphia, who were no longer in their first youth. They had built a beautiful house designed by Addison Mizner, called "El Mirasol," in the north end, very near the Harrison Williams's; but, sad to say, it's been torn down like a great many others because it was impossible to keep up. Fortunately, the gate house remains as a little monument to the day of that imaginative and beautiful Spanish style and can be seen at the entrance to the grounds of the present house.

I remember a big reception at "El Mirasol" when I was visiting a man called Edward Riter. Mr. Riter had given me a schedule of all the parties I was to go to, and one of them was an afternoon reception at the Stotesburys'. The day came, bringing with it beautiful weather, and "El Mirasol" seemed to have more of a fairy-tale quality than ever. There were lots of people there dressed to the teeth and to vulgarity, but lots who weren't, as well. On the receiving line, Mrs. Stotesbury, with jewels blazing in the Florida sunlight, was looking dazzling. She was very handsome indeed. The butler was announcing us all by name because it was a very large party with lots of strangers, and I was so happy to find two great friends, Stark Young and Wales Bowman, who were in Palm Beach visiting some friends who knew the Stotesburys. Just as Stark, who was in front of me, stepped up to shake hands with Mrs. Stotesbury, she raised her hand as if she had the mark of the stigmata and said in the most perfect, softspoken manner, "Stop. Somewhere on the floor there is quite a large emerald."

There was instant silence, which was no mean feat considering the number of people present. A large stone had fallen from the setting of her ring. Her words were the signal for Bowman, Young, and Baldwin to crouch on the floor, being careful not to break the emerald, and scurry and beat around under her skirts. It was soon found. "We may begin," she said, and the party continued.

Many years later I had the occasion to meet her son Jimmy Cromwell, after his marriage to Doris Duke. Doris and Jimmy had had an extensive honeymoon around the world, and everywhere they went they had bought like lunatics. They had a beautiful big house in Somerville, New Jersey, and, as they had to have somebody arrange it all, they selected Mrs. Wood. This came about because she was an intimate friend of Mrs. James Duke, Doris's mother. In fact, Ruby always called her "Miss Nanny." They knew each other extremely well and had been friends since they were young girls in Georgia.

The moment came when Mrs. Wood and I were to motor out to Somerville for lunch and see the loot. It was a terribly cold day, and I don't know how many coats Mrs. Wood had on. I know she had two black fox furs and a veil, and she never stopped smoking. She looked like a little pullet in an oven with the steam coming out.

We finally got to the house, were ushered in, and Mrs. Wood was carried to the ladies' room to thaw out. Doris was her charming self: kind, thoughtful, intelligent, the best of all the rich girls. Jimmy was not in sight. Pretty soon Mrs. Wood had recovered enough to peel off several coats, and she appeared with a sweater under an overcoat and her furs.

The drawing room was filled with animal horns and stuffed heads of wild animals. Every trophy had been shot by Jimmy and he was very proud of them. When Ruby, with those glasses of hers and wearing her fox furs, entered the room, she really looked as if they had imported her. I could see she was in absolute agony wondering how in the world she was going to arrange those things. The house was already quite full of beautiful furniture and very well done, and Mrs. Wood hated it because it wasn't done by her, but of course, on account of her friendship with Mrs. Duke, that was not to interfere.

Presently there came into the room, to all intents and purposes, a naked man. He had the physique of a superb artist's model: young, virile, and beautiful. He also had the most incredible suntan, and was wearing what I can only describe as the briefest loincloth, which looked like a jock strap. This was noon of a February day with snow covering the windows!

I did think that Doris looked just a little befuddled. At that moment the butler said, "Will you have a cocktail?" and Mrs. Wood said, "I certainly will, please. I'd like a martini, and I'd like it with an olive."

"Oh, good for you," said Jimmy, who was then presented to us as Doris's husband. You could see that Doris was quite mad about him. You certainly could. Very soon, the butler announced lunch. Mrs. Wood sort of looked over her glasses, Jimmy turned a little bit to the right, and Doris motioned us to go on in. As we got to the dining room door,

Jimmy turned to Mrs. Wood and said, "Mrs. Wood, I think we should have another cocktail, don't you?" Said Ruby, slowly looking him up and down, and dropping her furs quite a bit, "Yes. I certainly do think we'd better have another cocktail."

We had a very nice lunch while the snow piled up, and Jimmy sat there with his body glistening. Doris adored him, Ruby was mesmerized, and for once I didn't have a thought in my head.

Mrs. Wood had worked in Palm Beach for quite a while, and she loved working there because she simply despised the sight of one snowflake. She was cold in the middle of August on Long Island. Ruby got to Palm Beach as fast as she could whenever she had been given a job decorating someone's house, and of course I went with her, and we had the most glorious possible time because there were terribly attractive architects from all over the world there at that time.

When the vogue for the Spanish architectural imaginings of Addison Mizner went out, one of the first great houses in the British Colonial style was designed for the "Jell-O queen," Mrs. Vietor, by Marion Wyeth and his young assistant Bill Johnson. The house was being finished when I arrived in the summer, and the decoration was to be installed that autumn for occupancy by the Vietors, who would arrive in their splendid private railroad car to spend the winter.

Mrs. Vietor had a series of houses that all ended in the word *wood*. There was "Cherry Wood." There was "Happy Wood." There were all kinds of "Wood." She had a perfectly nice husband and two children, but nothing appealed to her as much as liquor.

When the time came, Mrs. Vietor, her personal maid, her secretary, butler, cook, and I don't know how many others all went down to Palm Beach in the private car, arriving in the late afternoon at the new villa, which she had never seen. She had not seen even one piece of material that had been chosen for her. It was the first time that I ever realized that there was something called "carte blanche."

One of the glories of the house was a long gallery, and Mrs. Wood had found an incredible Victorian wallpaper for it. The paper went from the baseboards up to a height of ten feet, and on it were, meticulously painted, the most beautiful series of garden vines. It was the perfect background for the simple bamboo furniture Mrs. Wood had selected, and her use of bamboo was the first it had been done in Palm Beach; she had earlier caused a sensation by putting plain, unlined linen curtains made from bedsheets in the houses of the Spanish style.

The drawing room of the Vietor house had walls covered with a pale, celestial blue Chinese paper with white flowers, and it was done in very comfortable contemporary upholstered furniture, all slipcovered in white linen. A huge white rug covered the floor. This decoration was very simple, absolutely new, and it was 1935!

Ruby did many houses in Palm Beach, and all of them had something about them. They almost denied the vulgarity of the people who lived in them. If anybody wanted to have a house decorated, Ruby could do it with all the pizzazz that anyone could have wanted, and she tried so hard not to fall into using vulgar, expensive-looking materials and furniture.

After the war when I was discharged from my defense work, I decided to stay in Palm Beach and continue my career there. I thought that I couldn't go back to that filthy city of New York, and I had to write to Mrs. Wood and tell her of my decision not to return. It was a very hard thing to do, because all through the war she wrote faithfully to me twice a week.

I had been offered a job by Mrs. John Jessup, who was a great friend of hers and who made most of the curtains and slipcovers for her decorating jobs there. I had a terribly difficult evening with the Jessups trying to figure out a way to ask them if they would take me on. They were absolute angels, which they are, anyway, and I was given a job on the spot.

Polly Jessup's taste is simply beautiful and quite unlike mine which is much more conventional. Her extravagant insistence upon quality, and quality only, has not been equaled, and her success has been without limit, and every bit of it is deserved. She is the most enchanting woman, and does, without question, the most beautiful curtains of anybody in America, or Europe, for that matter. They are terribly expensive and are made in a great outdoors sort of loft in West Palm Beach. Her patience and attention to detail is something to experience. Most of her work today is done outside of Palm Beach, and she has done an enormous amount of work for the Ford family. To list the decorators of America without mentioning Polly Jessup is only murder, because she is one of the very best that we have ever had.

Mrs. Wood was wonderful in response to my decision and said, "Of course I understand. I have an assistant who is in no way taking your place, but I do understand how you feel, if you want everything to be as peaceful and as attractive as possible. The rush and tear of New York might be a little too much."

Palm Beach was like a city being reborn. Everything was booming. The war was over, people were opening up their houses, and some people were building them. The most successful new houses were designed in a simple Regency style by Marion Wyeth and Bill Johnson.

Everything really went very well in many ways for me. There were certainly a lot of attractive people, and I had a couple of houses to do for Mrs. Jessup. The people were very nice, and they were also very nice to me, and it seemed a very successful idea.

However, it was very successful for everybody but me, because I was, after all, seeing only one kind of person, which was very limiting. Our clients were very rich, very chic, very bright; and when most of them either bought or built a house in Palm Beach they wanted to have a little something of pizzazz, and they wanted it to be different, but they all wanted the same kind of different thing. It was bamboo till you could scream and, always, those palms inside. If you took the palms out of Palm Beach houses, the decoration would collapse. They all had the same sort of very pretty colors and very little good furniture. So, in order to be a successful decorator in Palm Beach, you had to do a certain definite kind of thing, and that was that.

It did not interest me very much, and also there were too many things that were not in Palm Beach. There was no theatre, no museum, no opera, no symphony; and most of the houses were not by any means the best, and there were too many little chichi, expensive houses, and I knew it was not for me.

I lived in a tiny apartment on the top floor of a little white clapboard building that had an outside staircase off a garden on Worth Avenue. I thought it would be fun to be a little different, so I planted the garden with enormous sunflowers. I don't think there were any other sunflowers in Palm Beach at that moment.

Because it was so hot there, I decided to paint the entire inside of the apartment a very dark green, like the leaf of a gardenia. In fact, I gave the painter a gardenia leaf and spit on it and said, "This is what I want the walls to look like, including the spit."

I was able to use a few bits and pieces of the furniture that I had planned for my Bermuda house. The bedroom had two beds made of pale wood and covered with an English chintz, which was white with small snowflakes staffed in gold, and it had about ten different colors of green in it, and a very pretty rug which was to have gone to Bermuda.

Everybody was crazy about my ridiculous, almost New York apartment, and it really did not look like Florida. It was not too formal and was just a little different from the other Palm Beach interiors. I was blessed with the most marvelous maid, Lula, whom Mrs. Jessup got for me, and I must admit I was very content living there, but I was not happy.

After eighteen months of working as a decorator in Palm Beach, I just couldn't stand it any longer, so I wrote to Mrs. Wood asking her if it were possible to consider taking me back. She had a boy working for her whom I, of course, wanted to kill every minute. In my letter I said that I understood Randall had taken my place, but I hoped that perhaps there might be room for both of us.

A couple of days later the telephone rang, and it was Mrs. Wood in her whisper. "It's Ruby, Billy."

"Yes, Mrs. Wood," I said.

"I just want to tell you that I have been waiting for that letter for quite a while."

"Well," said I, "I know one thing, Mrs. Wood. It's not going to be the easiest thing in the world to find me an apartment."

She said, "It is, because I'm going to give you a much bigger salary. I'm going to investigate this thing about your past salary with Chalmers, and I'm afraid that I'm going to be embarrassed by how small it was. So I hope you will come back, and we will discuss it."

During this time I had become very friendly with a man called Albert Kornfeld, who was the brilliant editor of *House and Garden,* and before I could leave Palm Beach he called and offered me the job of decorating editor for *House and Garden.* He told me he thought I would be wasted in Ruby's office, and that Ruby would be very sympathetic because she, herself, had begun her career writing under the name of Ruby Ross Goodnow, and she had also worked on the *Delineator.*

I called Ruby to tell her the news, and she said to me, "Are you saying that you've reached the point in your career where you don't want to do any more creative work? Do you want to just be a critic of other decorators' work?"

Of course that is what I did not want to be. I wanted to be a decorator more than anything, and a decorator in New York.

She continued before I could answer, "Don't forget that you're talking to somebody who knows all about the magazine world, and I know that the atmosphere in those offices is almost entirely politics, the bitchery is beyond belief, and those women will be out to kill you. They're all going to hate you for one thing."

Ruby was relentless. She pointed out that, instead of having my own lovely brown office on 57th Street to which I could probably even walk to work when I found my apartment, I would be working in Albert Kornfeld's offices, which were hideously ugly.

"I'm telling you that I think it would be a ghastly mistake. The war caused you to be away from New York. *Only.* I don't think you've lost anything, and I hope you're going to send me photographs of the work you've been doing." Then, after a long pause, she added, "And certainly you'll come back just as soon as you can."

That was the end of our communication about my career, and I went home to New York and to Ruby.

"I'd rather eat a delicious meal on a tin dish than a dreadful one on a rare plate."

It was wonderful to be back in New York because of my work, my friends, and the prospect of moving into a new apartment. I had heard a rumor that James Amster had bought three houses on 49th Street in Turtle Bay and was turning them into super-deluxe apartments. That old boast again. I had admired Jimmy's shop very much and had bought quite a bit there to supplement the work I'd been doing before the war. The shop was on lower Lexington Avenue in a little private house that was painted black and white, and had enormous style and fascinating objects of all kinds.

So I telephoned him and said, "See here, I'm coming back to work for Ruby, and I don't know whether you like the idea or not, but if it's true about your apartment project, I've just got to have one, and I want the best one of all. After all, I've been away fighting for you."

Naturally there was a laugh and he said, "Listen, Billy, don't worry. I've saved one for you on the second floor of the prettiest of the houses. It consists of what was originally the drawing room, the dining room, the kitchen, pantry, and a little foyer."

He then told me the price, and I said, "Well, it's the most absurd thing I've ever heard in my whole life. How long is the lease?"

He said, "For three years."

Amster Yard, with dark gardenia leaf green walls as a tribute to Elsie de Wolfe. (Horst)

"Well," said I, "I doubt if I'll be solvent that long at that rate, but I'll take it."

"It's just as well," he said, "because I'd written you down for it long ago."

Harold Sterner did the architectural design of the renovation, and my apartment was used as a model for the others that followed in the Amster Yard complex, which consisted of four or five apartments and a shop for Jimmy.

When it came time for me to decorate my new apartment, I decided to use the same dark gardenia leaf green that I had used in my Palm Beach apartment, as a tribute to Elsie de Wolfe. When the painter finished, it seemed to me to be almost the darkest green I'd ever seen, but I told myself not to lose courage, and had the sofas upholstered in a flat cotton serge exactly the same color as the walls and had the curtains made in the same material. There were a few very pleasant simple Louis XVI chairs and tables, and I had some of the chairs covered in dark green needlework; others were upholstered in a bright green raw silk. There were no rugs at all. Jimmy Amster was so lucky because he had gotten a beautiful old parquet floor from Versailles; enough to cover the

Amster Yard. (Horst)

two rooms and the little foyer between them. After they were installed and polished, they were the most beautiful single thing in the apartment.

I had quite a few rather amusing pictures, mostly bought from contemporary shows and done by young artists. The pictures created splashes of quite bright color on the dark walls; my books, of course, were brought up from Palm Beach and put in a beautiful eighteenth-century bookcase. I also had the blessing of a wonderful Oriental screen that I had bought in a Baltimore antiques shop after the war; the shop owner had not the slightest idea of its value. Because there was always a flood of light from north to south in that apartment, it was simply wonderful the way the screen glowed and glittered in the dark green room.

It was a successful room and many people really liked it; it was a marvelous room for parties, and seemed to be sufficiently warm by night, and yet very cool by day. The year was 1946.

About five years later, around Thanksgiving time, I was so sick that I could not raise my head from the pillow, so I called St. Luke's Hospital and said who I was and who my doctor was, and asked for a room. I then called my doctor, who said he'd meet me at the hospital, where I was immediately put to bed; it was soon discovered that I had pneumonia caused by a staphylococcus infection.

I was kept in the hospital for over two weeks and the convalescing was most trying. Because I had been doing lots of work for Mr. Ambrose Clark, one of the great benefactors of the hospital, I had been put into an enormous room that looked out on Morningside Heights, which I knew was the den of crime of every kind and degree, but inside the hospital the nurses and the clientele were the likes of which I've seldom ever seen, and since then I've been in all of them.

One day I felt very well and decided to rearrange my room, so I got out of bed and was pushing an enormous chest of drawers across the floor when the head nurse caught me. She was furious and screamed at me, "Pneumonia! Get into that bed!"

After returning to my bed, at that moment I definitely decided to do over my apartment while I was in the hospital, and those were the wonderful days when you could do just that. I could certainly do at least one room, if not both, and have them really finished by Christmas. I had beside my bed a nice little swatch of orange cotton velvet; it was brilliant orange, and I decided to cover every inch of the walls in that orange velvet. The curtains and chair coverings were to be done with the same material.

My beloved and brilliant assistant, Edward Zajac, came to the hospital, and I told him my plan. He said, "We'll have it done," and everything was ordered. After that I had a lovely time, felt perfectly well, and recovered, but for fear of a relapse they made me stay on. However, all the details of my new scheme had been done, including lampshades, so I just spent the remainder of my stay in there relaxing. It had been the perfect time to redo my apartment while I was not in it, and Edward Zajac had made it work. The time came for my release, and back I went to Amster Yard.

Talk about a relapse! I certainly had it! I will never understand how I could ever have done such a thing. I had redone my apartment without thinking about the walls. It was just too much. The ceiling was ten feet high, and there was no break anywhere. It was a beautiful color indeed, but it had become absolutely overpoweringly dull in that room because in no way did it have a chance to do anything. I didn't have enough pictures and I didn't have enough mirrors. I thought, Well, I guess I just have to get some; but I knew that was not it either. It was just not right. That velvet was never meant for those rooms.

After I'd been home barely a week, and as soon as the doctor said I could, I began to entertain. One late afternoon when the curtains were all drawn, and there was an orange fire burning in the orange room, I asked Kitty Miller and her great friend Niki de Gunzburg to come and have a drink with me. They did, but I had said to them, "I'm going to warn you. You won't think you're home because when you get here you'll find that it's been changed a little bit."

At that time I was living under the care of my wonderful French servant, André, who was an incredible human being as well as cook, valet, and everything that you could imagine in the world. He was devoted to the Baron de Gunzburg and also to Kitty, and he made every effort to act as if my new decoration were just as it should be.

I had a lovely visit with Kitty and Niki, and they were charming about the rooms, although Kitty did say that she thought I had rather understated my warning that the apartment had been changed a little bit.

In less than a month I realized I couldn't stand it another minute. It had been a terrible mistake. It was like living inside a pumpkin in hell.

I decided that I could either use that orange velvet on a job or give it to a charity, and besides I had the perfect reason to redo my apartment. At that moment, Jimmy Thompson, with whom I had gone to Princeton, and who had gone back to Siam after the war, had returned with the discovery of the great glory of Siamese silk. Jimmy's intention was to import the silk for women's clothes, and he did not have the idea at all in the beginning of using the material for decorating.

He had asked me if I would take a moment to see his silk, so I told Mrs. Wood, and he came to see us and Ruby had a fit over it. I couldn't resist it either, so I bought enough of a bolt of yellow silk to have curtains made for the windows in my apartment and slipcovers for the furniture. Jimmy said he was not really sure he could guarantee the silk for upholstery, but he thought he could have a heavier weave executed, which he was able to do, and it was a wild success.

My apartment was to be painted all white but I thought that might be a little dull so I had Scalamandre make a copy of a Directoire silk from the Maison Decoratif, which I would put on the walls of the drawing room. It was of yellow and white stripes about an inch and a half wide, with a soft satin finish. The curtains were Jimmy's yellow silk, some of the upholstered furniture was covered in vivid yellow satin, and there was lots of clear yellow everywhere.

So from 1945 to 1951, I changed my apartment from the depths of the forest in green into the tortures of hell with the orange, and then to the clarity of white and yellow. Pauline Potter had hit New York by then, and she was fascinated by my goings-on, so I said, "Pauline, do you think it's disgusting? Do you think it shows a terrible restlessness, or that I just don't know what I want to do?" "No," she said, "not really. If you use your apartment as a laboratory, it's okay."

It was there that my André developed into a perfect prize in every way. He came to me when I moved to Amster Yard as a valet, and said, "Don't expect too much of me as a cook because I really am not one. I can always get your breakfast and I can do lunch at home for you alone. I can do an omelet, but I cannot do a meal." That was in the very beginning, and he soon changed his stance.

André was also quite insane. He looked like a wizened old man, and I think he was about forty-five. His feet were the size of a city block and they went flapping down with the most awful noise. His clothes were appallingly ill-fitting (his pants were much too short and too narrow); he was hardly presentable and looked like a clown. He was also intensely religious and he lived entirely for his mother, who was an ancient French lady living in Nancy. The terms of his working for me were that he would spend three months every summer in France so he could visit her.

Amster Yard, decorated yet again.

André was also deeply involved with a lady who was an authoress and who had a beautiful apartment in Paris. He worked for her when he was in France for the summer, but it was good for me as well because I knew he was mine from the autumn until the following spring. When I went to Paris, André could hardly wait for me to go see his lady there, which I did, and a deep mutual-admiration society was established among us all.

There was also a woman in New York who was a friend of both the authoress and André, and he decided that she and I should be friends, so he had her invite me for dinner to her apartment. I went, although she never came to my apartment. André thought he was in love with her French maid, but he wasn't really in love with her. God, he was crazy, but he was devoted.

I will say he could produce such food! Kitty Miller told me that if she and Gilbert were invited to have lunch with me on a Saturday, on the preceding Wednesday Gilbert would say he would not eat until then. Gilbert always ate like a pig, and came to look like one because of his enormous size.

I remember a ghastly moment when the Millers were at lunch one day and for some reason the Maginot Line was being discussed, and Gilbert said, "Those damn French are so stupid. They didn't prepare it at all. They just paraded up and down in front of it like little girls."

André said in a perfectly audible voice, "I'm sorry, sir, it is not true."

I didn't know what to do, because Gilbert shouldn't have said it. Kitty said, "Now, Gilbert. You eat your lovely lunch." When they left that day, I noticed that Gilbert wasn't spoken to by André, but Kitty was.

André said to me afterward, "How can I have my country spoken about in that way!" I persuaded André that Gilbert was an old fool and to pay no attention to him. André was wildly proud of his nation, no matter what, and I could not ever deny the fact that the food he produced by the recipes and methods of his country was certainly all right.

Among the fantastic luxuries that André brought into my life was a large glass jar filled with madeleines that he kept in the kitchen. Another of his specialties was a wonderful cake based on an almond filling called Dacquoise. He knew a perfectly extraordinary butcher who produced very small, and very inexpensive, quail. I don't know how he ever knew about the butcher. The way André worked over veal was a miracle. One day I had some people for lunch, and I thought the way he had prepared the veal was delicious. After my guests left, I went back to the kitchen to thank André, and found him sitting in a chair, wet with tears.

"The veal is impossible in this country," he said. "Nobody should buy it. Nobody knows what to feed it on, and I must refuse to cook it ever again because it does me an injustice." That kind of behavior was typical, but he did everything to perfection: he cleaned beautifully, he was a superb valet, and no one ever polished silver as he did.

A lunch menu André prepared for me was printed in Florence Pritchett Smith's column on Sunday, December 25, 1960, in *New York Journal-American:* "Rice Casserole, Cold French Lamb Chops in Jelly, Vegetable Salad, Hot Cornbread Sticks, Hot Baked Oranges, and Madeleines."

I was also quoted from that column:

The most important point in entertaining is to have a fresh atmosphere so the guests don't feel someone has been there before them. . . . Just before my guests arrive I light the fires in both rooms and then open the windows wide for five minutes. The clean cold air brings out the smell of the flowers in the drawing room and it is also a great stimulant to the appetite. I never turn on the steam heat and I insist there be no smell of cooking in my apartment.

I was also quoted as saying, "I'd rather eat a delicious meal on a tin dish than a dreadful one on a rare plate," a sentiment that I have had my entire life.

In regard to André and the glorious pleasure of his ability, I kept my little lunch parties to Saturdays and four people, because then everybody had plenty of time; not only the guests, but also André and I. They came around half past one and could stay all afternoon if they wanted to. My guests were mostly people who were working somewhere or another, who loved to eat, and who loved to sit around and talk after lunch. It would be hard to say that I could have had two more favorite guests than I did in Reed and Diana Vreeland. Reed was a real gourmet, much more than Diana, and he and André became fast friends.

I had other favorite guests as well. There was a man of terror to the chefs in New York City and that was Bill Paley. He adores to eat more than he likes to do anything else. All of the chefs are scared of him. Bill and Babe came to my apartment for lunch many times. Nothing in the world but joy filled me at the thought of her being there because of her great charm, and because she made everyone happy. André absolutely adored her, and he couldn't help but like Bill because he was in the highest praise of his food. André and I didn't ever have any difficulty in feeding Bill Paley.

The day after the preview of *My Fair Lady* — the production of which was owned by Bill Paley — he, Babe, Diana Vreeland, and Cecil Beaton were coming to me for lunch. We had all been to see it. I had gotten in by a fluke at the last moment, and thought it was enchanting. Well, the others really didn't think so, especially Cecil, who was joined very heartily by Babe in criticism of it. They thought the whole thing was old-fashioned and boring, that the audience of the day just wouldn't be interested in it, and really wouldn't care that much. Fortunately for the world, it didn't turn out that way.

As the years passed, André became almost impossible, and really a little cuckoo, so I told him I thought we had had a long enough time together. He said I was right, and he never returned after he went to France to spend the summer. It was after I had moved from Amster Yard and couldn't have had André in my new apartment anyway because there wasn't room.

CHAPTER EIGHTEEN

"Billy, I want you to promise me that you'll never allow yourself to have a corporation."

One of my friends with whom I renewed my friendship upon my return to New York was Herbert Esme Whiting, whom I had known since the early 1930s in Baltimore, where Esme taught at a private school. At that time Esme was one of those young men in America of whom there were many — intelligent, very humorous, a good athlete, and totally charming. Everybody who ever knew Esme was devoted to him, and I have to say that he gave me some advice that I have followed to this day.

Esme married Medora Roosevelt, the daughter of George Roosevelt, and he and Medora lived with her father and stepmother in Oyster Bay where the Roosevelts had a beautiful house. Esme was a most devoted husband, and everybody loved him; including his mother-in-law, who was almost a semi-invalid because she was hardly ever sober.

One weekend the Roosevelts had a large house party and there were quite a few people at their house. I was there, and Esme said to me, "I wish to God we could escape from all this somehow. It's so social it's driving me mad."

I said, "Well, we can. If you'd like to go for a swim we can go over to Mrs. Wood's house which is not far away. She and Chalmers are away for the weekend, but I know the pool is full, and I'll call and say we are coming."

So over we went. The pool was extraordinary because Ruby had had planted around it a quite high yew hedge, kept beautifully clipped, so that complete privacy was preserved. Ruby hated the whole idea of a swimming pool, and she didn't want to see it.

It was a very hot summer day and we ran into the beautiful yew enclosure, stripped off our clothes, and were standing on the edge to dive in when he said to me, "Billy, I want you to promise me that you'll never allow yourself to have a corporation." That meant a stomach.

Esme stayed in the army after the war and, in fact, he died in it. He was stationed in Washington, and he was in the military intelligence, which meant that there was a considerable bit of secrecy about his life. He had become a widower, and his life in the military suited him very much because he did not really care about society. He was a very contemplative man, but I saw him quite often when he came to New York for weekends.

At one point Esme worked at the reception desk in Washington for Americans in the entertainment world who had been abroad to entertain the troops. He told me that at one moment he was writing the names down of those who had to pass by his desk, and his eyes looked up, and he found them glued into the eyes of Marlene Dietrich. I think it was automatic double exposure, because very soon after that she had taken a house in Long Beach, and Esme spent several weekends there instead of with me.

One night after we had gone to the theater and we had returned home to Amster Yard, a frightening incident occurred.

It was very dark when we got up to the top of the steps and somebody disappeared into the darkness to go up the next flight of stairs. I had given Esme a key, and after we entered the apartment he said, "I don't think I can do this anymore. It's too dangerous for you." He told me that he was doing undercover work in the secret service, that his life was in danger, and he didn't want mine to be because of him.

However, Esme was a little bit crazy and it could perfectly well have been somebody going up those stairs to see somebody else — I never really knew for sure. In any case, I saw very little of him after that. Esme, by his looks, epitomized that period in a way for me, and he was very typical of the moment in which he lived.

I had certainly known Hattie Carnegie by name, and because of Pauline Potter I came to know her soon after my return to New York. She had been the only person on Seventh Avenue who had understood what Pauline had been trying to achieve with her dress designs, and of course,

Hattie Carnegie. (Condé Nast)

she hired her. Born of an inconspicuous and unimportant Polish family, Hattie was a woman of the most extraordinary taste.

She lived in a small ground-floor maisonette on upper Fifth Avenue in the high Eighties. The small entrance hall led into a ravishing Louis XVI oak-paneled salon which she had bought in Paris, and had measured and remade to fit the space in her apartment, of which there was luckily enough. This was not a cozy room, but it was comfortable, and over quite a number of years she had selected about six of the most beautiful French chairs that I have ever seen. It was possible in those days to do that. They all had very faded pale wood frames that looked almost like bones, and they were covered in marvelous bits of ancient tawny-colored damask. In that marvelous room were beautiful mirrors that were part of the paneling, and one or two eighteenth-century drawings that were sitting on tables rather than hung.

At the very first sign of winter there was a fire crackling behind the most beautiful andirons, which were miniature Chinamen, and that fire was always burning from that moment until spring was with us. There was always a profusion of very, very pale pink blossoms, and nowhere was there any intrusion of strong color; even the porcelain was of the very finest possible blanc de chine.

Hattie, who was extremely abstemious and very interested in health food, drank practically nothing, but she often had little parties for her friends after the theatre or opera or anytime she could get off from her work, which she never wanted to do because she really loved her job.

Her offices had the most beautiful boiseries, which turned into backgrounds for the little theatre where her clothes were shown. I never saw the dressing rooms, but I heard that they were perfectly beautiful too. She really cared about beauty as much as anybody in the business.

Hattie had a perfectly ridiculous idea and I'm sorry to say we all fell for it. In a moment of caprice, she decided that there were four decorators whom she really loved and whose work she loved, and she wanted to have a room done by each of them in the house in Redbank, New Jersey, where she lived with her husband, Major Zanft.

Well, that was all very well, and I said, "Now Hattie, don't you think you'd better tell us who the others are going to be because I think we then should compare what we're going to do."

That was not a bad bit of advice, because I had a very small sitting room to do, and James Pendleton was to decorate the big sun room that led off it. Jimmy had the most attractive shop in New York, which he furnished twice a year with beautiful purchases from abroad. He had unlimited money to spend and did he spend it! So twice a year he would telephone Mrs. Wood and me and say the shipment was in. Off we would go across the street to his shop. Mrs. Wood almost would have a stroke due to her excitement, because nothing drove her as crazy as the thought of a new shipment in a shop that she admired. When we arrived, there would be sawdust on the floors, and the nails would still be sticking out of the crates, but we really did have first choice of those shipments.

It so happened that not very long after Hattie had broached her plan to me, Jimmy called Mrs. Wood and me and said that a new shipment was in. When we got there, we all instantly discussed Hattie's idea about her house. Mrs. Wood said, "Thank God, I'm not the one. I'm glad it's my Billy." I said to Jimmy, "I think you and I had better get together."

I went to see Jimmy across the street because we decided I should bring my samples over to him and I would see his. They turned out to be exactly the same things. It wasn't surprising either, because Jimmy, Ruby, and I had very much the same taste at that moment; particularly because we were all doing clear, fresh, Matisse-like colors.

"Well," I said, "Jimmy, what shall we do?" He said, "Billy, I don't know what to say." I said, "I do. You stick to yours because I don't think you can change. You couldn't do anything better for that big sun room, and I'll find something else for the sitting room."

George Stacey was going to do a modern game room upstairs, and he told us it was going to become almost the living room because the dining room was on the ground floor and they would walk up a flight of stairs after dinner to play cards in his room, which meant bridge or gambling.

Another room was to be done by Hobe Erwin, who had become wildly successful and had done a beautiful apartment for Gertrude Lawrence.

A very pleasant result because of my involvement in this was that a great friendship was struck up between Chalmers and Ruby Wood and Major and Mrs. Zanft. I think it was just plain commerce between those two women. They both dearly loved their work, and I think both of them liked the idea that they could make fools of those very rich rich women if they wanted to. I know that Ruby once said to Hattie, "Darling, I know perfectly well that you think that you've got great control over your clients. Well, I suppose you have, but don't forget, I do the beds."

It was not long after I moved to New York in 1935 and was living on 54th Street that I met Horst. I would often see him playing tennis outside my apartment windows, which looked upon the Sutton Place tennis courts, and during the war I saw him at the Mayflower Hotel in Washington, but it was not until I returned to live in New York the second time that we became close friends.

However, soon after I first began working for Mrs. Wood, I met the whole *Vogue* family. At that time Horst was really entirely owned by *Vogue*. Mrs. Wood was very much involved with everyone on that magazine and had no use for *Harper's Bazaar* because she had had a quarrel with Carmel Snow, and because of her southern loyalty to Mrs. Chase, who was editor of *Vogue*. I was very lucky when I first worked for Mrs. Wood because, through her, one of the first people I met in New York was Edna Woolman Chase. Horst, of course, had already become one of her great friends.

It was only after many years that I was able to make it possible for Mrs. Wood and Carmel Snow to speak to each other. Carmel was very nice to me and in fact had me decorate her office, which I was very happy to do, and I thought she was very just because she thought I had ability; however, I do think she was also sort of getting back at Ruby.

Amster Yard, June 1947. Left to right: Unidentified butler, James Amster, Marian Hall, Ruby Ross Wood, Billy Baldwin, William Pahlman, Dorothy Draper, Nancy McClelland.

Horst and Natasha Paley.
(Hoyningen-Huene)

Mrs. Wood had the most enormous admiration for Horst. He lived in a very attractive modern house in Oyster Bay not far from her and Chalmers, and he became a great friend of theirs. Horst told me he thought Ruby had the best taste of anyone. He said he had been to Mrs. Wood's house in the spring one year and her big room was filled with large silver wine coolers in which had been put very low cut white apple blossoms. Nothing was more beautiful, he said.

Horst, with his wonderful taste, with his great knowledge, and his passion for everything beautiful, was the most extremely agreeable companion. He read enormously, he looked at everything he could possibly see, and he certainly added to the pleasure of a great many people because of his hospitality.

Horst was brought into the world by the great genius George Hoyningen-Huene. Huene discovered him in Paris when Horst was a very young man, and he directed his career by seeing to it that Horst went to the Bauhaus. Like all success stories, Horst had the stuff. He had the genius; of course he was influenced by Huene, but there was a very personal element to everything Horst photographed. His photographs in *Vogue* of lovely women in beautiful clothes had such charm and were so human that you hardly realized how great the fantasy was.

During the time that Horst was in Paris, Huene decided that it would be fun to make a movie, and that for the hero of the film, young Horst was the ideal choice. The dazzling beauty of her time, Natasha Paley, was to be the heroine. Natasha was the daughter of the Grand Duke Aleksandrovich, son of Alexander II of Russia, and was a Russian princess. She grew up in Paris with certainly not very much money, but she had everything else. She was married very young indeed to Lucien Lelong, the great dressmaker.

When I was a boy, I went to see my first Paris couture show in Lucien Lelong's beautiful shop, which was in a marvelous eighteenth-century house on the avenue Matignon, and the performance was extremely exciting.

The Lelongs were part of a wonderful group of extraordinary young people in Paris at that time who had wonderful taste, were enormously creative, very intelligent, and who really contributed immensely to the world in which they were born. However, they were soon divorced, and Niki de Gunzburg then became her best friend; I'm sure because of his Russian blood, and the fact that he gave those marvelous costume parties that brought them together daily. Niki and Natasha became friends with Fulco di Verdura in Paris, and in fact, there wasn't anybody in the world of fashion that they didn't know and were not respected by.

I've been told that at those wonderful balls it was the custom for a group of people to get together and plan an entrance, which meant that while the ball was at its height, it was interrupted by a series of processions of groups of people who represented historical events or personages, which looked like moving tableaux. I have been told by more people than I can even remember that every time the applause for Natasha Paley was thunderous.

In the meantime, along came a very attractive man called Jack Wilson who was a young and handsome American who spent a great deal of his time in Europe and had some money. He fell desperately for Natasha and they were married. It was not so easy because there had been this great friendship between him and Noël Coward; however, they all got along perfectly well, I suppose, and the Wilsons came to America where they had a nice apartment on Park Avenue and a very comfortable house in Connecticut.

Many years later my associate, Arthur Smith, had a house near the Wilsons'. I went to stay with him several times, and naturally went to visit Natasha, and I must say she still looked perfectly wonderful. By

Billy at Horst's country house for the weekend.

that time she was with Mainboucher as his head vendeuse. The Wilson marriage was a very sad one because Jack had absolutely no control over his love for the bottle. He was dead drunk most of the time. Pretty soon they got to see fewer and fewer people and, fortunately, he died from his failing and, also fortunately, left enough for Natasha to keep her apartment where she lived until her death a few years ago.

From the very moment that Horst got his house under way in Oyster Bay and it was possible to cook a meal, he began having people for Sunday lunches. He had that lovely gift of hospitality which I love. Later, when Nicholas Lawford joined him, there was the added pleasure of Lawford's charm and intelligence. Certainly nobody ever wrote better about Elsie de Wolfe than he did when he was in the British embassy in Paris.

I was very lucky because Horst and I became fast friends very quickly, which meant that he was kind to me and had me visit him and Nicholas for the weekends. There would usually be one or two other house guests, but when it came to the Sunday lunch, there would be six or eight more. Everyone that Horst had was famous. They were mostly foreigners, a great many theatre people, and all of the publishing world, which meant Alexander Lieberman.

It used to make me absolutely wild, if I had done a room I honestly did like, not to have Horst photograph it, but he was classed as a fashion photographer, not as a photographer of interiors. The great thing that changed all that was when Diana Vreeland became editor of *Vogue*. She designated Horst and Lawford her "warriors." Horst was to photograph interiors, very often with people in them, and Lawford was to write about them. That started a whole thing and eventually a wonderful book came out of it.

I recall so vividly the time that Nicholas met Horst at Mrs. Gilbert Miller's apartment. Kitty was having a very large cocktail party in her long, long drawing room. Originally the apartment had two large living rooms, but she tore the wall down to make one huge, long room, which was for her New Year's Eve party and for her annual good-bye party for about a hundred people in the spring when she went abroad for six months; she went abroad in April and didn't return until October, and the minute she got to London she would give her famous dinner dance. Kitty loved to entertain.

At this party, as always, was Margaret Case, who lived in an apartment above the Millers'. In fact, Gilbert paid Margaret's rent, which he should have because Kitty and Margaret were best friends and Margaret didn't have a dime. She got a miserable salary from *Vogue,* and she was also one of those poor women whom everybody gave things to. Anyway, there was the poor soul living over Kitty in a perfectly nice apartment with a lovely square living room, a square dining room, a square bedroom, a very nice bathroom, and a very good maid.

Cole Porter and I were sitting on a little sofa when she walked in. Cole said, "My God, here comes a woman with two dresses on." What she had on was a black taffeta top with a big skirt down to her knees, and then from her knees about halfway down was a white embroidered skirt so that it looked exactly as if she were wearing another dress under her top skirt. This was when Cole could be so stinking, because when she got near enough he said, "Miss Case, you know I just love what you have on." He hated her and he never once asked her to his apartment. It nearly broke her heart, because that was part of her job. I tried to sneak her in but failed, and once I was at a dinner where she was and she said, "Oh, Billy, I want to tell you how much I love Cole's apartment." I didn't say a word to contradict her because I knew it meant a lot to her, so I just said, "Oh, Margaret, you're so nice."

Margaret moved away from us and was talking to someone when I saw Nicholas Lawford come up to her. He had been at the party for a very little while. Nicholas was considered so brilliant and such a star in the British embassy then that it was said he was being groomed to succeed Anthony Eden as prime minister.

Margaret told me later that Nicholas had said to her, "My goodness, this is quite a gala, isn't it." She replied that it was and that it was quite attractive. Margaret was mad about Nicholas. He did have a terrible lot of sex appeal and he was the best dancer in town, almost. Margaret told me he suddenly said to her, "Who is that man over there?"

"Which one?" she replied.

"That blond man. Who is that?" he said.

Margaret said she told him that the man was very well known, and that she was surprised that he didn't know him. "It's Horst, the photographer."

She said Nicholas grabbed her arm and, pulling her in Horst's direction, said, "I wish to meet him at once."

So they went over, and as soon as Nicholas met Horst he just turned Margaret around toward some other people and began talking to Horst.

Horst told me later that he was never so bowled over in his life. After they left the party, he said Nicholas told him that he was ready to leave the British embassy right then. I don't think Horst has ever really quite gotten over Nicholas's feelings. He said, "Billy, you know, I've never had anybody say that their whole life depends on me."

Nicholas was all set to resign his position, but in a matter of days he was notified by his government that he was to be their representative in Thailand. Horst adviced him to accept this opportunity, but Nicholas refused to do it, and so it was decided that there was nothing else for him to do but move to Oyster Bay.

CHAPTER NINETEEN

"You'll be glad to know that what I want to do is to paint you in the nude lying on your stomach."

During the time I worked for Mrs. Wood after my return to New York I saw a great deal of Harvey Ladew, whom I had known since my early days in Maryland.

In Maryland there is a lot of beautiful hunting country, and one of the most famous hunts is the Elkridge-Harford. Harford County is beautiful country and the charming clubhouse for the hunt has always been very attractive, but it became enormously stylish due to the New York invasion of Mrs. William Goadby Lowe, Bryce Wing, Edward Voss, Tom Eastman, the Sanfords, and Harvey Ladew. All of them had hunted together in the New York area, and it was a fortunate thing in many ways for Maryland that they chose to become members of the Harford Hunt because they improved all the things that the land needed and also made a very attractive clubhouse. Many of them built small bungalows in connection with the hunt club and spent a good part of the year there. Chalmers Wood was one of the first people to be interested in it, and it is very likely that he was instrumental in telling Harvey about it because they had been great friends for quite a long time. Harvey was crazy about hunting and hunted not only in this country but also in England, Ireland, and France.

Once again my good fortune in life was directed by Edith Symington. Edith suggested to Harvey that he come and see me about the decoration of the house he had recently bought. I had almost finished decorating her house, and he was very impressed by it.

Harvey was terribly bright, and I think he found that there were not too many Baltimoreans up to his level of cleverness and awareness; but Edith Symington was, and she was devoted to him. Mr. Symington had to be away a great deal and it seemed to me that in an instant they had something beyond friendship; however, there was not by any means anything scandalous about their relationship. They hunted together, they danced together, and they did everything together. Harvey's dancing was really rather odd because of the way he pitched forward.

Harvey was, in every sense of the word, a great eccentric, a man of the highest possible taste, and practically a lunatic on the subject of anything having to do with England. His clothes were impeccable, done by the best English tailors, and aside from his hunting clothes, he was almost one of the best-dressed men I've ever seen.

He was also quite imposing to look at. When I knew him, he was no longer young. His hair was kept carefully controlled so that it was a very boyish shiny black, and he had a very extraordinarily small mustache as black as the hair on his head. People always said that a little bit of extra color was applied to the skin tone of his face, and I think it's likely true.

Although he did spend a great deal of his time out of doors in the hunting field, the only other form of exercise that he took was a mild game of tennis, and he did that only when he had his wonderful and hospitable weekend house parties.

He loved everything that you could imagine you might love if you had all of his money. He had delicious food, and he not only grew the prettiest flowers available, but he bought loads more to fill his house. He was wildly interested in the theatre, and music as well. Some of his interest in music may have been slightly self-conscious in that he thought that it made him more of a Renaissance man. He drew and painted extremely well, had a great talent for writing, and kept a wonderful diary that was never completed.

He entertained remarkably well and he lived in a very curious way in regard to people. For instance, the Duncan sisters were very popular in vaudeville in Baltimore, and Harvey thought it would be fun to get to know them, so he invited them for the weekend and they gave a performance. He immediately turned them into friends.

One of his eccentricities was that he was not interested in society, per se. Purely social people didn't interest him at all. He had an enormous number of friends from all over the world but mainly from England. He was a great friend of Mona Williams, whom he had known very well in Palm Beach, and they traveled together on a trip to Guatemala. He was interested in all kinds of people, and two of his best friends were Moss Hart and Edna Ferber, who stayed with him during the triumph of *Showboat*.

Harvey was the biggest snob I've ever met. He thought of himself as a southern colonel long before anybody really knew he was in Maryland. He was possessed by that idea, and there was the greatest excitement when he was made a member of the Bachelor's Cotillion. This was something not easily done in Maryland, because, quite frankly, the board which was made up of southern gentlemen was not particularly interested in a northern colonel.

He loved fancy dress parties, and he never missed an opportunity to give one or to attend one. He had quite a supply of scarves and odds and ends, so he could dress up at the drop of a hat.

His only near relative was his only sister, who married Russell Grace with all that Grace money, and they had three charming daughters. There was also quite a lot of Ladew money, which came mostly from leather. Mrs. Grace was very friendly with her brother, but Harvey and Mr. Grace were not friendly at all. I do not know to what lengths their lack of congeniality went, but I don't think that Mr. Grace had what Harvey would have called the proper interest in his house.

Mrs. Grace had exactly the same passion and wonderful taste in her houses that Harvey did. Her great rambling house in Westbury was simply one of the most personal and fascinating houses on Long Island. It must be said that Harvey and his sister really were their own decorators.

Harvey and his sister were remarkable look-alikes. If Mrs. Grace had grown a mustache, they really could have been mistaken. They also were very round around the middle, and they never walked — they trotted, leaning forward almost like the Tower of Pisa, and you always felt that their balance would fail them and they would crash headlong into a building or a tree. If you walked behind them down Park Avenue, it was a very odd sight to see the movement of their trotting round bodies.

After Edith arranged for Harvey and me to meet, he said to me, "Will I insult you if I ask you to be the person in Baltimore who will supervise, respect, and add your own ideas to the plans of a very bright young lady called Jean Levy, who is working for me and is from the firm of Elsie Cobb Wilson?" I was instantly impressed because there could be no higher recommendation from anybody than to work for Elsie Cobb Wilson, who was brilliant and had a spectacular shop on upper Madison Avenue. I had also seen the reception room in Elsie's shop that had just been completed by Jean Levy and was an absolute miracle of modern columns and mirrors.

I told Harvey that I was certainly not insulted, but that I was flattered, and that I could very probably learn a lot from Jean Levy. "Yes," said Harvey, "and me, too. You can learn a lot from me as well."

There was no idle jest in that because Harvey was constantly traveling, honestly remembering, and never forgetting anything he saw which made an impression. Consequently, the decoration of what had begun as an old unpretentious farmhouse turned into quite a remarkable performance.

It was the most wonderful experience for me to work for Harvey and Miss Levy. They were both very in love with the English eighteenth-century school, and they also had remarkable inventive ideas about color and materials. There was very little traditional chintz or fabric used. If he had a beautiful Chippendale sofa or other period upholstered piece (and he did), they would be covered either in a white leather, which was remarkable at the time, or in one of the brand-new linen serge textured materials in colors unlike the reds, blues, and greens typical of eighteenth-century furniture. I cannot ever associate Harvey with damask.

In his big drawing room there were two windows at each end. Once, when in England, Harvey's eyes feasted upon a miracle of material that he innocently bought for the curtains in that room. The walls had been painted a beautiful lemon color with a heavy glazing, and for the dado between the chair rail and the baseboard Miss Levy had worked out an extraordinary, almost chocolate-colored paint with a very soft glaze. The curtains were made of old bourrette, which is a form of heavy serge, and for the valances there were four pieces of eighteenth-century dark blue heavy needlepoint in the design of festoons with multicolored flowers, quite bold in color and in scale, with tiebacks of large wool tassels in the same colors as the valances.

In some ways Harvey had the most catholic taste of anybody I've practially ever known. For instance, on a table there would be a beautiful eighteenth-century box beside a lovely small drawing by Dali. One of his treasures was a painting by Johann Zoffany of the English actor David Garrick at his home in Chiswick. He also always had one or two modern French impressionists scattered around.

He had a remarkable collection of mirrors, and among his favorites were a pair of gilded Chippendale ones with a fox on the frames. He was very careful to keep the signature of the fox everywhere throughout the house, and had many objects with hunting motifs, all of which were interesting, but not necessarily always authentic.

Harvey didn't want to spend any more money than he had to. He was a wonderful buyer, but in many ways he was extremely stingy, and quite often knew that he was paying much more for something than he should have because the value was not really there, except for what it meant to him as decoration.

He spent quite a lot of time hunting in England where he had a very attractive flat and a vast number of friends. They would come and stay with him in Maryland, so there was a constant house party going on, engineered by the "Ladew Girls." The "Ladew Girls" were three very old women who worked for Harvey and adored him. Margaret was the chef. She was Scotch, almost completely deaf, and a perfect tyrant. Mary was the butler and Harvey's valet as well. Katie was a wizened little woman of indeterminate age because she was so old and she served the meals.

One weekend, Nicholas Lawford, Horst, and I were Harvey's house guests. It was a delicious warm day; Horst and Nicholas were having some fun taking photographs, and Harvey decided to have lunch indoors because it was so hot outside. The paneled dining room was painted an incredible dark yew green and had inserts of French hunting paper. We were eating lunch when we heard the most unearthly crash from the next room which sounded like what we thought was another Hiroshima, but not at all. It was simply that poor old Katie had dropped an entire tray of a complete set of Waterford glass which she had just removed from the dining-room table.

Harvey was a very naïve person, and he refused to believe anything that he didn't want to. The sad part about the episode of Katie and the Waterford was that she had been imbibing much too generously of the juleps before lunch. Harvey said, "Poor old Katie, she's just getting too old. I don't think I'll have her undertake this again." He never for a moment allowed himself to think of her as having been drunk. He also knew that he wouldn't be able to get anyone who would satisfy him to even carry the glass in as far as the pantry, so he simply had to blind himself to the fact that Katie was a menace from the point of view of breakage.

All three of those women adored Harvey and they, in turn, were adored by his friends. Katie died several years after that weekend. Margaret and Mary continued with Harvey and, in fact, survived him.

Just beyond the kitchen garden in which he grew French vegetables was a very large barn that had been turned into an enormous studio with a couple of guest rooms. Harvey used to give small dinner dances in the studio, which were wonderful because of the great scale of the room.

The house was like Topsy, in that it just grew. Harvey would decide to have a new room and he would simply have it built on to the house. One of his great triumphs, quite late in the house's life, was the addition of an oval Adam library. He had purchased an oval Chippendale partners' desk that was too large for any of his existing rooms, so he decided to build a room around it, and James O'Conner, the New York architect, helped him execute his design, which when completed was considered the masterpiece of the house. However, I liked the small Elizabethan room where we very often had breakfast just as well. The fifteenth-century pale pine paneling which was brought from England for the room always had great appeal to me.

In addition to Maryland, Harvey had a charming winter place, a "Pied à Mer" in Delray that was photographed by *Vogue*. The house originally looked Spanish, but Harvey knocked off the carving and gingerbread, ridding it of that influence. There was one bedroom that was simply wonderful because it was very much like the beautiful decoration that Oliver Messel did for *House of Flowers*. The whole room, including the bed, was curtained in bright pink theatrical gauze.

Harvey was not always practical because often he could not wait to have his various projects completed, and the actual construction of a project was sometimes not altogether secure. One day his great friends Mr. and Mrs. Gilbert Miller arrived in Delray from New York to spend the weekend. When they arrived, Harvey was in the swimming pool, which he had designed so that it looked as though it was carved out of giant rocks.

Kitty went straight up to her room, which overlooked it, and Gilbert went out to see Harvey. Kitty said to me that she was terribly amused and impressed by the fact that her room seemed to be practically in the sea, but was still very high. Curtains of fishnets fringed with shells hung at the windows, and to enhance the room, Harvey had selected several Regency chairs in the form of silver shells. Kitty noticed that only one window was open, and as she thought it was a little warm, she went to the window, which turned out to be French doors, and as she started to open them, she found that they opened inward. So she gave them a good pull. The doors and their frames fell down, surrounding her on the floor. The wildest screams were heard, and the entire staff rushed to her room to pull her from the wreckage.

At the end of their visit there was an embarrassing incident. Harvey had been very particular to have every possible seashell or sea horse motif placed on everything in the beach house, including the clothes hangers which he had had custom made at great effort and expense. After the Miller's left, he went up to check over the room and discovered the clothes hangers were gone.

He went into a wild rage, but he said he didn't see what he could do. However, as he had known the Millers chauffeur, Glen, from the time that he had driven Elsie de Wolfe for so many years, he decided to call him in Palm Beach where he had driven the Millers for their next visit. When he reached Glen, he said, "Glen, I have to know something right away. What happened to the clothes hangers?"

Glen said, "What do you mean, Mr. Ladew?"

Harvey said, "Well, they're gone."

"Oh," said Glen, "the Millers thought the hangers went with the room."

The hangers were returned, but Harvey told everybody about it, like a bad boy. Even though Kitty's maid packed for her, Harvey always believed Kitty told her to pack the hangers and that Kitty knew exactly what she was doing.

Harvey had a great lifelong friendship with Marian Hall, the decorator. One night in New York I went to the theatre with Chalmers, Ruby, and Miss Hall, and afterward had a drink with them. We'd seen the most exciting play called *The Country Wife* in which Ruth Gordon outdid herself. Oliver Messel had designed the exceptional sets and costumes. Oliver was a great friend of Ruby and Marian's, so he came to join us for a drink at "21." Before we had gone to the play, Harvey had telephoned Ruby to ask her if she could find out how to get him a candlestick that was on one of the tables in the set that Oliver had done, and that led to the subject of Harvey.

We were all in a very good humor and all extremely full of lovely "21" drinks when Marian said, "Ruby? I want you to be honest with me. You know that you and I have been very nice to Harvey, and you know that we've been to his house for weekends, even together. Are you willing to tell me in front of these people how much money Harvey has spent with you over the years?"

"I certainly am," said Ruby. "It's under five hundred dollars."

Marian said, "I could kill you. It's under three hundred dollars with me."

What Harvey would do very often was to borrow, in a sense, the ideas of others whose opinion and taste he valued, and then do the execution himself instead of giving it to the person who suggested it. To have known Ruby and Marian for that many years and to have spent only the sum total of eight hundred dollars between them can only speak for the loyalty those two women had toward him.

When Ruby had an exhibition at her Park Avenue offices called "Fantasy in Decoration," Harvey was one of the first to attend. It was really a display of well-known people's favorite possessions, and many of the objects were certainly unique. Ruby said to Harvey, "Now, Harvey, if you can get an idea from here that you can use, I want to be the first to congratulate you."

The exhibition really was fantastic and a column from *The New Yorker* magazine of the time describes a typical exhibit:

. . . the most fantastic exhibit was a white dog with eyes of blue glass, lying on a red velvet cloth with a bunch of flowers between his forepaws — the whole under glass. The dog was looking out from a fireplace at a clock shaped like a roulette wheel that played the "Marseillaise." A Mr. Baldwin, a gallery man, explained that this wasn't a toy dog but a fantastically neat bit of taxidermy performed on a purebred spaniel that had lived almost a hundred years ago. When alive, the dog belonged to a lady who lived in St. Marks Place. She had noted nothing unusual about him until one day she had happened to sing "No One to Love." Hearing strange sounds behind her, she turned and found the spaniel standing on his hind feet and swaying to the music. She put the dog on her lap and went on singing; the dog put his paws on her shoulders and began to yelp in rhythm, stopping to breathe when she breathed, holding a note when she held it. Thereafter, every time the lady would sing "No One to Love" the little dog would wag his tail and join in heartily; he'd be surly when his mistress tried to sing any other song. All this naturally made the lady very fond of her pet and when he died she gave him a resting place on her family mantelpiece. Nobody today knows the dog's name and Mr. Baldwin isn't even sure of the lady's. He says there's no doubt the story is true, though. On the chance that one of our subscribers might want to buy a stuffed spaniel, we inquired the price of it. Mr. Baldwin said it's not for sale. "I couldn't possibly set a price on it, anyway," he added. "It's a question of sentiment."

Harvey's taste was really much more European than American. He used lots of white which was Syrie Maugham's influence, and he loved the idea of lacquered walls, which he borrowed from the great English country houses. He was such a terrible snob about his own taste that he once said to Mrs. Wood when she was his house guest in Maryland, "Ruby, you're going to be in the guest room which is not quite finished, but it's comfortable, and I have a pad and pencil beside your bed so you can write down any suggestions that I should do for the room."

She was a little surprised. The room was lovely, and the walls had been painted a strong indigo blue. On the wall where the mantelpiece was, Harvey had pasted a piece of flowered eighteenth-century Chinese wallpaper with a blue background floor to the ceiling. He said, "Rubes, how do you like it?" She said, "It's going to be wonderful." The pale Chippendale furniture was covered in fabrics with very little color, and the blue of the paper was so strong that everything looked white beside it. He said, "You know, that wallpaper is very expensive, and I can copy it by painting it myself." That piece of paper was hanging on the wall ten years after he pasted it up, and was still there when he died.

The next morning we had breakfast sitting in big comfortable chairs around the fire in the oval library.

"Well, you asked for it," said Ruby, and handed him the note pad with her suggestions. Some were very funny. She had written: "Isn't it too bad that I have to walk ten feet across the room to get a light to read by when I'm in bed. Don't you realize you cannot have lampshades lined with blue taffeta if anybody wants to read. Please, for God's sake, consider the feelings of your guests before you bow to your snobbism. Buy some nice soft American toilet paper!"

Harvey had those wretched little tin boxes with sheets of English toilet paper, which have the softness of shingles, in all the bathrooms.

Ruby's lists were legendary, and one from her notes in 1952 recorded:

I have never —
Sat at the captain's table
Been presented at Court
Bathed at Newport
Played golf, tennis, or pinochle
Hunted
Shot at anything
Endorsed coldcream, mattresses or silverware

Stood on my head
Seen the inside of the Empire State Building
Read the *Graphic*
Had a diamond bracelet
Been suntanned
Liked purple orchids, oysters, liver or black sheets.

Harvey's selfishness was an eccentricity and just as legendary as Ruby's lists. Once he took Woodson Taulbee to lunch at Le Pavillon when it was at its height. Woody told me later that he would never be subjected to the embarrassment of being Harvey's guest in a public place again. When the check had been presented, Harvey had taken out quite a lot of bills, sorted them out, and left one dollar. Woody said he could see that the waiter was holding his fists to keep from hitting him.

That tipping incident was typical, but as a host he was terribly generous. There was no limit to the amount of money he spent on the things to eat. There was cavier all the time, and champagne flowed like water. Fresh flowers were everywhere. The last thing that I did for Harvey was a tiny flat in New York on 48th Street, and he spared no expense. The atmosphere and the things he had in it made you think that you were in a great London flat. It was an absolute knockout.

I watched him make a gem out of his house in Delray. He built a separate addition next to the beach house with a room that was copied from the proportions of his great oval library in Maryland. In Delray, he continued with his wild interest in topiary. His gardens in Maryland were already famous; in fact, in 1971 the Garden Club of America recognized Harvey as having the most outstanding topiary garden in America without professional help. On his death, the house and gardens in Maryland were left to the state.

Between the main beach house, which faced the sea, and the separate oval addition, Harvey planted an extraordinary garden that consisted of topiary whales. Each whale had a bright button where the eye would have been, which was lit at night with a quite bright light like a diamond, and a great spray of water jetted out of each head.

Not everything Harvey did was successful, and as I have said so often, if only rich people would stop doing things themselves. He was crazy about painting his own murals, so he painted an immense mural on a curve in the wall of the beach house, and it was an outrage it was so bad. It was just like Alice Garrett's painting. They, of course, were great friends.

Harvey Ladew.

One time when I was on army duty in Palm Beach, I spent the week-end in Delray with Harvey. It was one of those last late seasonal days, we had had a wonderful lunch, and I was taking a real siesta on the soft coral rocks at the pool.

Harvey at that time was painting everything he could lay his hands on, and that day he decided to paint a portrait of me. He said, "You'll be glad to know that what I want to do is to paint you in the nude lying on your stomach. I want you to spend the afternoon as though you were alone. First of all, I want you to get very comfortable so you won't have to change your position."

I said, "Sure, Harvey. But don't you think I'll get a wild sunburn?" That consideration didn't seem to bother Harvey, and the sun wasn't all that hot, so I posed and Harvey painted.

While he worked, I slept, lying with my head turned on its side. I got quite pink from the exposure, and when it was very nearly done he said, "I know one thing without doubt. Anybody who sees this who knows you at all will undoubtedly say, 'That is Billy Baldwin.' "

I got up and walked over to see it. The picture was small, about ten inches by twelve inches. My sleeping pink form was surrounded by white rocks and incredible colored hibiscus. In one of those moments where everything works, Harvey had caught me: the line of my shoulder, the line of my thigh, my head shape, hair, the whole thing.

I said, "Harvey, I've never asked you to give me anything, but I would love to have that portrait."

Harvey said, "Oh, William. I couldn't do that. It's going to be one of my treasures."

"Can you do another?" I asked.

"No," he said. "It's been done."

It would have been fun to have because it was a very amusing thing. He painted very well; not as well as he thought, but still it was as amusing as the dickens. I often wonder what became of it. After Harvey's death and the Delray house was sold, I'm sure that it was probably sent to an auction house where it was sold, or it might simply have been destroyed and is in ashes.

"... keep Whitney Warren and Kitty Miller from ever setting foot on Nantucket ..."

J met Helen Hull very soon after I came to New York in 1935, but it was not until after the war that we became very close friends. Of all the country houses that I've seen or known by photographs, the most dramatic and personal of them all was hers.

She was born Helen Huntington, her family had long lived in the Hudson River Valley, and after her divorce from Vincent Astor she decided she wanted to remain in her native country. Vincent promptly agreed to build her a house on her family's property.

The result was a beautiful, very personal, and totally original concept of a large country house, built in the shape of a crescent moon. It was quite big and very subtly curved until you came inside, and then you were very aware of the gently curving walls of the house; especially in the library on the first floor.

During the time when the gardens were in flower it was almost impossible to see the rooms downstairs because of the incredible flowering plants that were brought in from the greenhouses.

Helen had a faithful and loving gardener who sometimes met her guests at the Rhinecliff station nearby, which had been added to the line especially for the Astors by the railroad company. On one particularly beautiful summer day when he met me there I asked him how Mrs. Hull was. With the most enormous affection he replied, "Mrs. Hull is

wonderful as always. You know, Mr. Baldwin, my madam really cares only about two things in the world, her music and her flowers."

That was really a true statement. Her love of flowers was constant. That love was clearly seen in Nantucket where she went for the summer every year after she had married Lytle Hull. Opposite the front door of her simple clapboard house there was an apple tree surrounded by quite formal little square beds of flowers, which were kept in constant bloom. Before her arrival on the island, she would send the gardener on ahead with an enormous truck full of flowering plants from her gardens on the Hudson. Those flower beds were a mass of color from late spring until after Labor Day.

The house in Rhinecliff had the immense advantage of being furnished with furniture from her other past houses. She had a great deal of antique painted furniture, Venetian in style, quite a lot of English lacquer, and lots of slightly old-fashioned upholstered chairs and sofas covered in materials patterned with faded bouquets of flowers. One could not help but instantly notice the beauty of the floors, all of which were of parquet inlay in the most intricate and beautiful designs.

Everything in her rooms was so unobtrusive that your eye was never caught by any one thing. There was no sin of that kind. There were no great paintings, and there was no great furniture. The flowers were the only really great things. Everything was full of charm and had merit, but above all, it was loved by Helen. I do not remember ever having seen any house more filled with personal things.

One end of the big drawing room looked out onto a great lawn going down toward the Hudson River. At its foot was a brilliant border of flowers like an English garden against the background of the river. There were many immense elm trees by the house, and Helen used to say to me that every time she looked at them she prayed that they would not be struck by the Dutch elm disease.

At the opposite end of the drawing room in front of a group of windows there were two grand pianos back-to-back, and it was there you recognized her passion for music. Helen played the piano very nicely, and one of her favorite guests was Merton Powell, beloved by the musical and fashion world of New York. He was a professional piano teacher and they often played duets together. I had met Merton through Mrs. Wood. He had been a friend of Chalmers Wood and thus became Ruby's friend. In fact, she took him abroad for his first trip to Europe when he was a young man, and there was a photograph of him in a sailor suit during the war, in her library.

One of Helen's best friends was the pianist Rudolf Firkušny. She was devoted to him and it was wonderful for her because he was always there so she had someone to practice with at the drop of a hat. She was in love with him and thought that she was going to marry him, but instead he married a young woman and they had two children. Helen, like Alice Garrett, had the wonderful quality of hospitality; she took care of her musicians, and provided a very attractive cottage on her property where the Firkušnys lived for part of the time.

Every year Firkušny played a sold-out performance at Carnegie Hall, and I was very lucky because several times I was able to be with her in one of the boxes she took for the concert. A day or so before, Helen would have a dinner party for maybe twenty people, and we sat at little tables scattered throughout the house. After dinner, Firkušny would just sit down and run through his program. It was, in a word, a dress rehearsal.

Helen was a woman of immense vitality although she had a crippling illness, and in her last years could hardly walk. She simply never knew where her feet were going to go. She and Elsie Woodward were the two women in New York who really looked like grandes dames. Helen was tall, she wore very old-fashioned, beautiful clothes, and when she put on the jewels, they really were jewels. During the twenties and thirties she took on more than any of the young ladies of her time or any of the women we know today. She ran her husband's, Vincent Astor's, enormous establishment on the Hudson River, a large and beautiful house on 80th Street, a house in Newport, a house in Paris, a house in Bermuda, and the *Nourmahal,* which was one of the biggest yachts in the world. These were all big establishments with a vast number of servants, and she ran them all with the utmost calm and humor. She did indeed have a delicious sense of humor, and also had the real qualities of loyalty, affection, thoughtfulness, and generosity. She was not snobbish, but she was very strict with her friendships, and very kind to people that she liked.

There was absolutely no doubt that Mrs. William Woodward was the other grande dame of New York society. Born one of three beautiful triplets, she ruled her life according to her own wishes. In her enormous and elaborate house in New York's upper 80s she entertained constantly and royally. Elsie and her husband had three daughters and one son, but she and her husband were really not at all congenial although there was never any public statement to that effect.

At her parties she usually had her guests sit at two immensely long tables of twenty people each, and Cole Porter once said to me, "Elsie considers she's entertaining High Bohemia." She was the most faithful of all Cole's friends during his illness when he lived at the Waldorf, where she had moved after Mr. Woodward's death.

I had known Mrs. Woodward very slightly in Baltimore because of horse racing. Mr. Woodward owned the Bel Air stables outside of Baltimore. I had gone to several of her parties in New York, but I was overcome with pleasure when she said she wanted to see me on business. This was to tell me that all of Mr. Woodward's racing paintings were being given to the Baltimore Museum of Art, and that she was in charge of the building of the wing to house them. She felt that I, as a Baltimorean, should be given the honor of helping her, and a nice coincidence was the fact that the architect was a great Baltimorean friend of mine, Francis Jencks.

The Woodward Wing was added to the Baltimore Museum during 1955–1956, and as the building progressed Mrs. Woodward and I went more frequently to Baltimore. We always took an early morning train and had breakfast together. It must be admitted that she was very stingy and careful about tipping.

Sometime before the beginning of my project with her, I was spending the weekend on Long Island with Horst and Nicolas Lawford. On the Sunday of that weekend they told me that Ann Woodward, the wife of the Woodward's only son, William Jr., wanted to see me about the decoration of a house they had just bought nearby.

I had known young William who was a man of enormous charm, but, alas, this could not be said for his wife, Ann. I was instantly and primarily impressed by her toughness. Certainly, Elsie had nothing in common with her, and Ann was nowhere popular in any way. She asked me to send her samples of materials for several rooms in the house. I was very pleased because I could see that her taste could be influenced in the right direction. Several weeks passed and not a word from her. I telephoned and asked her if she had made any selections or should I start fresh.

She exclaimed that she felt badly because she had intended to call me to say that they were doing nothing about the house at the moment because they were going to India to visit a maharajah who was going to make a tiger hunt possible. She said she felt a little worried because she was by no means a great shot.

Later, the following happened as it was reported in vast national newspaper coverage. Quite sometime after their return in November of 1955, they were at a big dinner party and someone there told her that there had been a night prowler in the neighborhood and to be prepared. They went home and were going to bed. William Jr.'s bedroom was a little bit beyond her bedroom, but connected by a short dark corridor. Ann Woodward heard a noise in the hall. She opened the door and saw the dimly outlined figure of a man. She had armed herself with a pistol, fired, and instantly killed her husband.

In spite of all the horror, Elsie took the time to ask me to go ahead with decisions about the wing in Baltimore, and that she would send for me to come and see her as soon as it was possible.

The scandal of this tragedy became a topic of conversation with everyone, every stranger on the street, and with every taxidriver. You were even asked by taxidrivers if you would like to drive past the house of Mrs. William Woodward, Sr. Elsie behaved with the utmost courage in her defense of her daughter-in-law, primarily because of her two grandsons, the young sons of William Jr., and Ann.

I did as she instructed about Baltimore, and it can be imagined that the story had reached enormous proportions there. Elsie, however, was determined to protect her grandsons, and there was never a hint that her son's death was other than that as described by her daughter-in-law. Indeed, Elsie was very much the grande dame.

The great sorrow in Helen's life was that Vincent could not have children. This, of course, was confirmed in his two subsequent marriages which were also without issue. Not long after her divorce from Vincent, he married Minnie Cushing, and when they were divorced he married Brooke Marshall. Helen and Vincent had a very amicable divorce; in fact, Helen and Brooke were great friends.

I remember Helen said to me not too long after the marriage of Vincent and Brooke, "I simply cannot get those two married in my mind." Helen and the Astors had quite a few mutual friends, and whenever either household had weekend house parties, they visited back and forth. Very frequently the Astors and their guests would have lunch at Helen's house, and then Helen and her guests would be invited to dinner at Brooke and Vincent's.

During the time that Nixon was campaigning, Helen brought her house party to Brooke's for lunch, and we were sitting outside having drinks and Brooke said, "Billy Baldwin wants me to tear down the squash court and put a garden in its place. It would be a fine idea because we would have another view of the river, but to tear it down alone would cost forty thousand dollars." Looking slightly guilty, Brooke said almost directly to Helen, "I just don't know what to do because I feel as though I should probably give that money to the Nixon campaign."

Helen, looking like an angel, said, "Why not both, Brooke dear."

I do not think that Brooke Astor ever really felt altogether happy at Rhinebeck in Vincent's house, and the moment that Vincent died, she disposed of it. Helen, on the other hand, loved the Hudson River Valley from the time of her birth, and it was there she chose to live.

Her marriage to Lytle Hull was one of those divinely happy marriages, and afterward he moved into the house on the Hudson. He was full of charm, good-looking, and mad about sailing. Consequently, they had to find a place to go in the summer, and luckily for me they decided to come to Nantucket. Helen bought property on the harbor side of the island at Wauwinet, and built a house with a view of the Nantucket Harbor, which was alive with sailing in the summer. It was ideal for them, and was really a haven for Lytle. After he died, Helen told me she thought that she would not be able to come back to Nantucket because she couldn't believe that she could live without seeing his boat come into the harbor every afternoon. But being sensible, she did return and found that she could live.

In 1975, when I was living in one of the Chanticleer cottages in Sconset, I got a call from Helen, who said she had to speak to me privately. I went to her house for lunch and didn't think she seemed quite as usual. Finally, she said to me, "My dear boy, you know I've only asked you to do one thing for me, which was to keep Whitney Warren and Kitty Miller from ever setting foot on Nantucket, but now I've got to ask your help again." Helen hated them both. She hated Whitney more because she thought that he knew better than to behave the way he did, in comparison to Kitty, who didn't. They were both out of bounds as far as she was concerned.

Helen continued, "Prince Rainier and Princess Grace are to be my guests for several days here and I need your help."

Helen's life was music, and that was exemplified in her constant year-round work in fund-raising for the New York Philharmonic. There was to be a series of benefit balls at the Waldorf-Astoria, with members of European royalty as guests of honor. These guests of honor either visited Helen or she gave a dinner for them, but she refused to receive the Windsors because she didn't like them, and they were not accepted by the royal family, whose side she had taken. I don't think it's possible to estimate how much money Helen actually raised for the New York Philharmonic.

She told me that the Grimaldis were to be the guests of honor that year, and that she had not only invited them to be her guests in New York, but that she had asked them to visit her in Nantucket.

She said, "They have accepted with pleasure. They're coming here, and I'm terror struck. I really should not have invited them to Nantucket because I haven't got room for them, and I also know that the Astor reputation and the Rheinbeck reality are both very grand and misleading compared to Nantucket."

She told me that they were bringing with them one of their daughters and their son, and that one of the principal reasons for their tour was to find an American school for their son. They planned to be in Nantucket for a long weekend, and would have a lady-in-waiting, her husband, and a male secretary with them as well.

Helen said, "I can take care of the children through the kindness of a neighbor who lives not too far from me who said she would love to take them in. I'll put the lady-in-waiting and her husband in the hidden guest cottage, which is near the house, and I'll put the male secretary in Stanley's room and God knows where Stanley will sleep." Stanley, a very handsome Englishman, was Helen's butler, and he, with his wife who was Helen's cook, really ran Helen's house in the most perfect possible way.

Helen told me that the most important aspect of the visit was that there was to be no publicity. They were traveling incognito under assumed names, and their wish to be completely anonymous was to be respected at all costs. She had been told that they wished to come to the island and leave absolutely unnoticed, and that under no circumstances were there to be any photographs taken.

"Now Billy, dear," Helen said, "I want you to do two things for me, and if you will, you really are going to be my savior. First, I've never met Mrs. Melhado, but I know her house is the handsomest house on the island. Do you think," said she, cocking her head, "Mrs. Melhado would mind giving a dinner for the Grimaldis?"

I said that I didn't think she would mind at all.

"Well," said Helen, "there is no possible way that I can have a dinner party for them at my house because it's too small. Do you think you could call Mrs. Melhado and explain the situation, and if she agrees, I'll ask her to lunch so we can decide who to have for the dinner party."

I said I would be happy to call Mrs. Melhado.

"The second thing I want you to do for me is to give a luncheon for them at my expense at the Chanticleer."

I said that I would be happy to do that for her.

The next day I received a telephone call from Louise Melhado, who said, "Well, dear Billy Baldwin, aren't we going to have fun with our little secret."

I said, "Well, I think we're going to have fun, but I don't see how we are going to keep it a secret."

Louise said, "I think we can. I know that I won't say a word to anyone and I know you won't."

The dinner party was a smashing success and the event was indeed kept a secret. That night at the party, Roswell Gilpatric, Mrs. Melhado's son-in-law, offered to take the young Grimaldis on his boat to the island of Tuckernuck the following day. His offer was eagerly accepted.

Princess Grace wearing a turban. (© Laura Pettibone)

My luncheon at the Chanticleer was the next day. I had made all the arrangements with Jean-Charles and Anne Berruet, the owners. I had told them of Mrs. Hull's insistence that privacy was essential for the luncheon, and Jean-Charles and Anne said they would put a sign at the entrance of the Chanticleer saying it was closed for a private party. They also said they were going to invite a few of their best clients for lunch so our luncheon would not be in an empty restaurant, which I thought was very thoughtful of them.

Princess Grace and Prince Rainier arrived very promptly and they were crazy about how pretty the restaurant was. Princess Grace had her hair tied up under a turban like a laundress, and she was quite disagreeable. She was also very disagreeable to her husband, who was enchanting, witty, and polite. He sat next to Helen and they had a very good time. Princess Grace was on my right and we got along quite well until she started to talk about decorating like a boring housewife. As we were finishing lunch, Helen asked me if I would show Princess Grace my

Billy's Chanticleer cottage.

little cottage, which was next door to the restaurant, and I said I would be happy to do so.

Before we left the Chanticleer, the Berruets asked if they could take a photograph of their guests. "Oh, my heavens, yes," said Princess Grace. "We were wondering where the cameras were." She had not liked it at all that there were no pictures being taken!

So Jean-Charles, looking perfectly grand wearing his big white chef's hat, came out and took photographs of them. After that Princess Grace walked with me over to my cottage. She walked in and said, "Oh, I like those lamps. I think I'd like to buy two. Send them."

I said, "They're not for sale. I'm retired and there is nothing for sale here."

Paying no attention, she spotted a little table and said, "I'll want that too, but don't be too sure he'll let me get it because he's so stingy. I'm trying to get an apartment furnished adequately in Paris, and he won't let me do what I want because he won't spend the money so don't count on it." She told me she had had a lovely day, and then she left.

Helen was thrilled that everything had gone off so privately, and I was pleased that I had been able to help her. I heard the next day that after they left, when they got to the boat the captain recognized her and said, "That's Grace Kelly! How about a picture?" I understand she was more than happy to pose.

The living room of Billy's cottage

I am so glad I met her because I've been basking in her light for over forty years.

J t is almost inconceivable that I must admit that I cannot remember the exact moment, the hour, the place, or any detail of when I came face to face with Diana Vreeland.

I do know that it happened through Mrs. Wood and that they were never friends. This could possibly have been due to the fact that Ruby was a very down to earth southern girl who was not totally at ease confronting a bird of paradise from Paris and London.

One of the first times I did certainly talk to Diana was a weekend on Long Island when the Woods and I had lunch at Carmel Snow's enchanting house, which was only about five minutes away from the Woods' house. Diana had not been at Carmel's house before, and she was fascinated by its immense romanticism. She has never been exactly in love with high price, high style, great French furniture. She is far more interested in the eccentric, the personal. As for her own houses, half of the furniture is made up of tiers of shoeboxes taking the place of chests of drawers, but color does matter to her, and that is what she surrounds herself with.

At Carmel's I deliberately made myself as charming as I could to Mrs. Vreeland, so at the end of the luncheon I could say, "Goodbye, Diana. I hope I may see you."

Diana Vreeland. (Louise Dahl-Wolfe)

She said in a very loud voice, as though I were a mile away, and not looking at me, "Of course, you must!"

It meant nothing. I saw Diana at least a month or so later at a big party somewhere, and somehow we got to be really intimate friends. I don't know how we did, but we did. Perhaps it was that I was exactly the right age to be a friend of her's and her husband Reed's.

There never was a more attractive man than Reed Vreeland, and Gilbert Miller used to say of him that he was the only gentleman in the entire city of New York. It was a well-known fact that Reed was really the housekeeper in their wonderful flat, which was the first one that I went to before the one she is in now.

They gave the most enchanting dinner parties of anybody in New York. They had a wonderful Spanish cook who could cook anything, and two little tables where they could seat six or possibly eight, and the most wonderfully selected guests. The menus were all entirely planned by Reed.

Reed had a great many devoted rich friends, but nobody could ever quite figure out why because the Vreelands were not rich at all, and his friends were very rich indeed. There was an extraordinary mixture of guests at their parties, but one thing was certain: there were always two or three beautiful girls. Diana never minded looking at beauty and was interested in seeing what they had on. Reed was crazy about beautiful girls, and what they had on, or not, was not the point. It must be understood that Diana and Reed were a very happy couple, and it was because of her real infatuation for him and his great appreciation of her that they sailed this wonderful boat so beautifully together. Until the time that he went to the hospital to die they slept together in an enormous double bed.

Do not think that in their early years Diana and Reed were flying around in Biarritz, Cannes, or any other of those wonderful summer places abroad. They weren't. Summer after summer they took rooms at the Meadow Club in Southampton where they were enormously popular.

There was nothing very common then about Southampton. It was a very attractive summer colony started by people who didn't want to dress up that much, and wanted to have a simple life as opposed to the marble palaces of Newport. Cordelia Biddle Robertson, the Wolcott Blairs, in fact, about the most chic group in America at the time lived in Southampton in their huge old-fashioned gray shingled houses.

The Vreelands were invited everywhere. One weekend I was a house guest of Adelaide Leonard's. Adelaide always had a huge Sunday luncheon for thirty of forty people, and it was the ambition of almost everybody to be invited to it. We were all sitting around outside having cocktails, and Adelaide said to me that she thought we would have to begin lunch in spite of the fact that two of her guests had not arrived.

Suddenly, tramping over the dunes with the sea behind them, appeared Reed and Diana, looking as though they had come out of some other world. They were late as usual, at the very least an hour, and dressed exactly alike in gray flannel knickers, suede waistcoats, and silk cravats. They were wearing the most incredible shoes and carrying golf bags. There is no doubt about it that Reed and Diana were very notable figures in Southampton as well as in New York.

One night I had been invited to the Vreelands' in New York, and one of the guests was Mrs. Henry Parish. Sister Parish was really my great friend although most people in New York didn't believe it. She was a serious competitor, we knew a lot of the same people, and we would sometimes even be working on different rooms in a house belonging to the same person. There was never anything bitchy about our relationship at all.

She is an enormously entertaining woman, and I have to be forgiven if I say once more that her point of view of a woman's bedroom and its decoration is the best thing that has ever been in the history of the art. There is no doubt about the fact that she knows how to please a man from the point of view of where he's going to eat, sleep, and be.

That night at the Vreelands' I was sitting beside Sister and she said, hoping that we might even have a little quarrel, "Don't worry, Diana. Don't change the seating." We really could not have argued because we always just roared with laughter.

The time came for her to turn to the lucky man on the other side of her, and she spent quite a little time with him, but she did turn back to me and said, "You know something. While I've been talking to my friend on the other side, I've been looking at Reed Vreeland. I've seen all that they say about his charm and his looks. It's all there, but I think there's an awful lot you can see through."

I said, "What do you mean?"

She said, "Well, I'll tell you exactly what I mean. You and I should not be flattered by being here tonight. This is no first-rate dinner."

I said, *"What are you talking about?"*

Sister said, "Well, you have a look, too. You can tell it's not first rate because Reed has not taken the trouble to shave his sideburns."

It takes a little while to be bright enough to be with Diana. There are these extraordinary statements that she makes in quite a broad voice with quite a broad gesture of the mouth. They are made with no uncertainty, and you think, Of all the nonsense in the world, that's it. To your great surprise and sometimes dismay almost, an hour later or maybe a day later, you realize that she has uttered pearls of one hundred percent wisdom. In her remarkable lingo she is speaking what she believes to be the truth and it almost invariably is. There is no affectation. She believes entirely in those remarkable hurdles, curls, and gymnastics of speech that she indulges in. She does not indulge in cruelty nor in self-indulgence for pleasure. She just simply sits there, telling you what she thinks. I think she practically always has. She has done this by permitting nothing second rate. She will not bear to subscribe to an opinion that she doesn't totally believe in. *She is a warrior.*

One of the most touching and tender elements in Diana's daily life, and which explained so much the devotion of her husband, is the spellbound admiration she has from bright young people. She is surrounded by people many many years younger than she is who hunger to hear her opinion about anything at all that is of interest today.

She is never so happy as when she is talking to some bright, creative American or European boy or girl about their work and what they are doing. She hangs on every word that they say, and vice versa. Diana gives them more than is possible, with great warmth and enthusiasm. The word *blasé* is something Diana does not know in any language. Her trust and her hope in the young is overwhelming.

She opens the world's eyes to everything, as has been seen in her remarkable shows at the Metropolitan Museum in New York. She has an immense wealth of sympathy and enthusiasm, and she is unwilling to put up with being bored because, like a great gardener, she throws out the weeds and is interested only in cultivating the flowers.

A pleasure that Diana gives to those who know her, and one which I'm not going to say is not self-conscious, is to see her walk down the streets of New York. It is a marvelous sight. She walks with all the grace, beauty, and charm of a ballet dancer. She studied ballet when she was a young girl, having been exposed to it by Nijinsky and all of the Diaghilev stars who were friends of her parents in Paris. She also, in that way, became very familiar with the scores for the ballet from the Spanish of de Falla to the French of Ravel and Debussy.

My greatest possible privilege with the Vreelands was in getting them into the little apartment that Diana lives in now. It gave me almost an entire winter of pure satisfaction and pleasure. We were all working: Diana, Reed, and I; even though Diana and I didn't know what Reed was working at.

We did not have a moment during the week for anything but our own jobs, and therefore Diana would say quite meekly but with the strength of a lioness, "Of course I don't know whether you would like to or not, but we would love to have you lunch with us on Sunday."

That would mean my being spic and span, and clean as a whistle for Sunday lunch all during that year at either half past one or a quarter to two, which was as early as Diana could make it. I do not know why the captain of the restaurant was still smiling at us at four o'clock, because we would still be sitting there deep in conversation about the apartment.

Diana and Reed drank very slightly. Reed usually had one martini and Diana maybe drank a little straight vodka on the rocks before lunch, but that was it. So our conversation was not prolonged by alcohol. There was plenty of prolongation on the part of Diana, but it had nothing to do with drinks. It had to do with her wonderful imagination, which she translated into reality in such a way that it really was quite hard to tell sometimes what she was doing. But in the end you would not be fooled because she wouldn't make up something just to make it up. She might add a little something to it in the way of a word or two, but it was a word we all knew.

After lunch, sometimes in a deep blizzard, or sometimes on a spring-like day in late March, we would go to their Park Avenue apartment. It was entirely Reed's idea one day that we should eliminate the hall altogether in the apartment. That meant that we turned the living room and the dining room into a curious and remarkable L-shaped room which is still without a fireplace.

Diana said some pretty strange things about shapes, about what she wanted to do, where she wanted to sit, where the light had to hit her, where she must be quiet; and it was up to me to do it. She threw me some very difficult problems, but with Reed, we always managed to solve them. There were never any questions about money. There wasn't enough room to spend too much money anyway, but Diana attacked the whole apartment as though it were a perfectly divine little palace.

The spirit of the apartment sprang from what Diana said to me one day just before I went abroad: "I want this place to look like a garden, but a garden in hell. I want everything that can be to be covered in a lovely cotton material. Cotton! Cotton! Cotton!"

I found the perfect material for her in John Fowler's shop in London. It was a scarlet chintz covered with brilliant Persian flowers.

And so we began. She said, "I've got those big crates that look like nothing whatsoever, but they are so marvelous for holding my treasures, which are my scrapbooks and certain letters. They can be pushed around and made to fit the spaces. I don't want you to show me one Chippendale chair or one French commode. I don't want anything like that. I want lots of flat space for photographs of my beloved friends. I want plenty of room for flowers everywhere, growing plants as well as cut flowers, and I want plenty of space for ashtrays because I smoke. At one end of the room I want banquettes and at the other end will be my sofa. Don't you forget, Billy B, that I once heard Pauline say to you and me that there are only two things of any real importance in a woman's life, and those are her bed and her sofa."

She continued by saying, "I know that you know me well enough to know that I adore *things*. I realize that you have hardly enough room to put your cigarette in an ashtray because there's hardly any room to put an ashtray on the table. Another vase of flowers on the table doesn't bother me if the flowers are divine. I know you can barely get around the chairs, but when I am in a room, I want to sit close to somebody. I never do really feel crowded; especially as you know that you can arrange anything comfortably and with a sense of space if you know how."

Diana got her wish. At the wall farthest from the living room was a corridor that led to the bedroom. The floor of the apartment was covered in solid wall-to-wall scarlet carpet, which continued through the corridor back to the bedroom. This achieved the effect of having it look like one large space rather than looking like several cut-up areas.

The bedroom had an entirely different point of view. It was a room that they spent a great deal of time in; Diana particularly. Even in her busiest days she did not get up until quite late. The great double bed was always dressed as if it were going to go to a ball. There never were more beautiful Portault flowered sheets than there were on that bed, as well as several kinds of bed covers, knitted afghans in beautiful colors or brocades, or any little fantasy in the way of material that happened into Diana's life. We didn't really talk much about that room until we

Mrs. Vreeland in her apartment before it was decorated "to look like a garden, but a garden in Hell." (Cecil Beaton photograph courtesy of Sotheby's London)

more or less got the concept of the living room finished. Diana had not decided on the chintz for the bedroom walls, but we knew that whatever we found that looked like a beautiful dark garden would be marvelous.

I also knew that we didn't want another garden in hell again for a bedroom, and I really didn't know what she did want. I showed her many materials, and naturally they were to be figured. It's very difficult

Mrs. Vreeland in her "garden in Hell." (Horst)

for Diana to look at a piece of plain material; in fact, practically impossible. I showed her dozens and dozens of samples and finally one day, which came like a day after a terrible drought, the rains fell. I showed her the same pattern as the living room. It was the color of a deep but brilliant blue like the depths of the sea. She said, "Just a minute, please. That's it!" So the walls of the room were covered with this extraordinary material of the most beautiful blue and quite a lot of green, again with Persian flowers.

I decided that when she was lying in bed she would see the ceiling, and perhaps we'd better do something about it rather than just cover it with the fabric of the walls or a plain material. The living-room ceiling was done in very much of an off-white, so for the bedroom we got the most wonderful material that was a combination of blue and green in a rather abstract design.

There was a beautiful Chinese screen, a little red lacquer dressing table, some smaller Chinese lacquered tables, and a very comfortable chair for Reed to sit in. At certain times they would eat there. She would have dinner in bed and he would have his dinner sitting in his chair.

You have to believe me when I say that there were two windows in the room. There was one opposite the bed and there was one to the left of the bed. The one to the left of the bed was closed up. No lovely sunlight could enter Diana's bedroom at all. The one at the foot of the bed has a blind so that it can be entirely blacked out if necessary. It is the window, however, where the air-conditioning is, and the air-conditioning runs with the delicacy of a butterfly's wing so that there is nothing more than a hint of a beautiful coolness.

The door to her bathroom on the bedroom side has a very brilliant, strong, clear, thick mirror over which is hung a stark naked light bulb of a wattage that God alone knows. That is so when Diana has her hours with her dressmaker, she can stand in front of the mirror and be illuminated as if she were in the sun.

The bathroom was an absolute triumph because it was left in the most pristine state of white tile. The carpet had a pattern of blue, green, and red triangles. Clinical is the way that room looks; except for the colored walls, which were done for practical reasons.

The closet in the bedroom was taken up entirely by Diana and in it were the most beautifully made shelves for shoes, many of which she had had for several years and were unworn until they had been polished year after year so that they would have the quality of eighteenth-century leather.

Across the hall was Reed's bedroom where he never slept because first of all there wasn't a real bed in it. There was a very chic daybed which could be used in case of illness or in any wild crisis when one of her two sons might happen to be there, but that happened very rarely as they both lived out of town.

In his room we built something that looked like a mausoleum for a pharaoh. It was a double wardrobe for Reed's clothes. I think he did have every good reason to want it, because in it hung some remarkable clothes and I suppose certainly the most beautiful overcoats and topcoats of any man in New York. The wardrobe was very tall because he was a very tall man and his coats went to its floor. There was a big double Chippendale desk, a chair of considerable great comfort, and many many many plants all blooming beautifully. Off that room was a bathroom; simple to a degree except for a big-scale wicker chair.

Over the daybed was a very old-fashioned and very attractive pastel portrait of Diana wearing a turban, which was done in the late twenties or early thirties. However, the portrait of Diana I have in my mind transcends time. Her great vitality and spirit not only enriched my life then, but continue to do so today.

CHAPTER TWENTY-TWO

"I just want you to know that when I die, you're not going to collect one cent and not one thing either."

One morning in 1945 after I had arrived at Mrs. Wood's office on 57th Street, the secretary told me that I had a personal call from Mrs. Gilbert Miller. I confess that I was impressed, because Kitty Miller represented one of the reasons that I wanted to be in New York. I admired her taste enormously even though I had never met her, but I had seen many photographs of her houses in London and in the country in England, her New York apartment, and her father's, Mr. Jules Bache's Palm Beach house.

I said, "Hello, Mrs. Miller."

She said, "Hello, young man. Are you rivetingly bright? Because if you are, I want to know if you can possibly find time to help me."

I said, "Of course, Mrs. Miller, I'd love to do anything you would like."

"Well, she said "It's not really for me, but for my niece, Mrs. Warren Pershing. The job is not going to be enormous, but I will not have her mutilate a very nice apartment. She has no taste and neither does her husband, and she's so stingy that she's going to embarrass me in front of you. How about it?"

I told her that I would adore to help her, and we agreed to meet and hung up. I was very pleased but sort of scared, because Mrs. Wood had said some rather unpleasant things about Mrs. Miller. I rushed into Mrs.

Wood's office and said, "Guess what, Mrs. Wood? Mrs. Gilbert Miller has made an appointment to see me about a job for her niece."

Mrs. Wood made one of her stone faces and said, "Well, I'm not impressed. I've always tried to avoid that woman. I know she has beautiful taste, but God knows anybody with that much money should have. I also know she has a lovely house in London, and gives the best parties there during the season. So go to it, darling."

Kitty Miller was really very rich because she had inherited a vast fortune from her father, Jules Bache, who had had only two daughters; Kitty being one; the other married a man called Richards by whom she had three daughters. There was a constant war between Kitty and her two nieces, Mrs. Pershing and Mrs. Michel. Kitty's third niece, Dolly, died very soon after I got to know them.

Kitty and Gilbert had lunch nearly every Saturday with the Michels. I was included occasionally, but by no means regularly, and it was enormous fun except that Gilbert usually got a little drunk on the wine, and there was always a slightly tense atmosphere.

Kitty put up with the Michels because of Bache and Company for whom Mr. Michel worked, and she put up with the Pershings because Muriel's marriage to Pershing was quite a social asset for the Millers.

There certainly was not a man in America who was not glad to have the Pershings for lunch or dinner, and in the eyes of Kitty, Muriel had done a very fine job by marrying the son of the great American warrior general. My mother told me that when General Pershing came to Baltimore, at the end of the war, as a guest of the Bachelor's Cotillion, all anyone could hear were the screams of the debutantes being pinched by him. Kitty also told me that the general was perfectly awful.

Kitty really didn't like anybody. There were very very few people that passed her judgment without some great drawback. She was a wonderful friend if it suited her, and her generosity to Margaret Case of *Vogue* was very attractive. Gilbert through his kindness made it possible for Margaret to live in an apartment in the same building by paying a good portion of her rent. Kitty was wonderful to her, although it must be stated that very often some of the hand-me-down clothes which she gave her did not exactly fit, and they were not always suitable for Margaret; however, Margaret was loaded with castoffs from Mainboucher, Givenchy, and other favorites of Kitty's.

The friendship between Kitty and Margaret was an extraordinary one. They both gave to each other enormously, and of course, it was the most marvelous thing for Kitty to have Margaret on tap by elevator

Margaret Case, Billy, and Woodson Taulbee.

anytime she wanted to see her. If Kitty were going to be alone for dinner, which was very rare but it did happen, or lunch or whatever, the telephone would ring in Margaret's apartment and Kitty would say, "Sweetie, come right down. I'm by myself. We'll have a little drink and a little talk." Most of the time it was accepted, and believe me, her invitation had better been accepted because Kitty was not at all pleased if she said no. On the other hand, she was wonderfully kind to her, but Margaret was there all the time to keep Kitty from ever being lonely.

Gilbert worked, and he was very often frightfully busy producing his plays, which often meant out-of-town engagements. Kitty was very important to him in regard to the clothes that were worn by the actresses and actors, and she finally did select the clothes in all of his contemporary productions. Her total involvement in this began when Gilbert produced *The Reluctant Debutante.*

Three nights before the play was to open in New York, Kitty was in England because she had decided that she wanted to go to a ball in

London, but she flew to New York to see *The Reluctant Debutante* two nights before it opened. She went to the dress rehearsal and said, "I will not allow one single dress that I see here to be worn in this play. I won't allow it!" New clothes were ordered for everyone immediately, and the cast hated her, of course. It wasn't so difficult to newly outfit the cast except for the little reluctant debutante herself, who was Raymond Massey's daughter. Kitty went with her to two or three of the best American couturiers and did not find anything that she liked. She called Diana Vreeland, and Diana said, "Darling, there is a young man called John Moore who is a friend of Norman Norell. You will adore him, and I'm sure he's got a couple of dresses just waiting for you." They went, the dresses were selected, and worn with huge success. That was a typical difficulty that Kitty solved with Diana's advice.

Margaret was not only Kitty's loyal lady-in-waiting, but she served as a sort of ambassador for her as well which was not easy to do because of Kitty's colossal snobbism. However, if somebody was attractive like a good-looking young man or a pretty girl, Kitty would automatically be for them, and God help them if they were ugly because even if they were geniuses, she would not see their light shining through.

At that time when London was a beacon of joy, creativity, and wild popularity there appeared in New York a young man called Antony Armstrong-Jones. At this time in London it was the thing to do, no matter where you appeared, to wear blue jeans or extremely downbeat clothes. Jeans were being worn somewhat in New York, but not quite as much.

One day Margaret called Kitty and said, "Kitty, I've got the most enchanting young man who knows all about you and knows you by reputation in London and is simply dying to meet you. He's here because of *Vogue*."

"Oh, God!" said Kitty. "That's bad news."

Margaret said, "He doesn't want to photograph you. He's not here to do that. He's to photograph young people."

"Oh, really," said Kitty. "Well, we must not bother him, then."

Margaret said, "He really does want to meet you. He doesn't want to come for a meal. He just wants to see where you live because he hears it's very attractive and he wants to see you."

"Well, darling," Kitty said, "fine. Why don't you bring him for a drink tomorrow afternoon. It won't be any party. I'll have on my negligee between tea and dinner, but I'd love to see you for about half an hour."

They arrived the next day, exactly on time, and Margaret told me that he looked very sexy and was very good-looking indeed with his lovely blue eyes and sweet charming manner, but he was dressed in blue jeans and was wearing boots, which somehow looked odd in Kitty's drawing room.

By that time Tony had made himself very popular and knew almost everyone that Kitty did, and they had a very good time.

The next day during their morning conversation, Kitty said to Margaret, "Now listen, darling. That was all very well done, Mr. Jones was charming, but don't you ever dare, as long as you live, bring anybody into my house wearing those clothes."

Margaret, squashed by Kitty, called me and told me what Kitty had said. She was abashed and in tears; however, several days later his engagement was announced to Princess Margaret, an event about which Kitty was curiously subdued.

As a young girl, Kitty was never attractive. She was too fat and she was not pretty. Furthermore, her fundamental jealousy and resentment of being Jewish were circumstances for her to get over. A great deal of her early life was told to me by several women who were mutual friends of both of us and who had gone to school with her. She had a perfectly good figure, although at school the girls called her "La Vaca," which means cow in Spanish, and she was not popular because she was sour.

This characteristic became more pronounced as she grew older, and at times she could be very sour and very bitter. She absolutely did not like to pay a compliment. On the other hand, most of her judgments were correct, but she wasn't tactful. I don't think she ever tried to make anybody feel better. One of her great pleasures, I'm afraid, was in tearing down, and a special target was other people's food. The curious thing about this was that she did not really serve by any means the best food herself. She always had a well-known chef, usually Italian, from London and brought to America, who was just sort of a not quite. The food served at Kitty's lunches and dinners, whether in England, Majorca, or in this country, was not all that memorable. The most outstanding food that she had was served in her house in Majorca. Once in Majorca we had gnocchi for lunch. I was delighted when it appeared and said, "Kitty, I absolutely love it. I don't think we've had it before." She said, "Eat up. You'd better because I hate it, and we'll never have it again."

Kitty built the house in Majorca with some money that she got her hands on as the result of some kind of business merger at Bache and Company, and she built it solely because of Gilbert who was mad on the subject of Spain; he had gone to school with the Duke of Alba, an association of which he was very proud.

I decorated her house there and it was quite a sensation because almost everything I used came from that island; an opportunity that no one else had taken advantage of at that time. Kitty had told me before I left New York to come there to see about the decorating, that there were no materials to be had, and that I should bring samples for her from which to choose. That was ridiculous, because Majorca had the most beautiful cottons ever. At first, Kitty, of course, didn't want that because she wanted what everyone else had, but I convinced her that she would have something in her house that nobody else would have, and she liked the idea. I used different cottons on everything so that there was not one material the same, and the rugs were cotton, made there. All of the furniture was wicker from America, and the final result was a triumph.

Gilbert spoke English, French, German, Italian, Spanish, and Hungarian perfectly well, although not always perfectly as far as the pronunciation went, but what he could do was to think devastatingly in them and that enabled him to produce translations of European plays which he brought over straight from London where he owned a couple of theatres. He was, indeed, a transoceanic producer. I remember the day he asked me if I had time to do a set for him. It was a moment of enormous excitement for me, and the set for *The Reluctant Debutante* was a happy result. The play opened on Broadway on October 9, 1956, and I received the highest praise from Brooks Atkinson, the drama critic for the *New York Times,* in his review in which he wrote, "the fashionable London drawing room shines extravagantly." I did the sets for another play Gilbert produced called *Patate,* which unfortunately closed almost immediately.

Ironically, Kitty couldn't bear the theatre and she openly told the actors and actresses that she hated them. She just couldn't stand actors. One of the greatest successes Gilbert had was the incredible production of *Victoria Regina,* starring Helen Hayes, in which he spent without stinting. Kitty said, "I have to admit that little woman was very good in it, but of all the bitches that ever lived, she is it, and she's just a little chambermaid."

Gilbert treated Kitty as though she were a bad animal, and he absolutely slew her with vindictive criticism, but he respected her enormously for her taste and intelligence. It was rather pathetic when he would be sitting at the end of one end of the table at lunch almost every Sunday in New York, and she'd be there at the other looking marvelously groomed, and he would yell down the table to her, "What year did we go abroad on the *Mauretania?*" She would answer in her very attractive voice with the exact date and hour of the sailing. Her memory was absolutely flawless, because she just simply remembered everything she saw or did.

I certainly know that as far as I'm concerned, she was the best-dressed woman I have ever seen. I can quote with perfect safety Bill Blass, who said of her, "She just could not go wrong."

Niki de Gunzburg once said to me, "Billy, you know this thing about clothes is all very interesting, but our dear friend, Diana, whom we respect enormously, doesn't know one-tenth as much about clothes architecturally, structurally, or in any other sense, as does her grand friend Kitty Miller." It was true. Diana, in comparison to Kitty, in regard to clothes was the poor relation.

Kitty always looked like a million dollars, and the one thing that she really loved was clothes. It was what she knew about, and she used to discuss the details of every dress she ordered with each of the great dressmakers of whom she was a client.

She adored Bill Blass, and she liked nothing better than to talk to him about the design of his clothes. She just didn't want to look at a dress and say nothing. She really knew what she was talking about, as an architect would in discussing a building.

Two of my assistants, Arthur Smith and Edward Zajac, both said to me at different times, "You really feel that when you go to see Mrs. Miller at twelve o'clock for an appointment that she has dressed herself as if she were going to a ball."

Kitty never did anything but dress to the teeth. She was immaculate in her grooming, and she looked as if she had dressed for a celebration. It would never have occurred to her, not even once in her life, to think of being seen without being perfectly and beautifully dressed.

As she grew older and gained weight, which she did because she was not well, she still would take herself every spring to Paris and buy a few numbers from Givenchy. These consisted of beautiful tea gowns which she adapted for formal or less formal use and wore every night. Kitty dressed for dinner every night of her life. She dressed for breakfast every morning of her life, and she also dressed for lunch. I know that when she had breakfast served in bed she was fully made up, wore a beautiful negligee, and was weighed down by her necessities, which for her meant being dressed with her jewels. She never allowed herself to be seen without them. She invariably wore a pair of gold and diamond earrings,

Kitty Miller looking like a million dollars. (Cecil Beaton photograph courtesy of Sotheby's London)

a gold necklace every day, and a gold and diamond necklace at night. She wore at least two bracelets, one on each arm, and there was usually a diamond and gold pin somewhere.

After her sensational robbery in London, she called Jean Schlumberger and said, "Johnny, my dear, all our little trinkets are gone. A few things have not been recovered, one of which is my diamond necklace, and alas, the beautiful diamond that Gilbert gave me. So you'll just have to get to work, and reproduce them."

Johnny told me he wanted to kill himself when he heard that, because she knew so much about jewelry. He said that if she was interested in something she really made a study of it and she *knew*.

I agreed with him because it was the simple truth. She knew more about the design of eighteenth-century houses in England and France than anyone I have ever known. She knew what had been in those houses, from the fabrics to the flatware, and she also knew about living in the houses of the eighteenth century.

Kitty saw, and she understood what she saw. She was a violent sightseer. She rushed at the first possible chance to a new exhibition, and she invariably bought something from it. She really knew what she was looking at, and furthermore, she knew what she didn't like, and she hated a lot of things, a great many things.

Kitty adored everything pretty. She liked having around her things that belonged to her and which were pretty to her. Duarte Pinto-Coehlo, the greatest decorator in Spain, was visiting her in Majorca where he had decorated the house next to hers on the same beautiful stretch of land. He was crazy about her and he said one day at lunch as we were sitting and drinking Bloody Mary's made with fresh Majorca tomatoes, "Kitty, may I just do something? Tell me if you don't want me to, but may I expose you? May I look through the contents of your bag which is lying on the table here beside me?"

She said, "Of course, darling."

Duarte said, "You know, what a lady has in her bag tells the whole story."

Kitty said with a big smile, "Go ahead, kid."

Out came the most wonderful, brilliant-colored enamels made by Jean Schlumberger: a cigarette lighter, cigarette case, powder box, lipstick, everything that you could imagine. Therese, Kitty's maid, had carefully put them in the beautiful canvas bag for her mistress for the day.

Kitty's bags as well as their contents were changed for every occasion. She would no more have used the same evening bag and its contents that she had used the night before than she could have been a wild animal.

Her smoking paraphernalia was beautiful and it gave her great pleasure. She smoked quite a lot, and she also smoked beautifully. Her hands were not very pretty because they were too fat, but she managed getting the cigarette out of its case and into her hands, and the lighter to light it, and offering a cigarette to other people with the utmost charm and

Duarte Pinto-Coehlo.

calm. She made a thing of it, almost like a ritual, and it was appealing and attractive.

During the uncountable hours of business and pleasure I spent with Kitty, there was never one moment of boredom. Her enthusiasm, her knowledge, and her experience made her the most delicious companion. If you happened to be in England visiting her at her country house on a day when her gardener was there, you were in for a perfectly wonderful time discussing gardens. Peter Coats, one of the great horticulturists, had such respect for her, as did everybody who worked for her. The curtain man respected her knowledge about the correct length of what a curtain should be, and the painter of a wall knew how to get the color because of her instructions. Her directions were always correct.

It also seemed when you were with her that everything was so personal. She really cared about your feeling for the sandwich she ordered to be taken on the picnic. She simply cared about your interest in what was around you.

As for her humor, you couldn't beat it possibly; it was perfectly extraordinary. She was not a giggler, but someone with a smile ready to break at any moment. If she thought you deserved it, she was very quick in giving you the nice gentle reprimand. She was very witty, but the difficulty was that very often her wit was unnecessarily cruel. She could have gotten along just as well if she hadn't been quite so mean.

Kitty was one of the great hostesses, and the New Year's Eve parties she gave became legendary. She and I had grand times decorating for those parties. In effect, it was as if Kitty gave two enormous parties on New Year's Eve, which were the wonder and admiration of New York City. First of all, at eight o'clock there was a dinner for fifty people in her apartment. After dinner the guests were taken out of the dining room and spread around the rest of the apartment so that by a quarter of twelve just before the New Year, the dining room had been transformed into a room with little tables around its edges, and a huge buffet done by Le Pavillon restaurant had been set up.

About one hundred people were invited to come in after dinner, and among them was Arthur Rubinstein, who used to stand opposite the buffet where there were these marvelous Hungarian sausages and just eat one after another. He looked perfectly divine — just eating — and he would say to me, "I'm so glad to see you every year, young man. So sensible, eat!"

Ailsa Bruce with her delightful friend, Lauder Greenway, always came in after dinner to Kitty's New Year's Eve party, and Kitty was mighty proud of that little feather in her cap. Ailsa was not a beauty, but she had real looks, and Kitty always used to say to me, "Well, she makes my party look better than anybody."

Ailsa was tall and slender and when she decided to wear her jewels, everything else in New York looked like tin. Without doubt, Ailsa had the most beautiful stones I ever laid my eyes on. She had a parure of emeralds, which consisted of huge emerald earrings and a great broad flat necklace with even larger stones. She had the same thing in sapphires, and I guess that only God and Ailsa knew what else she had.

She looked as though she smelled something terrible all the time. Her nose was always in the air, and she might just as well have been blind

Ailsa Bruce. (Condé Nast)

because she never spoke to anybody; including me, and she and I were great friends.

A typical performance of Ailsa's occurred at a dinner party given by Lauder Greenway at Le Pavillon. At the time I lived near Le Pavillon and I arrived very on time. In a few minutes in came Ailsa with our host, Lauder, who took Ailsa's coat, and she came and sat down beside me. There were to be twelve of us and we were seated at the table, but not at our final places, and Ailsa said, looking as though she were dying of agony, "Lauder, for God's sake, a martini!" So a martini was brought. In the meantime, Lauder went to the captain to see about the dinner that he had ordered, and while he was away a marvelous-looking young man came up, bowed politely, and spoke to Ailsa, and then said, "How do you do," to me.

I knew that I knew him, but I couldn't remember which of my clients he was the son of. Ailsa, without even a smile, looked straight through him as if he were invisible. So just as the boy was looking embarrassingly desperate, Lauder returned to the table and spoke to him. I heard the boy say, "Lauder, how lovely to see you," and he walked away as if he were stunned.

Ailsa said, "Lauder, dear. Who was that?"

Lauder said, "That is your nephew and godson. Didn't you recognize him?"

That was Ailsa's usual pattern of behavior. She had a table at the Passy restaurant almost every day where she sat with maybe one or two friends, and people would go by her table whom she knew and whom she played bridge with after lunch, and she would not speak to them.

Basically the reason for her behavior was that she was shy, much more so than her brother, Paul Mellon. She had a real phobia, a real fear, and she was paralyzed by it, which is probably the reason she couldn't even focus.

Ailsa also could never make up her mind. She had a lovely house on Long Island and in it was a very fine English Georgian pine-paneled room. It had a couple of rather nice paintings, maybe a Renoir and a lovely eighteenth-century Lawrence, and I was possessed to paint the room a warm butter yellow, and have chintz curtains; therefore, making the room look more cheerful because at the time there were woven wool curtains, which were dated, and the room was dull. For years, every September, Ailsa would say to me, "We are closing the house now, and it's going to be yours to open and do the room by May."

So every fall she had an estimate from me for painting her drawing room, but the years went by, and Ailsa could never quite make up her mind to have the room painted. Her indecision was maddening; in contrast to her sister-in-law, Bunny Mellon, who was electrifyingly efficient and would have something done before she even heard the question. Ailsa really hated Bunny for her decisiveness because Bunny's ability made Ailsa look even more as though she didn't know what she wanted. The room was never done because Ailsa died soon after a minor operation for hemorrhoids during which it was discovered that she had cancer.

Kitty's parties in London were just as famous as those she had in New York, and one of the reasons that made her so sought after, especially abroad, was the annual party usually given the weekend of July 4th at the Savoy Hotel in London. About one hundred were invited for dinner, and many people came from Paris, Madrid, and New York for the event.

After dinner there were an equal number of young people invited in for supper and dancing. That last little plan was the miracle, because it meant that after dinner when you left the dining room you walked into the ballroom where all the young people were drinking champagne and dancing around like young people, and not like a lot of old fogies. I don't think I ever saw so many good-looking young men and women in one room in my life.

If someone in London society had not been invited to the party, they were certainly fighting to be, and there was a wonderful remark that somebody made at a very grand party in London about a month before the invitations were sent out. The person said, "My God, we hear that nobody is going to be invited to Kitty Miller's party unless she has been to their house for a hot meal."

There were quite a few prominent hostesses who couldn't remember whether they had had Kitty for a hot meal; so they looked it up in their date books, and the grills began to sizzle. Kitty told me that she never in her life received so many dinner invitations in a period of two weeks.

One lovely delicious June I was visiting the Millers in London. It was a year when everything seemed to be at its best.

I had been told by Kitty in a letter before I went to London not to bring my white tie because it would not be necessary as we were not going to any big balls while I was there. However, to my horror, the moment I arrived, Kitty said, "I'm terribly sorry, but you've got to go and rent yourself a little white tie to wear to the Schwarzenberg Ball." That really meant no problem because everybody did that at Moss Bros.

Kitty's chauffeur, Tony, motored me down to that wonderful establishment, and he was chuckling because he had a silent bet with himself that I would not find a white tie to fit. He was right, because I didn't! Every single garment was tried on, *everything,* and the establishment of Moss Bros. was horrified because their reputation was that nobody would ever have any difficulty in being fitted. Well, I did!

I said to Kitty when I returned, "Kitty, dear, I'm sorry, but I just can't go because I can't get a white tie, and that's all there is to it."

"Well," she said, "let's think it over."

Kitty had a few people in for dinner before the ball, and I was dressed in my little black tie. I felt terrible because Gilbert, who was a stickler, didn't want to do anything wrong or have a badly dressed guest, but he said to me after dinner, "Now come along with us. It's perfectly all right. It won't matter."

The Schwarzenberg Ball was held in a lovely house in Belgrave Square that served as the Austrian embassy. The delay in getting into the house was considerable because the night was so beautiful that everybody was receiving each other in the balmy air before going inside.

A superb staircase wound itself, it seemed, to the very top of the house, and from the bottom to the top, it was solidly banked with red roses. There was no stopping the fragrance, which filled the air. Everything had been removed for dancing from the second floor at the rear of the house, and the drawing room on the first floor had been set up for the buffet.

I was standing beside Kitty, who was politely introducing me to everybody, and I must say I was very proud. She never looked more wonderful. She was wearing the best possible heavy white Balanciaga dress and her spectacular Schlumberger diamonds. She said, "Now you have to be a good boy and sit with me, and I will show you all the beauties, and believe me, that's going to be quite a job because this house is filled with nothing else tonight." It was true, everyone there seemed to glow with an especial radiance.

One of the fascinating sights was the arrival of Lady Diana Duff Cooper, who was appearing in public for the first time since the death of Duff Cooper. She was dressed in yards and yards of black tulle and looked breathtakingly beautiful. I had met Lady Diana two days before at a very brief luncheon given by Kitty's neighbors in their garden which abutted Kitty's garden on Hill Street. After I had been introduced to her, I said, "How do you do. I have a message for you from Diana Vreeland."

"How kind of her," said Lady Diana, "I've never met her."

Upon Lady Diana's arrival, she spied Kitty and me in the throng outside the house while all the "How do you do's" were going on, and she came over to speak to us. Leaning forward a little bit, and staring at me, she pointed to my black tie, and said, "Not good enough."

Sadly, more and more frequently as Kitty grew older, she had too much to drink. She really couldn't hold her liquor anyway because it went right straight to her head, and then you really had to look out because she was incredibly cruel to everybody. She became forgetful, and she was no longer any fun, which was a kind of tragedy because she had always been so much fun; the truth was that her behavior was a real curdling. She directed such moments of cruelty to poor Margaret Case, to whom she had always been enormously kind, so that you wanted to kill her and say, You must be merciful.

Late in life Kitty was fortunate to have a great friend in Jo Hughes, who was a most loyal and wonderful companion, but her friends did not all stand by, and when Gilbert died, there was quite a difference in everything. She gave up the house in Majorca because she found it was too difficult to maintain, and another difficulty was that most of the people whom she depended upon to come and visit her couldn't afford to any longer; especially the English with their restricted amounts of money. She also sold her property in England, and moved back to America, where she bought a more than adequate house on Long Island to spend her weekends in. She kept her apartment in New York, and rented a house of considerable size every winter in Palm Beach where she could entertain.

There was always the glorious thing in Kitty's life of the staff. She simply took it for granted that there would always be around her a full retinue of servants who would keep her life flowing smoothly. Therese, her personal maid, who had been with her for about fifteen years, must have been the super maid of all time. She and Kitty fought like women in the fishmarket; in fact, it was sometimes very unpleasant when their quarreling could be overheard. Therese was a poor old maid who had beautiful taste, and Kitty was always pleased to have her admire her clothes. She said that Therese was the best maid that she had ever had, which must have been something. Before Therese, Kitty had an adorable one called Angel, who had once been part of Elsie Mendl's establishment.

Kitty's last chauffeur was a devoted, young, very handsome Englishman called Tony, and he was absolutely wonderful with her and to her. He made her very happy by always driving faster than he should have. Kitty loved nothing better than to go speeding over hill and dale with Tony driving. He was never late, and he was never anything but polite. Tony was devoted to her, but some people felt that he was a bit fresh, which if he was, was entirely Kitty's fault.

It must be admitted that she got more and more difficult as the seasons went on. It really got to the point where she could not tell the truth, and she made up some dainty little lies just to make the world a mess for herself and her friends.

She had a perfectly ridiculous house in Palm Beach one year that had a rather pretty loggia that connected with her bedroom. Her bed was quite far from the door and when she got into her room, with her back to the world, she was unable to see that she could be observed from the loggia.

One day on the loggia she was talking to me before lunch and to my total dismay she said, "I'm sorry to be disagreeable, but I feel cross today. I think I do quite a lot for my friends, and I'm not so sure that they always do so for me, so I'm in a very bad humor. I'm telling you so that you can be prepared, because I'm going to say it to the whole bunch of them at lunch today."

I said, "You just have a little Bloody Mary."

"No," she said, "I'm not going to have a Bloody Mary. I'm cross!"

She walked away to her bedroom, with her beautiful cane, and when she was not too far inside, she stopped. There was a pretty little French table close to her and I saw her look it over to see what was on it, and after she decided that there was nothing too valuable, she gave it a good shove. There was the most terrible crash, and then I saw her lower herself to the floor beside the wreckage and begin screaming, "Oh, help! Help! Poor me!"

Well, that was not the only one of those little incidents I saw. I saw several, and after seeing one of her self-imposed falls which was particularly absurd, I said, "Don't do that anymore. It's not becoming." She looked up at me exactly as though she were a great mongrel and I'd beaten her. However, she was dressed in a purple satin evening gown that evening, and in reality, she looked like a baked potato, with two beady black eyes surrounded by purple aluminum foil.

Close to the end of her life, she gave us all a little warning. One very happy weekend in Palm Beach I was sitting by the pool with some of our mutual friends when Kitty appeared; immaculate as always, dressed to the teeth in a wonderful bathing outfit, and wearing her bathing jewelry. Unfortunately, I can't begin to describe her feet, except to say they were hideous, because they were the most terrible things I have ever seen.

She sat herself down with great difficulty because by that time she'd gotten quite fat and was having trouble moving. When she got herself settled and was comfortable, she looked at me, and said, "Well, darling, I'm going to tell you something. I just want you to know that when I die, you're not going to collect one cent, and not one thing either."

I said, "Well, Kitty, I don't see any reason why I should. First of all, you've been marvelous to me. When you think of the number of years we've been working together, and I'm not even going to guess the amount of money you've spent with me because I don't know, but I'm sure that my books will show you've been quite generous. I have to admit there were times when I worked for it, but most of the time, it was a pleasure, probably because of two things: one, the fact that you were always such fun; and second, because you always made your mind up instantly. And sometimes you make up your mind a little too quickly, as you so often do with people."

One of the major difficulties in visiting Kitty during the last years of her life in Palm Beach was that she didn't let you out of her sight for a minute, and you really couldn't go out of the house to see your other friends. Another difficulty was that she became increasingly rude.

I visited her the first season she spent in Palm Beach after Gilbert died, and we were invited to a party. She looked splendid, dressed in a wonderful scarlet outfit, and she was in a very good humor as Tony drove us to our hosts. When we got there, she said, "Just find me my seat, and then go on and I'll see you later," which I did, and when we went in to dinner I saw that she was going to be seated next to a man who I knew was going to be bad news. He was an American who lived in the south of France, he was very dull, and Kitty didn't like him one bit. I was seated across the table from them and took my soup spoon and gave it a little wave at Kitty, who was glaring like a fury. At that moment the butler came to me and said, "Mr. Baldwin, Mrs. Miller is leaving."

So I got up and went over to her, and before I could get her out of the dining room she said in a very loud voice, "You don't think I'm going to sit beside that deadly bore! Get me out of here." I took her home and she had some more whiskey, and said, "I will not be insulted by being seated next to people like that." She did that kind of thing more than once, and it was terribly embarrassing.

When Kitty was in New York, I often took her to lunch, which invariably meant going through a ritual. I always got to the apartment at twelve o'clock, and at exactly five minutes past twelve, down the long hall corridor would come Kitty wearing one of her six or seven sable coats. When we got as far as the little bar in the library, she would always stop and say, exactly like a bad child, "Aren't we going to have a little nip?"

It was the fatal thing, and I would say, "Why? Tony is outside waiting for us in the car, and Quo Vadis is just a block away. Do we have to?"

With the firmness of the law she would reply, "Yes, we have to." Well, the trouble was that that little nip was a great big snort of whiskey which she bottomed up, and it would go immediately to her feet. Even with her cane she would start to stumble, and by the time we got to Quo Vadis it was very hard for her to walk. The minute we got there she would have another huge drink, and more often than not, a third.

Toward the end of her life, one evening after dinner in New York, I took her home and she insisted that I have a nightcap with her, which she certainly did not need. She was more than wound up that night, and being rather disagreeable. We talked and I decided that it was time I left, but she demanded that I get her another drink, which I refused to do because she was hopelessly drunk. With that she said she would get herself one, and with great difficulty she tried to raise herself from her chair before I could help her, and slid to the floor and burst into tears.

I helped her back up to her chair, and she said to me, sobbing wildly, "Billy, you've been my friend for more than half my life. Do you think I'm a lady?"

"Kitty," I said, "you, of all people, know that some questions don't deserve the dignity of a reply," and helped her to her bedroom.

I'm afraid that not all of Kitty's outbursts could be blamed on drinking. She had plenty of them throughout her life even before she drank too much. One of her worst scenes occurred in Paris at Givenchy's atelier.

Kitty was a great supporter of Hubert's, and every season she always bought many dresses from him. Bunny Mellon was also an ardent client of his. Kitty absolutely hated Bunny although she had never met her. It happened that one day both Kitty and Bunny were at Givenchy's at the same time. While Kitty was in her fitting room she heard one of Hubert's assistants say that Mrs. Mellon was in another fitting room and needed the advice of Monsieur Givenchy. Luckily for Hubert, at that moment he was with neither Kitty nor Bunny.

Kitty rushed from her room and went to the room where Bunny was and opened the door without even knocking. There was Bunny standing in the middle of the room being pinned in more ways than one. After taking a good long look at Bunny, she said in a loud voice, "Who is this woman? I don't know why she deserves so much attention; after all, I spend a lot more money here than she does."

Of course that statement was totally off the mark in so many ways because Bunny buys all of her clothes from Hubert; even to the extent that in Antigua her maids' uniforms, which are different colors and patterns for each day of the week, are designed and made by him.

One of the last winters that I visited Palm Beach there was also a very attractive woman from England called Bat Stewart, who was a constant attendant of Kitty's. Bill Blass was there, and we were all invited to go to the Loel Guinnesses' for dinner on a Sunday night.

Kitty said, "Now this is not going to be terribly dressy." So we all said, "All right, Kitty. Black tie."

"Now we must not be late," she said, "because Gloria doesn't like to sit around and drink for hours. So please be on time."

So later I got myself all dressed up and went down to the loggia, sat down, and then decided to get up and have a drink. I had on no socks or shoes because I was going to put them on before I left. Just as I rose to my feet there was a crash, and I put my foot into the shattered glass of a bottle of Campari. It had fallen to the floor and was quickly mixing with my blood. It was, I have to admit, agony, and I said, "Oh my God, it's my foot!"

Kitty burst into shrieks, Bill picked me up and put me on the sofa, the chauffeur came in, and Bat began to put cold compresses on my foot. Kitty said, "For Christ's sake! Call the hospital and see if they can take him in the emergency ward." Because it was Sunday it was impossible to get a doctor, and someone called the hospital and they said to bring me right over.

Kitty said, "I'm going to call Gloria and tell her to go ahead with dinner. We'll come if we can or not, whatever she wants us to do."

Tony carried me to the car and took me to the hospital, and it was incredible because in no time a very bright young doctor had put sixteen stitches into my foot, and I felt perfectly fine. We returned to Kitty's, and she called Gloria who said that there was no rush and to come when we could, which was all right because in spite of my accident we were not going to be very late at all.

When we got to the Guinnesses', two of their footmen carried me down to the pool where drinks were being served, and I noticed that Rose Kennedy was standing beside Gloria. I heard Kitty, who was coming along behind me, exclaim, "My God! It's Rose Kennedy. Gloria could not have done this to me!"

I knew it was going to take more than a miracle to make Kitty behave, so I turned my head to her and gave her a look, which was not easy to do because of the awkward position I was in being carried by the two footmen.

The Guinnesses' house was a triumph and it had been designed and built by Gerald Lambert, a Beaux Art architect, celebrated yachtsman, and father of my good friend Bunny Mellon. I saw that we were to be eight for dinner: Loel, Gloria, Kitty, Bill, Rose, a young man, who was a friend of Gloria's, Bat Stewart, and me. It can be said without exaggeration that Gloria served the best food of anyone. It seemed that all the ingredients were there for a perfect party: a beautiful setting, attractive people, and delicious food. We had a very pleasant time during cocktails, although I noticed that Mrs. Kennedy and Mrs. Miller had not spoken to each other.

When we went into dinner and were seated, I saw that Mrs. Kennedy was seated exactly opposite Mrs. Miller. Our dinner began with a heavenly cold cream sorrel soup. It was delicious and Mrs. Kennedy asked Gloria what it was and she told her. "Oh," said Mrs. Kennedy, "I've never heard of cold sorrel soup."

Kitty exclaimed in an absolute bellow, "Imagine that! She's never heard of cold sorrel soup."

After a brief silence, Loel Guinness, who is the world's most charming and best-mannered man, said to Mrs. Kennedy, "Rose, dear. How is everything? How is that son of yours?"

Well, Mrs. Kennedy was very polite, I must say. She talked quite a lot, and we found out it was Ted Kennedy's birthday. The conversation came around to politics a little bit, and Mrs. Kennedy enthusiastically told us her son was very busy with the primaries. Then Mrs. Kennedy, leaning forward in the most polite way, said to Kitty, who had her face in the soup by that time, "Tell me, Mrs. Miller, what are you doing about the primaries?"

Kitty said, "The *what?*"

Mrs. Kennedy answered, "My dear, the primaries."

"What is *that* woman talking about?" said Kitty to Loel, and without waiting for an answer she continued, "The primaries! I've never heard of the primaries," she said sarcastically. "What's that?"

Mrs. Kennedy said, "Imagine that! She's never heard of the primaries," and that ended the intercourse between Mrs. Kennedy and Mrs. Miller.

I will say one thing for Kitty; either one way or the other, she never let you down.

Kitty had cancer at the very end of her life, and she never spoke of it to me but once, and then it was typical. She was not at all well, and though she continued to complain about almost everything, she did not complain about her health. In spite of there not being much hope she underwent a series of radiation treatments which were far from pleasant, and she told me that the only reason she had them was because her doctor was astonishingly good looking and he made her smile.

*Kitty Miller wearing her favorite red dress by Givenchy at her last
New Year's Eve party.*

She decided to wear a red dress, which she had gotten from Givenchy for her last New Year's Eve party. It was one of her favorites, but Therese did not think she should wear it because she felt it was not suitable for a woman of her age. They fought like banshees about it; of course, Kitty had her way, and in spite of everything, Kitty looked grand that night and was her old self.

After she died a letter was given to Therese. Therese was devastated by Kitty's death and was overcome with tears to receive what she thought would be comforting words from her mistress whom she had served for approximately fifteen years. Not at all; the letter gave instructions to Therese about how she should be dressed for her funeral. She wrote that she was to be buried wearing the red Givenchy dress, and she added: You won't be able to do anything about it, and you can't sass me now.

Whether or not it is true that Kitty wrote her own obituary for the *New York Times,* I do not know, but I do know that she ordered and paid for all the white flowers that were placed on the altar at her service.

It is true that in the material sense, Kitty left nothing to anyone; not even to the servants who had been with her for years. No one should have been surprised. Without apologies or explanations, Katherine Bache Miller was an absolute.

CHAPTER TWENTY-THREE

. . . he had a heart of beige.

I can say with perfect certainty and with no delicate touch that when I came to New York in 1935 most of the leading decorators were ladies and most of the taste was set by them. It really was at that time a ladies' profession, and was dominated by Mrs. Brown of McMillen, Diane Tate and Marian Hall, Elsie de Wolfe, Syrie Maugham, Elsie Cobb Wilson, Dorothy Draper, and Ruby Ross Wood.

In spite of this fact, there were a few men who were creeping in as parts of decorating firms or as great influences, but surely even before that, there was the strong influence, thank heavens, of William Odom. He was a brilliant man who was sort of a silent partner of Mrs. Brown's, and he lived in Paris where he managed the Parsons School. He always bought beautiful furniture, which was sent to New York and sold through McMillen. There were certain people who unjustly objected to the fact that the Parsons School was too intimately connected with Mr. Odom and therefore with McMillen. That was absolute nonsense because Mr. Odom was simply the person who bought furniture for McMillen, and there was no earthly reason why there should have been any connection between his management of the Parsons School and his buying furniture for Mrs. Brown. Mr. Odom had beautiful taste, which was imminently suitable for the kind of decorating that was being done then. The French taste was *in,* but I do not mean the use of the elaborate side piece: I mean the use of the attractive small-scale Directoire usable chairs, French furniture with a country influence, and of course, the beautiful town furniture.

Another man who had remarkable taste, great knowledge, and a passion for decorating was George Stacey, and when I first came to New York, he was absolutely the king. At that time he was working for three women who were considered to be the epitome of taste, and they were the three Cushing sisters: Betsy, who was Mrs. James Roosevelt and later married Jock Whitney; Babe, who was Mrs. Stanley Mortimer Jr. and later married William Paley; and Minnie, who was Mrs. Vincent Astor and later married James Fosburgh. It honestly is true that those girls had a kind of monopoly on taste.

George was remarkable in an idiosyncratic way because even when he had a very rich client he used to be proud of selling them material for drawing room curtains which was very inexpensive. This fact became a sore point in Mrs. Gilbert Miller's life. She was about to have George make some curtains for her drawing room and it was just after she'd asked me to come and see her so that I could help her niece. I went to see Mrs. Miller and I will say I can't understand why George wanted her to have a really very cheap brown curtain material for her beautiful drawing room. She said to me, "Look what he's doing. It's an outrage. Tell me why that pill wants me to buy this cheap stuff which won't last at all, and which will look cheap. He knows that my clothes are not made of material like this, so why should I have junk at the windows? I'm going to tell him to get out of my house." And Kitty did just that.

It made no difference to George because he was so successful, and he continued to sell fabric by the thousands of yards for curtains and slip-covers to the chicest women in New York who could perfectly well pay for the same thing in a material that would have really been a little better looking. George made so much money that he had to leave the country because his income tax was so colossal that he couldn't afford to stay in America. He got himself a lovely little château in France, but he still kept a very attractive apartment in New York.

George was prematurely bald, and this fact upset him to the point of eccentricity, so he never ever took his hat off. I remember so well going into Mrs. Wood's office one day and seeing George sitting there. They were great friends because he was a witty, attractive man, but there he was sitting in her office on a nice winter day wearing quite a large brown felt hat. She said to him and to me, "Look at him. How can I let him get away with it? Take your hat off, George!"

George had been a brilliant student at the Parsons School, and one of the results was that he and Van Day Truex didn't like each other at all, but I think that George had extremely good taste, and I regret that I was never able to stay with him in France. Don't think he let this pass unobserved. "Oh, I know," said he, "you can't possibly come to stay with me in France because when you're there you must stay with the Windsors." He knew perfectly well that I was not really at all a friend of the Windsors. He simply adored teasing me. However, I wish I had stayed with him in France because he was so much fun and he made such marvelous martinis.

George also had an enchanting little house on Long Island that Mrs. Davison, who had a beautiful house there and was married to the famous Trubee Davison of the American Red Cross, had given him to live in for the duration of the war. I did spend the weekend there with him, and could not have had more fun.

The house that Mrs. Davison had given to George had been an indoor tennis court, so the windows were God knows how high from the floor, and not one structural change had been made. There was a sort of balcony at the end of the room where there were two very comfortable beds and a chest of drawers. That is where you and your host slept. Downstairs was a great long room which served as the living room, dining room, and kitchen. A number of drawing-room chairs were scattered around the room, and the whole thing was made into a fascinatingly attractive house. The bathroom facilities were slightly odd in that the shower was outside in front of the house; consequently you had the advantage there of showing off to everybody.

A young man called Van Day Truex, who was absolutely smothered with taste, appeared from out of the west. I consider without a doubt that he was the best-dressed man that I have ever seen, and he always had the prettiest apartments, which he was constantly changing for one equally or even more charming either in Paris or New York. He was also constantly redecorating them so it seemed as though he lived in a moving mobile. All of this was supposed to have been done on no money, but I think it was done on a remarkable economy. Van was a very good cook, and I consider that he managed his little luncheons in his apartments with the greatest possible charm. He could also take a bolt of material from London and carry it under his arm down to Italy

Van Day Truex. (Condé Nast)

where he would have the most beautiful suit in the world made at one-tenth the London price.

Van really did honestly make the thing of one flower in a vase not look poor or affected, and his apartment was always scattered with tall thin glass vases with a brilliant single anemone in each of them. He did exactly the same thing in Paris.

Van's food was delicious and the apartments were always delightful, but he had a heart of beige. He literally could honestly only love to have himself surrounded in beautiful beige materials. It would have been impossible for Van Day to wear a colored necktie. He saw, without question, the brilliance of browns, beiges, whites, and blacks, but he used his apartment to experiment with, and he nearly always started with a burst of red as a background, or even dark green, and finally even a very dark brown as a wall color. All of these experiments in color were very successful, but not enough of that happened for very long. Always, somehow there was a return to the beige.

Fortunately, for us all, he was an extremely good artist. He left behind him the results of many annual exhibitions of drawings: of Provence, Paris, and also Greenwich Village in New York. His drawings were very inexpensive, which was a wonderful thing because it gave younger people who did not have a great deal of money to spend on names the opportunity to purchase charming first-class things. His shows were always sold out on the day of the opening.

In contrast to his beige world he had the most delicious humor, and was not the slightest bit solemn. Van Day was laughing all the time, wishing everybody to be happy, and adding enormously to the gaiety of the world. Because he was a semi-invalid, he didn't mind at all going to bed early; in fact, he insisted upon it, and he always left every party at ten-thirty, but we all knew perfectly well that was not absolutely necessary. Van Day had had terrible trouble with his lungs when he was young, and as a result he loved the simple life, which was in contrast to his very busy life in New York and Paris as head of the Parsons School in both of those cities. He loved visiting his great friend Helen Hull in Nantucket because there was nothing to do there but to enjoy the climate, and it was wonderful having him there on the island because he required no possible entertainment.

The sad thing was that Van Day died of a heart attack just as he was about to buy the first house he had ever owned in America. He lived in Provence in the summer and his apartments in Paris and New York in the winter. I think Van Day suddenly felt that perhaps he should own something in his own country — some of his own land — but unfortunately he never lived to see this accomplished.

After a certain period of time he severed his connections with the Parsons School and became the art director in toto of Tiffany's, where he put new life, beauty, charm, and inventive imagination into creating a totally new Tiffany look.

He did very dashing things such as having prominent New York decorators design table settings, which were then displayed at exhibitions at Tiffany's. In 1957 I designed a table setting for a luncheon called "Four in a White Room." The other decorators who designed table settings at that time were Mrs. Henry Parrish, Mrs. Russell Davenport of McMillen, Inc., Marion Hall, William Pahlmann, and Van Day Truex.

Very often some of Van Day's decorators were really quite unknown, and honest to God, many years ago, Andy Warhol, who was not as well known then as he is today, designed a child's table for one of Van Day's exhibitions and in the middle of the table was a stuffed cat. It was one of the few that had died of the forty that Andy had in his apartment where he lived with his mother. I am not a cat person, and I remember very well going back to the exhibition one day and seeing to my great relief that the stuffed cat was not there. I asked a very nice attendant in the show room, "Where is that pussy?" "Oh," he said, "somebody had a fit, so we had to remove her." However, I became fond of Andy, and when he asked to draw my feet for a project of his, I was happy to let him. I have often wondered what ever became of my "Warhol feet."

It is not possible for me to overestimate the truth, the importance, or the pleasure of what I can now say were some of the happiest moments of my life when I was lecturing at the Parsons School under Van Day Truex. I was terribly flattered that he chose me to do a series of lectures. Van and I had had a great deal of fun shopping together or going to exhibitions, which we did nearly every Saturday afternoon after lunch in the winter, in New York, and his approval of my taste could not possibly have been more sought after by me; however I felt that sometimes he was a little strict for me. There were times, I am sure, when I was more flamboyant, and in regard to color I was quite generous, but I don't think my concept of color was ever as consistently pure as Van's was. He had perfectly beautiful pure taste, but there were moments when I think that he was a little conventional.

Van, looking very serious, said to me one day, "There's something that I want to ask if you would be interested in doing for me, but let me say here at the first moment that it has nothing to do with money. You will be making nothing out of it, and you may also find that you're just too busy; however, I cannot bear to have your ability be appreciated only by those who can afford to pay for it, and I want you to be connected with my school. Now don't jump, because you always do jump too soon when making a decision. Just listen to me."

I said, "Of course, I will."

"Well," he said, "I want you to be frank and truthful and tell me what you think because what I want you to do is to lecture to the students. Have you ever done any lecturing?"

I said, "Well, I've done a little, and I'm not exactly shy."

"I should hardly call you shy, Billy. What I want you to do is to lecture to the class who will be graduated in June. There may be as many as sixty kids, and they're not all kids either because there are some old ladies. But before they finish their three-year course I want you to come to the school, and tell them that they're not worth a goddamn thing, and that they are entirely unexposed to the only important thing, which we can't give them, and that is contact with the human being. There is no way for us at the school to do it, and the only possible way for them to know what it will be like is to hear it from a person who is a decorator. I want you to figure out the best way you can to tell them how they can get the most for their money because many of these kids are paying the last cents of their lives to learn a profession. They come from all over the east, north, south, Europe, everyplace, and you've got to help them."

"Well," I said, "let me think, but the answer is yes. I'll do it, of course."

So I began thinking, and I have to say that I was given a great deal of confidence and a great deal of patience from Woody Taulbee.

He said to me, "I think Van's right. He's giving you a wonderful chance, and he's also giving the students a chance."

I decided to call my little project, "Forever," and the students were given three weeks to complete it. Their assignment was to decorate a specific room in a specific house to serve people with specific tastes, needs, and interests.

Lecturing to the students was extremely intense for me, and I never ever knew any student's name or even what they looked like until after the test was over. At the end of the three weeks the students submitted to me what they had done, and I then gave them a critique of their work. Never have I had such satisfaction in my life as I had in helping sixty students further their careers and find jobs.

I started lecturing at the Parsons School in 1946, and continued on and off until 1952. I had become Baldwin Inc. in 1950 after Ruby died, and during the following time my clients made increasing demands upon me and I could no longer continue my lectures, but my Parsons years were totally rewarding for me and I also never had more fun or such a good time.

It was also in 1952, because of my friendship with Anne Kinsolving Brown, who was married to John Nicholas Brown, the commodore of the New York Yacht Club, that I was engaged by him to design a column for the America's Cup, which I did. At that time the cup was simply sitting on a table and we all thought it should be properly displayed.

Another person, who fortunately for me became a great friend, was Roderick Cameron, a man of the most remarkable taste. Van Day and Roderick were indeed great friends although Van was considerably older than Rory. Van had actually been a friend of Mrs. Cameron, Rory's aunt, even before he was a friend of Rory's, and Rory was always known as "the nephew." His mother, Lady Kenmare, was an Australian beauty and twice a widow when I first met him. Lady Kenmare and Rory with a combination of American and Australian money had bought a property on the Riviera which was a wreck due to damages done to it during the war. This remarkable building was known as "La Fiorentina," and it certainly did have, for one thing, the most beautiful views and sights on all of the Riviera. It was clinging on to the tip of Cap Ferrat, and surrounded by perfectly fantastic gardens, terrace upon terrace, most of which had remained in pretty good condition in spite of the war.

The restoration began and it was lucky for everybody because Rory was a young man of enormous taste, great enthusiasm, and plenty of money. Together with his mother, they bought a great deal of the furniture for the house and turned it into the most beautiful house on the entire Riviera. The restoration was by no means an exact copy of what it had been before the war and before the bombing; instead, Rory brought the whole thing into the present time with a remarkable clarity, a great feeling for textured materials of the day, a lovely absence of color in that most of it was rather bony or very pale, and the introduction of contemporary French furniture, most notably tables by Jean-Michel Frank, who was the last great cabinetmaker in Paris.

Lady Kenmare even painted murals, and she painted a wonderful one for the dining room which looked like a tapestry of leaves and foliage. Everyone was full of enthusiasm for "La Fiorentina" and I, for one, adored going there.

She died at a very ripe old age, and Rory suddenly felt bored with all of France, including Paris. He just somehow wanted to get out. He also didn't know what kind of place he wanted to go to, and he made a very quick and unfortunate decision to go to Ireland, only because there was a lovely house there that he wanted. It was one of the best examples in the world: never buy a house somewhere just because of the house — you must as well buy the place, the people, and everything about it. Rory took all his furniture with him to Ireland and his house there was a distinct failure. I never saw the house, very few did because he got bored with it and eventually moved back to the south of France where he built himself a great edifice very near Van Day Truex's.

"My name is James Woolworth Donahue and my father was the president of that dime store that I know you must have heard of."

It may seem odd when I say I'd never met Jimmy Donahue during my early years in New York because we had in common many many mutual friends in Paris, London, and New York. As far as I'm concerned there never was a more controversial figure than Jimmy. He had a perfectly outrageous reputation for every kind of misbehavior. He was almost a criminal, and he lived a totally selfish life for himself alone, but in 1957, when I began working so diligently with him on an enormous house in Old Brookville on Long Island, I learned that he had incredible qualities of goodness, generosity, intelligence, and kindness. I have never worked with anybody who endeared himself more to the workmen associated with the decoration of a house. It was an enormous red brick Georgian performance, and had been built during the time when there was such luxury as very attractive sunny basement rooms for guests' visiting valets and other personal servants. In many ways it was more like a great English country house than almost any I ever worked on. Not for a moment was Jimmy stingy about the way he lived in his house or the way he ran it. He was truthfully and easily the most extravagant client I ever had although I have found myself saying that about quite a lot of them.

Cole Porter was responsible for Jimmy's calling me not too long after I had finished his apartment on the thirty-third floor of the Waldorf

Towers. I have no hesitancy in saying that that job gave me more joy by far than any other I've ever done. It is true that when Cole went to Europe he gave me carte blanche to do his apartment, but it was more than that. He totally believed in my creativity and integrity as a designer, and as a result I created a brassbound library for him. I designed bookcases for him made of brass piping, and had the walls of the apartment covered in tortoiseshell leather. It had not been done before and it was a great success. From that great success we became really unbelievably good friends. His gratitude was beyond expression, and I enjoyed him as a brain and a charmer as much as anybody I've ever known.

I met Cole at a performance of the ballet at the Metropolitan Opera House during the intermission. I was walking up the staircase going to the bar with Howard Sturges and I suddenly heard a voice like a little bird say, "Is that the great 'Billy B'?" I looked up and there was Cole hanging over the end of the railing like a hummingbird. Howard was saying to Cole, "It is indeed, and I want to introduce you."

"Well," said Cole after Howard introduced us, "I hope you feel very well and strong because I must see you as soon as possible, and I want you to come for the weekend to Williamstown. I am moving the contents of my wife's house down to the new apartment I have taken at the Waldorf. Before her death, my beloved wife, Linda, said to me in a letter which I am mailing to you: 'Please get yourself a beautiful apartment at the Waldorf, and have Billy Baldwin do it.' "

After it was done, I have to say it was a wild success and Cole invited everybody there. He gave a luncheon party twice a week for about twelve people. He had a staff of his own, in addition to the employees of the Waldorf Hotel, and his own chef prepared the most unbelievable food made according to Linda's recipes from Paris. I supervised the arrangement of the flowers for his apartment, which were beyond description and price. Fortunately, I never had the shock of looking at the bills.

Several months after I had decorated Cole's apartment, he asked me to come and have lunch with him there, alone. I went, and he said to me, "You can see how happy I am here."

I said, "Yes, and I envy you. I think it's the most attractive thing the way your European friends love to come here for lunch."

"They like it better than anyplace in New York," he said.

"Well," I said, "I will never forget the other day when I was here, and in came as a first course an enormous iron dish filled with great chunks of crushed ice, and scattered over it the freshest raw clams and oysters."

"That was the way Linda used to do it in Paris. Now," he said, "Billy B," a name that was taken up by a lot of people in reference to me, especially by Margaret Case, "I am sure you know Jimmy Donahue, and don't faint."

"I don't, and I won't," I replied.

"Well," he said, "I feel certain you can cope with my suggestion, and there is no reason, if you handle it in a purely businesslike manner, why it cannot help but be a great financial success for you. Quite simply, Jimmy Donahue has decided that he must live by himself, and be in the country although he's going to continue to live in his apartment next door to his mother's on Fifth Avenue. He has bought Alfred Gwynne Vanderbilt's estate on Cedar Swamp Road in Old Brookville, Long Island, and he wants you to decorate the house."

I knew the Vanderbilt estate, which was an imposing property of approximately one hundred acres with beautiful gardens.

Cole continued, "Jimmy's mother, Jessie Woolworth, has been a friend of mine for many years, and she is one of the nicest women I know. I always see her in Paris and I see a lot of her in New York where she lives in an appalling apartment. It's crammed full of English eighteenth-century furniture and paintings, although lately the French curse is seizing her and she is now having the whole thing painted in the French manner and the Louies are sneaking in."

I said, "It's true that Jimmy and I have a great many mutual friends, and in the spring of 1954 I redecorated a suite at the Pierre for his cousin, Barbara Hutton, after her marriage to Rubirosa was over. I also know Mrs. Donahue because I see her every year at Kitty Miller's New Year's Eve party, where I also have the pleasure of seeing you."

"Oh, my God!" said Cole. "You know I think she's the most evil woman I have ever met. I know she has great style, is a great hostess, and Gilbert is a brilliant, brilliant man, but I can't possibly like her. I just think she's evil."

"Well," I said, "now, Cole, I'm not surprised to hear you say that because unfortunately it seems to be a popularly held opinion. However, I've been working for Kitty for quite a while with the greatest possible pleasure, and I know people are bored with her taste because they think it's terribly conventional, but I can't see it that way because I think how terrible her taste might well have been."

I told Cole that I would be happy to talk to Jimmy about his project, and Cole said he would tell Jimmy, but time went by and I did not hear from him.

That New Year's Eve, we were all sitting around at Kitty and Gilbert's, drinking before dinner, and I had arranged to have the good fortune of sitting on a little stool by the sofa where Cole was. There Cole sat being mercilessly witty like a little king, holding court with all the prettiest women circling around him. Diana Vreeland was next to him, looking more extraordinarily frightening than ever, and just across from us, but, thank God, not within hearing distance, was Jessie Donahue.

Mrs. Donahue's flesh was one of the most extraordinary things I've ever looked at. It was of such creamy beauty, and her bosom was like something out of Holbein. Her breasts were just sitting there, and on them were resting a matching pair of emeralds of the most beautiful color imaginable, and somehow it seemed so right. Diana said, "You know something. The happiest things in this room are those two emeralds on Jessie Donahue's bosom."

When we went into dinner, I happened to be seated next to Mrs. Donahue, and she said to me, "I hear that my son wants you to work for him, and I think I'd better tell you that I've offered him all the furniture from my house in Newport, which I've just sold, if he wants it. I have to tell you that you look like a very nice young man, and I think you'd be a fool to work for him because there will be nobody in that house but the biggest bums in New York, and it will be a waste of your time. I don't say a waste of money, because God knows he will spend *that!* I don't know about his taste or how much he knows about housekeeping, but he will have plenty of servants who will help him with that, and maybe you can control his taste. If you do work for him, I certainly wish you luck, and I want you to know if you have any problem with him, please come to me and talk to me about it."

I thought that was awfully nice of Mrs. Donahue because she totally adored him, which she should have, but she had no illusions about him.

After dinner, Cole asked me what Jessie and I had been talking about through dinner and I told him. He said, "Well, I'm going to talk to Jimmy tomorrow and tell him he'd better stop dillydallying and call you."

One morning a few days later the telephone rang and a nice quiet little voice said, "Is this Mr. Baldwin?"

I said, "Yes, it is."

He said, "My name is James Woolworth Donahue and my father was the president of that dime store that I know you must have heard of."

I said that I had, and that just recently I had seen his mother at Kitty Miller's.

"Did you see her this past New Year's Eve?" he asked.

I said, "That is exactly when I saw her."

"Did she have on two emeralds?" he asked, and I told him she did, indeed.

He said, "Whenever she goes out to dinner she always lets me see her so that I can see how she looks, and that night I said, for God's sake, Mother, take one of those off, or you'll look like the five and dime."

I was to learn that Jimmy always had dinner with his mother unless she went out, which she did a great deal. He also acted as his mother's host when she gave a dinner party, but if she were alone, they had dinner together, and he remained with her until a certain television program went on. Then he would leave her and go out on the town. He would say to his friends that he would meet them at one of his favorite night spots where he gathered together some of the most decorative young men in New York.

When we first began to work together, it meant that I went nearly every afternoon to his apartment for quite a long time. It had a separate entrance, but adjoined his mother's apartment in the same building on Fifth Avenue. I would go there about two-thirty or three o'clock, and Jimmy would appear from his shower-bath, smelling marvelously clean and fresh. He would have just gotten up because he never went to bed before six o'clock in the morning, and one of his little habits was taking friends back to his apartment after everything had closed.

Jimmy had no instinctive taste whatsoever, but he saw that he must listen to me because I was a practicing decorator, I knew what was in the market, and I knew what was suitable for a young man and not for an old lady. His interest in art didn't exist, but what did interest him was acquiring the best possible seventeenth- and eighteenth-century English furniture for those vast rooms in his country house. He was very interested in Queen Anne furniture, which at the time not too many other people were because it was not very practical. With this furniture he wanted bright clear color, and a modern point of view. Because of this point of view, what would have been simply a great number of opulently furnished rooms became instead a remarkably interesting interior in which to live. As he had vast amounts of money and total freedom in every way, we were able to create exactly what he wished. We got beautiful old, but still brilliant needlepoint rugs, which complimented his furniture perfectly. He was crazy about porcelain and acquired one of the best collections ever. Upon his death it went to auction and the sale was patronized by all the important collectors and top porcelain houses.

Very often he would call me at the office around lunchtime and say, "Duck, when are you going to be here?" I would reply, "Don't you want me at about half past two?" He'd say, "Yes, but hurry, love. I felt lonely yesterday afternoon and bought the most beautiful Meissen cock you've ever seen."

After the house was finished, Jimmy would come into the city every Monday afternoon and return to the country on Friday morning. He was the best housekeeper of anyone I have ever known, and his house was run in the most incredible order. I must admit that part of the remarkable performance of running his establishment was due to the fact that money simply didn't even exist when it came to doing what he wanted done. Nobody ever served better food, had nicer servants, nor treated his guests with such kindness and generosity. He loved flowers and the house was always full of them although he hated roses, and he said to me once that he never wanted them around because he thought they were common.

In the beginning when we started working on the house, he said, "I just have to tell you something that I want you to do. You're a little bit too gentlemanly with me in some ways, and you've got to be tough. For instance, I know you think my mother's apartment is perfectly ghastly, and I know you know that she has no taste whatsoever, which is true. So let's avoid having any of her taste rubbed off on me in my house. You know I love red velvet, so if I say, Can we have that chair covered in it, and you know it's perfectly awful; you must say to me: Plushy! Plushy!"

So that is exactly what I would do, and I tried so hard not to let him see anything that could be considered at all plushy, but every now and then he would slip away to the wholesale houses, which I didn't allow him to do, but he did anyway. He would then call me and say, "Now, listen. I've got to see you tomorrow because I've borrowed some marvelous samples from a firm you've never taken me to, and I'm only allowed to have them twenty-four hours because they are so expensive. Can you come a little early?"

So, of course, I came a little early, and the samples would be absolutely ghastly, very expensive copies of old tapestries, but hideously ugly, and I would say, "No. This is the plushiest thing ever. So cut it out."

About six months after I had been working for Jimmy, Cole called me and said, "Billy B, how are you getting along with Jimmy?" I told him that I was getting along very well and that I was crazy about him.

Cole said, "Well, I'll tell you something. He's terrified of you, and he said to me: I like that little man so much, but I'm scared to death. I don't want to do anything to hurt him, but I've almost gotten so I can't say anything and I don't want to do the wrong thing because I know that Billy is selling me not prices, but what is the best, and I trust him implicitly."

I said, "Well, Cole. Jimmy should trust me because I honestly have saved him a great deal of money."

I must admit that in most things Jimmy was very good at following the advice of those who knew best. I am not a landscape gardener, but he had extremely good advice on that subject from the gardener whom he had inherited when he bought the property. The gardener lived in a cottage on the estate with Jimmy's valet, who was also the gardener's lifelong friend.

Jimmy also had a devoted companion, Joey Mitchell, who lived in the house with him, and who attended to some of the business ends of running it. Joey had his work cut out for him in keeping the house running smoothly because he never knew what to expect. He told me that one night Jimmy got very cross with his butler and fired him in the middle of the evening. Jimmy said he could have a Carey car take him back to New York, and he would give him his check, which he did. The car came, and the man was sent back to New York. The next afternoon he called Jimmy and said, "Mr. Donahue, I'm very sorry, but the check you have signed is no good because it is signed 'Beautiful Baby Jimmy.' "

Unfortunately, one of the things that Jimmy did best was to embarrass you to the point that you practically had to leave the house. I went out to his house many times for the weekend, but I usually tried to avoid it because those weekends were too complicated, too drunken, and much too dangerous. More often than not, I would go out only for dinner. He would send a Carey car for me, and keep it there until two o'clock in the morning if I wished to return, but I always tried so hard to get out by midnight.

There were usually several Carey cars there that had brought his guests out for his parties, which normally consisted of twelve to eighteen people. His dinner parties were nearly always stag affairs, which consisted so often of boys and young men who I don't think in many cases had ever been inside a house like Jimmy's, although in fact, there weren't very many houses like Jimmy's to be inside of.

He had a fantastic collection of records that he played in the library during his parties. It was filled with wonderful books that he had read, and there was no show-off about him in any way in regard to that. He dressed terribly and wore the corniest neckties I've ever seen. He had the best sense of humor, couldn't have been wittier or more charming, and had the most beautiful manners; that is, when sober, but when drunk he was beyond the pale. Then he loved to do a strip tease until he was naked and dance, which was mild compared to what else he might do or say.

Some years before, in a state of drunkenness, Jimmy circumcised himself with a penknife, and he told me that never in his life had he suffered such pain and agony. As a result, he was grotesquely scarred and painfully sensitive.

The only time there was cavier was when I was there, and he would say to me in front of his other guests, "This trash doesn't even know what it is, and I've got just enough for you."

One of Jimmy's intimate friends was Ethel Merman. After his house was finished, he arranged for her to be brought out to the country on a Saturday night, spend the weekend, and go back on Monday morning. Jimmy was thrilled because she was in a big hit, and he begged me to spend the weekend too. I really didn't want to go because it meant that you had no idea of when you could get to bed. He never thought of going to bed until the sun was shining brightly, and he wanted his guests to stay up as well. Also, whenever I spent the weekend I was always given Mrs. Donahue's room even when a lady was there, and I didn't know what Ethel would say about that.

Jimmy had invited nine or ten people to greet her on her arrival and maybe three or four others to spend the weekend. While we were waiting for her, everyone got as tight as a tick, but I admit, I did not. Woody Taulbee was there. Jimmy was devoted to Woody and Woody went out there quite a lot because for some reason it fascinated him, but as a matter of fact I always thought that Woody went there much too much.

Ethel arrived quite late, after her performance. She walked through the huge living room to get to the library where she was to be entertained, and sat herself down next to me and quite a lot of champagne and my cavier. After a brief little while Jimmy said, "Now, darling, I'll take you to your room whenever you want to go."

Ethel said, "I certainly am not going to bed yet!"

Jimmy said, "I want you to see the dining room and the other rooms on the floor."

"For Christ's sake! I'm not going to buy the goddamned joint! I want to have a good time," she said.

Ethel off stage in contrast to Ethel on stage was like night and day, and so it was that I spent another long, long night waiting for the dawn's light so I could go to bed.

Jimmy first met the Windsors in Palm Beach in 1950, but he was still going abroad a great deal at that time, and he saw them in Paris frequently, where his great friendship with the duchess first began to blossom.

When they were living in New York at the Waldorf-Astoria, they went many weekends to Jimmy's house in the country, and he always entertained a very representative group of their friends. Nearly all of the Windsors' friends accepted Jimmy's invitations, but there were a few who didn't because some husbands didn't approve of Jimmy, and they had a perfect right not to.

One glorious summer night Jimmy gave a beautiful dinner dance for them. He had a tent erected outside to dance under, there was a very snappy band, and some of the most respected people in New York City and on Long Island were there. The duchess was having a perfectly lovely time in the library where all the excitement was going on. There was a big low Chinese coffee table in front of the sofa, and on it, scattered around as if they were nothing but popcorn, was a collection of priceless eighteenth- and nineteenth-century gold snuff boxes.

Miraculously, in the long history of Jimmy's countless friendships, only one was ever stolen, and he even recovered that. Over a year after it was stolen, Jimmy was in a late-night supperclub, and out of a boy's pocket came the gold snuff box, which he was using as a cigarette case. Jimmy said, "Listen, young man, you just give me my snuff box or I'll have the police right here." The boy said he was terribly sorry and that a friend had given it to him, as he quickly handed the box over to Jimmy.

One of the first times that she and the duke went to spend the weekend at Jimmy's house on Long Island, Jimmy played one of his practical jokes, and the joke was on me. He said to the duchess, "I want you to see something now. It is the only thing that Billy Baldwin has done for me here, and I think it is only fair for me to show it to you." The duchess told me later that she thought it was rather odd that Jimmy hadn't mentioned me at all in connection with the rest of the house.

So Jimmy took the duke and duchess and two other couples who were also visiting there to the basement, which was really a superb, extraordinary work of architecture. In it were a series of rooms that had originally been built for visiting valets and maids. There were two charming separate suites which each had a bedroom, bath, and a small sitting room with a window looking onto a little terrace.

When I first began work for Jimmy, he had said to me, "Now listen here, I want to have you design the most divine valet's rooms in the world."

To be perfectly truthful, they were not for that purpose at all. He wanted them for young men who were too drunk to go home. When they really couldn't even make the Carey car, they were to be rolled into the beds of the rooms downstairs.

"For the first room," he said, "I want you to think of it as someplace that Diana Vreeland would be very happy in. I want it all to be red, red, red. And I know that you've done that for Diana, and I know that you can do that for my little valet's room. It can look as Oriental as you want, but I want the best bed, and the best bedding. I want the most expensive upholstered chair, and I'd like to have some sequins for the (quote) 'drapes,'" said Jimmy, swishing. "I just would like to have it so whoever is there would never want to leave it."

Across the hall was the other suite. Jimmy said, "This I want to be a greater triumph. This must be absolutely Moorish. I want it to have black walls, black curtains, a black bed, and indirect lighting. I want everything black. All I want to be able to see is their teeth and their eyeballs."

So I hung the ceiling and the walls with black velvet like a tent. There was a daybed covered in black velvet with lots of brilliant black sequin pillows on it, and the carpet was thick black pile with a black bearskin rug on top of it. There were a few paintings on the walls and they, too, were black. However, for the connecting bath, I insisted that there be normal lighting.

So I did Jimmy's red and black rooms and that is what the duke and duchess and the two other couples were shown as an example of my work before they retired for the evening.

I saw Jimmy several days later after the Windsors' visit, and he told me what he had done. I said, "Jimmy, I'm sure that you didn't do that!"

He said, "You're stinking mad."

I said, "You're perfectly stinking."

"Well," he said, "you did do those rooms."

I said, "I know I did, but I honestly think I did more than that."

"Well," he said, "the duchess was very impressed."

The following spring I went to Maryland for the Maryland Hunt Cup and stayed with Wallace and Eleanor Lanahan. The Windsors were also at the Hunt Ball where they had two tables and I sat at the table where the duke was seated.

During the preceding year not long after they had seen Jimmy's house, they had also seen Cole Porter's apartment and they were crazy about a pair of lamps that had been made for him from old Empire columns.

One afternoon after the Windsors' had had lunch at Cole's I received a call from the duchess's secretary. She described the lamps and asked me to please send a pair to the duchess by six o'clock that afternoon. I explained that I didn't think I would be able to do so because they were old and not readily available. The duchess got on the telephone and said, "Billy, I've got to have those lamps. They're for the Mill and I want them to go with us on our evening flight."

I told her that I didn't think it was possible, but that I would try. So I got one of my assistants who ran all over town trying to find them, but couldn't. I sent the Windsors a cable saying that I would need a week or so, and I would do what I could. I did finally find a pair, and sent them to France. That was the time when the Windsors were not supposed to have been paying their bills, but I got paid at once, and I must say the Crown sent a very fascinating check.

That night in Baltimore at the Hunt Ball the duke said to me, "I do want to tell you that the two lamps you sent us for the Mill are beautiful."

I don't know if he had rehearsed saying that or not, but he said it with his beautiful, beautiful manners, which he certainly did have.

I don't think that Wallis had what I call taste in regard to the decoration of houses. The Mill was perfectly terrible, and was plastered with a lot of cheap American wallpaper, mostly from Katzenbach and Warren. The only thing about it that was ravishing was one great room which had been taken almost verbatim from Fort Belvedere, his house in England. In it was a huge equestrian portrait of the duke, and some lovely English furniture. That room was attractive, but most of the Mill was awfully tacky, but that's what Wallis had: tacky southern taste; much too overdone, much too elaborate, and no real charm.

One of my real regrets in this life is the fact that I am five years younger than the duchess. If only I had been five years older, I know I

The Duchess of Windsor. (Condé Nast)

would have been dancing at her side every minute. She was a friend of the most attractive people in Baltimore, and she had two or three young beaux who were the outstanding bright boys there.

When she was a young woman she made all her own clothes because she had no money whatsoever, and my mother said she was the best-dressed woman in Baltimore although not very many of the Baltimore ladies approved of her clothes because they weren't fancy southern ruffly dresses, but the passing years have proven Wallis to have been one of the best-dressed women of her time. As she became older she often wore gloves because she had very unattractive hands; that she got straight from Elsie Mendl.

Wallis Warfield's family were very attractive-looking people. One of her relatives, Edmund Warfield, was one of the most marvelous-looking men I've ever seen, and one of her female relatives who was a raving beauty married a Polish count; she had a faint little black mustache — very chic! Wallis's mother, a very striking woman, had a lover, and he slept openly in her house, which was impossible for the Baltimore ladies to accept. Because of that, when Wallis came out she was almost déclassé, and she had a very hard time making the grade.

After she came out in Baltimore she married a man who was stationed in China, and while she was there with him she learned many things from the Chinese.

Wallis could tell the most wonderful entertaining stories, and even in those days she had beautiful manners, which she continued to have up until the last time I saw her. I never saw her very much because she and her friends were a little older than I was and there was never any reason for me to see her as a client. She did become a great friend of Kitty Miller's, and although she was a bit critical of Kitty, she respected her judgment and taste.

There were two elements in Wallis's life in which she excelled and in which she had no peer: those were her clothes and her knowledge of food. Both of these things were far better than her taste in decoration. It may simply have been another case of being *nouveau riche* because she didn't really have any money at all until she married the duke. She knew all about comfort and extended it to a degree. She was a brilliant hostess, and she served the best food of anyone. I can never forget being in her house in Paris for a meal that was fit for the gods.

I have to state that the Windsors were Café Society if there ever was such a thing. I did not spend much time with those people, but I worked for them gladly. I never thought that the so-called Café Society was made up of terribly interesting people. In the end, the Windsors didn't care whom they saw, and they would finally go anyplace if anybody asked them to come for a meal; they just had no discrimination whatsoever.

Jimmy used to talk to me at great length about the duchess and her charms. There can be no doubt about it, the duchess had charms, and that's all there is to it. Her career is not exactly marked by charming events, but she's done one thing that no American has ever done, and that is to marry a king of England.

The great thing about Jimmy and the duchess was this. There was a little restaurant just off Park Avenue on 59th Street which is no longer there. My office was at that time on the corner of Park Avenue and 57th Street, and so I used to lunch nearly every day at that little restaurant because it was quite pleasant, not expensive, and filled with nice people, many of whom were employed in the decorating business in one way or another.

To my great excitement one day, I heard an absolute roar of laughter from the entrance of the restaurant, and into the room, like two children, rushed the duchess and Jimmy. They didn't see me at all, and rushed right past my table back to the farthest corner in the back back back back of the room where there was practically no light. It was at the time the duke was writing his book, so she and Jimmy would go there nearly every day, and after lunch they would just quietly go to Jimmy's apartment. The duchess was always well behaved, but a couple of times I saw that she was rather tight, because she liked to drink. They were inseparable in New York, and I know that during that time in her life she had more fun than she had ever had before. In a strange sense, Wallis had never had a beau, and Jimmy became her beau and treated her like a young girl.

Jimmy said to me one evening before dinner, "I just want to tell you something about your little duchess. She's the best I've ever known. She's always considerate and adorable, and she never hurts me as almost all the others do."

Jimmy died on December 6, 1966, in his apartment at 833 Fifth Avenue. That night he went out on the town with his lover. They went to a great many night spots, including Regent's Row where I saw him early on, and it was said that he drank an inordinate amount, something like thirty drinks. Finally, as they were about to go back to his apartment, he met another boy. He told his lover that he was not to come with him, but instead he was taking the new boy home.

Much later I was told that when Jimmy and the boy got to bed, the first thing the boy knew was that Jimmy was dying. He got his clothes on and got the hell out of there as fast as he could, and I think he either phoned the doorman or spoke to him on his way out. Well, that was that, and the next thing we knew was that Jimmy's funeral was to be at St. Vincent Ferrer on Lexington Avenue.

Every spring during the last five years of Jimmy's life I placed the order for the flowers that he sent to the Church of St. Vincent Ferrer. It cost thousands and thousands of dollars and the whole church was solid with white lilies. In connection with the church he campaigned on the radio to help unfortunate children, and he offered to match any contribution that was given. So it was very suitable that Jimmy's funeral was held there.

Woody Taulbee and I went to his funeral, and I am ashamed to admit I don't know whether I saw Mrs. Donahue there or not. During the service, in the middle of the eulogy, the most embarrassing thing happened. Up stood one of Jimmy's friends, dressed in black and looking extremely handsome. He said, "I don't think what you're saying is true." He was sat down mighty quickly before he could say anything else.

It cannot be difficult to imagine the disparate and incongruous persons who were at the funeral. I don't think that New York ever had in one place so many prominent, very respectable people together with some real honeys whose likes were not often seen.

"I do not want to sit here having some man look at that goddamned bridge. I want him to look at me."

It is very gratifying as life rolls along to discover that one has realized a great ambition. I have had several of these rewarding experiences; two of which I really didn't work very hard for, but which I think I would have done almost anything for. They were working for Ina Claire and for Whitney Warren.

My real passion in the theatre was Ina Claire. Never will I forget her. When I was living in Baltimore and had no real hope of ever becoming a citizen of New York City, I saw Ina in a play called *Polly With a Past*. Chippie Reynolds did the sets as a brilliant adaptation of Elsie de Wolfe's style of decoration, and Ina's clothes were sensational.

One dress she wore in the play was made of salmon pink velvet pulled skintight across her tummy, and it had a colossal bustle at the back which was made of a flaming mass of feathers the same color as the velvet. *Oh yes,* there was a matching fan.

I had followed Ina through everything that I possibly could, and not long after I moved to New York and began working for Mrs. Wood I learned that she and Ina were great friends. They were friends because they admired each other so much professionally, and also because both women at that time had more or less settled down.

Ruby had married Chalmers Wood who was a well-liked New York society man, popular among men, a fox hunter, and when he wasn't

Ina Claire. (Condé Nast)

interested in hunting, he was interested in having dinner at the Brook Club with his somewhat stuffy friends, but the thing Chalmers loved the most was being in love with Ruby. The other great part of his life was his son, Ben, by his first wife, whom Ruby simply couldn't bear; and because Chalmers and Ruby were childless, Ruby took Ben on as her own son and they became devoted to each other.

Ina had married a perfectly nice man who was as conventional as Chalmers. It was one of those times that Ina, in a way, had decided to try one of her "temporary" retirements from the theater. So Ina and her husband and Ruby and Chalmers got along very well indeed. It was only after Ina divorced her first husband that Ruby admitted that Ina's husband was tiresome and an ineffectual bore. Ina's divorce later paved the way for her marriage to John Gilbert, which created a sensation.

Ina told me that she had no business getting married at all because she was lousy in bed. She said in her perfect diction and looking at me with her marvelous eyes dazzling, "I just get hysterical and laugh."

The dissolution of Ina's marriage to Gilbert left him wide open for Garbo, who became rather serious about him. One day Ina and I were lunching with Miss Garbo, and the subject of John Gilbert came up, which was very entertaining, but not to Ina, however. I could see that little foot of hers tapping on the floor, and I can still hear that strong little voice of hers saying to Garbo, "Shut up, you damned fool. I married him!"

Ruby was a friend of a great many decorators who were mutual friends of Ina's, but nobody had done very much work for her because she was always on the road. One weekend I was having dinner with Ruby and Chalmers at "Little Ipswich," their house on Long Island, and Ina was there. It was at the moment she was living in a very attractive apartment that Hobie Irwin had done for her at the Pierre Hotel. Hobie was enormously admired by Mrs. Wood as a decorator and he had always been one of my idols.

At dinner that night, apropos of nothing, Ina said to me, "Now listen, baby. You've just got to help out Miss Ruby. I'm here, I'm rehearsing for a play, I've just unpacked my belongings again and they're all over the floor of my apartment at the Pierre, and you are to please make it beautiful for me to live in. Here's a chance for you, dear boy."

I was quite excited, naturally; in fact, I thought I was going to die of a heart attack of pleasure.

After dinner Mrs. Wood said to me, "I have to have a little talk with you later."

The next day Mrs. Wood had her little talk with me. She said, "Don't get yourself too excited. I adore Ina, she's a good Irish girl, but she's absolute hell because she cannot make up her mind. As you know there is no greater sin or handicap that anyone can have as part of their character when they're decorating."

Ruby smiled at me over those glasses of hers like a devil and continued, "Of course I have got, still, a little reputation which you do *not yet* have, and I might find it easier to just knock her down and tell her to make up her mind and that's it.

"Don't be alarmed if your sleep is disturbed at three o'clock in the morning and you hear her lovely voice over the telephone saying, 'Billy, this is Ina. For Christ's sake, you can't put that goddamned pink lining on those lampshades. I'll look like a rummy if you do that!'

"If you can keep her mind on her work, you will have a lovely result. She's always lived in charming places, and she can go into an antique shop and pick out the prettiest thing every time. She has strong feelings about flowers and how to arrange them, and she's always dressed so beautifully for the room she lives in. No," she said, "Billy, I'm not going to worry about you. I think it will be perfectly all right."

Ina had bought a lovely apartment with an enormous living room and I was to go see it on a Sunday, but the morning of that day her maid called me and said, "Mr. Baldwin, Miss Ina says not to come and see her today or anytime ever today. She's got something real mean to tell you."

I said, "Thank you very much," wondering what it could be and wondering what I was going to tell Ruby. Ina didn't call for about three days and I was wild! Woody thought I was going to go crazy.

At last she called. "Dearest Billy B," she said. She was one of Margaret Case's disciples too. "The whole thing is off. It has nothing to do with you, but it has to do with the fact that I've canceled my contract with the play, and it's not going to be done at all. I'm about to be in the movies, and I'm going out to the coast to see my beloved genius, George Cukor, as fast as I can. The movie's called *Ninotchka,* and it's Garbo's first comedy. George tells me he's going to get Miss 'G' to laugh."

Ina asked me to come over and see her right away because she wanted to discuss something with me and not over the phone. When I got there she told me that she felt terrible about having to cancel our project, but she said, "I'll tell you what I want to do. I hope that some of the things we discussed for the apartment and planned to order can be used in another place. One of the first things I'm going to do when I get to

California is to get a divine apartment, and you will decorate and furnish it in the same way we planned here."

That excited me almost more than decorating an apartment for Ina in New York because it meant I would be introduced to California by Ina. Not bad! So in 1938–39 I realized a dream by working for Ina Claire.

Ina went to California and did everything she said she was going to.

Again, in 1960, I was sent for. She had bought a ravishing apartment in one of those lovely old-fashioned buildings with very high ceilings and enormous windows which had a spectacular view of the San Francisco Bridge and Bay. The apartment presented every opportunity for a wonderful result.

One of the first things she said to me when I entered the apartment was, "For Christ's sake! Don't talk to me about the view. I do not want to sit here having some man look at that goddamned bridge. I want him to look at me. Everyone who has a view out here wants the chairs lined up and facing it as if they were going to a movie. Just forget that! I want somebody to come in and be mad about me."

In my *whole* life she was the only person I ever heard say something about the view in that way. The apartment, which was completed in 1961, turned out beautifully. I found an Aubusson rug that was the basis for the peachy pink and yellow sunlit room that was to be filled constantly with flowers and Ina. Of course, the windows were covered in curtains from the ceiling to the floor, which when drawn blocked out the view.

Through the years my affection for Ina did not decrease, and my admiration for her judgment increased; however, she had *no* possible idea about housekeeping. It was all scenery. The flowers were divine, the chintz was lovely, her clothes were enchanting, but the food was all brought in from the best restaurant around the corner. She didn't know how to order a meal. Ina never had the slightest idea of how to concentrate on anything remotely bordering on the practical.

Ina was witty to a terrific extent, and she was madly intelligent. Stark Young once said to me about her, "The tragedy is that she hasn't done every play by Shakespeare. Comedy to tragedy. She's better than any of them." I certainly know that I will never forget her in the last act of *End of Summer*. There were more times when Ina could make you dissolve into tears while laughing than any tragedienne I have ever seen.

To my great surprise, and I think to hers, she suddenly decided to get married to a man called William Wallace who was very attractive and of a suitable age. He'd been in love with her when he was a student at Yale, but then so had an entire regiment of men, including Vincent Astor, and Ina had turned him down. I suppose because Ina was older and was thinking about the happiness of Ruby and Chalmers and a few other marriages, she just decided to do it. Among other things, Bill Wallace was a saint. He adored her, and I'm happy to say that he became a great friend of mine. He had enormous looks and she idolized him. I think he represented to her the perfect gentleman, which he wasn't.

The trouble with Ina and what interfered enormously with her life was that she *absolutely* could not stop talking. It was a continuous flow and there was never a moment, no matter where she was — in a car, in the air, in a restaurant, no matter where — that Ina was not talking constantly. I know there was a moment when Truman Capote, who adored her and thought she was a brilliant actress, wanted her very much for *The Grass Harp,* but he said to me, "You know something, I couldn't stand listening to Ina talk while the rehearsals were going on."

Truman decided not to do it and Ina always said she didn't care. I suppose she didn't really care all that much when you consider that she turned down without any reservation *The Madwoman of Chaillot.* There are things that make you wonder about her until you realize the very strange quality she has.

Ina loved clothes and she knew how well she wore them. I've heard more than one woman say that Ina wore clothes better than anyone. Kitty Miller and Margaret Case were two women who killed, murdered, and slaughtered other women in what they wore, but they both said that nobody dressed better or could do more with the addition of a scarf or a flower than Ina could to the clothes that she bought and wore. Kitty and Ina heartily disliked each other, but Kitty said to me, "My God, if I had those looks and wore clothes the way she does, I don't know where I would have ended up."

Chanel always longed to dress Ina, and she launched several of Chanel's most popular dresses on Broadway. Her love of clothes closed her eyes to doing anything but being in a play in which she was to be a very chic, beautifully dressed contemporary woman.

Unfortunately, she was in a production of *Barchester Towers* based on the novel by Trollope, which was a wild failure because there she was in a setting of the last century stuck in a wheelchair. I always thought it was a silly idea, anyway, but she was brilliant in *The Cocktail Party,* and was overwhelmingly ragingly successful in *The Confidential Clerk.*

I have heard more playwrights say that they would rather have Ina act in something they'd written more than any other actress because her ability and talent made the whole thing into something that went beyond what was there. Cole Porter used to say the same thing about Ethel Merman. He said her diction was perfect, and I think he liked her diction and the way she sang his songs more than he did the lyrics of his music. Cole felt that Ethel was not going to have the audience miss anything. Nowhere in the world were there two more different people than Ina Claire and Ethel Merman. Ina was the quintessence of chic, style, and intellect; Ethel, glorious as she was, could hardly be called that.

San Francisco really did open up her golden gate to me, and in 1960 I was asked to help Whitney Warren move into his glorious new apartment, which he was having built on the top of Telegraph Hill. It was an extraordinary building of five floors, all designed by Gardner Dailey, one of San Francisco's brilliant architects. Whitney was to occupy the top three floors, which had the most glorious view of the bridge and the harbor. There was to be a drawing room, three floors in height, which was copied from his father's apartment in New York. There was luxurious garage space in the basement, and what was between Whitney's floors and the basement was to be rented as apartments. At the time, Whitney was living in a place that was made wonderful by bits and pieces from his father's New York Park Avenue apartment of the twenties.

The Warrens were a most notable and attractive family and in many ways really more European than they were American. Whitney's mother was a petite elegant little beauty and his father always dressed in nineteenth-century clothes with enormous capes and flowing bow ties. Mr. Warren's great friend and mistress was no less a person than Cecile Sorel.

As children and young adults, Whitney and his two sisters spent at least half of the year in France, and they spoke French as fluently as they spoke English. Whitney was brought up as the only son, and he was called "Brother" by his sisters for that reason.

One of his sisters later married a man who had been the mayor of Bernardsville, New Jersey, and lived very happily. His other sister also married happily and later bought the Harry Payne Whitney house in Newport, tore it down, and built herself a very reasonable little French house that now belongs to her son. This property also included Mrs. Harry Payne Whitney's famous tea house, which has been recently restored by the Preservation Society.

Whitney inherited his father's very French, very beautiful taste, but as he was growing up in New York City, he did not want to be known simply as the son of the great Whitney Warren, Sr., of Warren and Wetmore, who had to his credit such incredible achievements as the New York Yacht Club, Grand Central terminal, and many of the great town houses of New York; many of which, sadly, have been destroyed to make way for luxury apartments.

So for a time, Whitney became the real playboy with money to burn and no thought of any kind of responsibility except his wild desire to have a good time. Whitney really did have a lot to do with what was called Café Society, which essentially meant that you went out and had dinner in public in a restaurant. A lot of that occurred at the beautiful oval dining room in the Ritz Hotel, which was a creation of Whitney's father. Every night, the young people came there for supper after the theatre. They all had money, looks, talent, charm, and they were certainly having a good time.

At this time one of the things that hit Whitney hard was his great devotion to Jeanne Eagles. She was at that moment at the height of her fame and starring in *Rain*. It was his custom to call for Jeanne before curtain time, and let her stop at her doctor's before getting to the theatre.

Many people have told me that in those days in New York the Warrens were like royalty. As they spent half the time in Paris, they were terribly sophisticated and very aware of the world and they were not overly impressed with New York City as so many were. Whitney often spoke to me about his New York life then.

One time to my great interest Whitney asked me if I had ever met Kitty's mother, Madame Bache. I told him that I hadn't. He said, "Well, I wish you had because she was the most extraordinarily chic, the best-looking, and most exciting woman of all of them."

Madame Bache was accepted in Paris society because the Jews were, but not so in New York. He told me that he would never forget hearing about a great ball given in New York at that time. "You know I was up the next morning at twelve o'clock and I went to see my mother who was just getting up because I wanted to hear about all those dresses."

So he said he asked his mother about the ball. Mrs. Warren said, "It was beautiful and I got home at dawn." Whitney said he was sure of that because his mother was very popular, very naughty, and wore the most beautiful clothes of anybody. "And oh," she said, "Whitney, dear, of course the belle of the ball was Madame Bache." Whitney said his mother then spoke in great detail and at length about Madame Bache's captivating charm.

Whitney adored his mother. Mrs. Warren's last years were quite sad because she lost her mind to the extent that she was seen constantly walking up and down Fifth Avenue having the most violent arguments with herself. Sometimes she would even slap her own wrist in disagreement, but she was perfectly harmless, and she still was dressed better than anybody else.

Whitney really had no home for himself in New York, and when he moved to the West Coast he carried on with his wildly gay attractive life in San Francisco. He then decided, which proved he had a pretty good brain inside that sometimes silly head of his, that he could not simply continue being the second-rate son of a famous architect. So he put himself two years before the mast, ending up working with Sir Thomas Lipton for three and a half years on a tea plantation in India where he realized that the whole thing for him in life was the soil. He said to me, "When I first dug my nails into that soil on the tea plantation, I knew that's what I was supposed to be doing."

He came back to this country and went to a school in San Francisco where he studied agriculture. Soon afterwards, he bought something like fifty acres of bottom land just beyond San Francisco in the Sacramento Valley, which was overshadowed by snowcapped mountains. This resulted in Whitney himself spending the hours from six in the morning to six in the evening on horseback going over his land, working on it, and living in a very rustic cabin, but it must be admitted that he had with him a wonderful cook.

Very soon he built a house like a Basque peasant farmhouse there, and it had the most enormous luxury. All of the baths had the most beautiful tiles I've ever seen, as did the floors of the main house where his bedroom and two or three guest rooms were. He had a marvelous kitchen in which the wife of the Chinese couple who lived on the ranch cooked some of the best French, German, and Italian food I've ever tasted. She could cook anything and was one of the best cooks ever. Her husband was Whitney's gardener and he had the assistance of three or four others because the gardens were quite vast.

There was also an extraordinary overseer. An absolutely fascinating and typical Warren trick was the schedule that was religiously followed no matter who was staying at the ranch. He never had more than two or three friends or a couple visit him at any one time, and I don't think that he ever had more than four people at the table. The ranch was run on a very early time basis, and we would meet at six o'clock and drive a short distance to the overseer's apartment where Whitney would go over the business of the day. The overseer was an American boy to whom he had given the opportunity to run his ranch. He had a splendid wife and son who was going into the army when I knew them. Sadly, the son was to die.

Whitney left San Francisco every Tuesday morning at about ten o'clock and motored up to his ranch. He always took marvelous sandwiches and plenty of martinis, and he would arrive around two or three in the afternoon.

He very seldom had guests because there was nothing much for them to do. The walls of the big room in the house were lined with his collection of volumes and volumes of drawings and photographs of the architecture of Europe. He also had wonderful records for his hi-fi. So what you had to do was sit down with a book and listen to music or you'd go crazy. Dressed in comfortable casual clothes, usually blue jeans, you would have a super six o'clock martini and then a very early dinner.

You left on Saturday morning to go back to San Francisco where he had arranged to have a dinner dance for approximately twenty to forty people, or maybe a series of two or three very small dinner parties. One whole car completely packed with flowers was always driven in with him to the city so that his apartment could be filled with them. What Whitney did was simply to reverse the usual pattern most people had in leaving the city on weekends.

I think his gardens on the ranch are some of the most unbelievable in existence. They are a remarkable creation: of Italian design, taken care of by a brilliant Chinese gardener, and filled with all kinds of western flora.

I happened to have the great experience of being at the ranch one year when his Chinese tree peonies were in full bloom. I do not know when I've ever seen anything so glorious; in fact, I do *know* that I've never seen anything so beautiful.

They had the most curious Edwardian look. The entire peony garden looked as if it had been done by Worth, the great designer, who was of the period of Whitney's father. The colors of the peonies went from the darkest, darkest red velvet to the palest pink. You could have taken the flowers from an entire plant for a vase to be filled for the week in town and nobody would ever be aware that any flowers had been taken at all. He won a great many prizes for his tree peonies, but many other kinds of flowers filled his gardens too. He loved flowers, and I mean really loved them. Whitney could not step over the threshold of anyplace that he lived without preceding himself with a bunch of flowers.

After Gardner Dailey designed Whitney's apartment, and it was built, I helped him move in. The apartment had some extraordinary wonders in it; one of which was a Florentine gilded door frame eighteen feet in height, which was on the inside doorway of the drawing room. There was an extraordinary fireplace, and the windows of the apartment were very modern with very large panes of glass. He had a much smaller library with a lower ceiling, which he used for intimate parties and after-dinner coffee, and there was a glassed-in terrace that had huge trees on it and overlooked the harbor. When he built his apartment he was determined to have the most spectacular view in San Francisco, and I must admit, he did. One of the interesting things about Whitney's taste was its eclecticism. It went from a present-day drawing back to a piece of velvet from the Renaissance. He loved everything that seemed to him to be beautiful, and he had immense knowledge of the things he loved.

Whitney became active in the San Francisco Opera and, in fact, became a member of its board. He was also interested in the arts, and had a lot to do with the city's galleries and museums. There can be no doubt about it that Whitney became a rather remarkable citizen of San Francisco.

He was extravagant to a degree but never without reason. If Whitney served caviar by the ton five times in succession, you knew it was perfectly all right, and that it was fresh. He was accustomed to the wildest luxury, but he was the most un-*nouveau riche* person I've ever known in my life. There was never any splurging. It was awfully amusing to me to know the way that Whitney traveled, for it gives an idea of the character of the man. Every summer he would go abroad and take only a certain amount of money to indulge his whims and purchases. When that was spent, he would come right back to this country.

It is perfectly understandable that Whitney adored the work of John Singer Sargent, and it was tragic for him that he had never had his portrait done by him. At one point, he heard of a man who was at the St. Regis Hotel with a collection of twenty or more Sargents for sale, and of course Whitney went to see them.

He called me that night when he got back to his room at the Pierre Hotel and he was really hysterical with excitement. He said, "Billy, I've seen something today that I can never get over and never will, but I'm very upset because I honestly can't quite afford it. It's a picture by Sargent and the cost is against my principles because it's about five thousand dollars more than I would intend to spend. I don't know what to do, but I can't help it, and I know I'll never be happy until I have it."

I said, "Well, in that case, you must get it."

The following season I saw it hanging over his bed in San Francisco. The size of the picture was about eighteen inches by twenty-four and its subject was that of a young woman in a yellow damask ball gown lying down on a white satin sofa, and over her head was an iron hoop covered with very fine black netting. In India before dinner these contraptions were used by people so that they would not be mutilated by mosquitoes. Sometimes they were designed to cover not only the head but the hands and arms as well. The mosquito netting was transparent enough to reveal the face, so here was this unforgettable portrait of a young woman wearing an enormous yellow damask dress with her head covered in mosquito netting. Whitney said to me, "Well, what do you think?"

I said, "I have to tell you what I honestly think. I would rather own it, and have it hanging in my room, more than any picture that I have ever seen."

At the time I saw it Whitney was redecorating and I knew that picture could go anyplace, but that was not to happen because he gave it to Jacqueline Kennedy for the White House. I think that Whitney liked that picture more than anything he ever owned because not too much later he said to me, "I could kill myself for having given it away now."

San Francisco certainly in no way let me down, and I had the remarkable good fortune of meeting, knowing, and working for Helen Crocker Russell, who was born a Crocker of the famous California family.

Ina adored Helen as did so many people, and Ina said to me in no uncertain terms, "It's just a damned shame she wasn't born a man because she's got much more sense than most of the Crocker men have."

At this time I was in the middle of the job I was doing for Ina, I had agreed to work for Whitney, and Helen had asked me if I could help her, too.

Ina said to me, "If you work for Helen Crocker, I'll never speak to you again."

I said, "What's the matter?"

"No," she said, "You have enough to do. It would just prove to me that all you do care about is money."

I said, "Now, Ina, listen to me. I don't think that's true. What I do think is true is this. I'm mad about San Francisco. You say you will not allow me to come out here and live because it would be my ruin, but I want to."

At that moment I wanted to sell everything in New York, and move to San Francisco. I told Ina that I felt that way very strongly.

I said, "I don't want to lose your friendship so let's not discuss this until we get your job done, but I really mean it when I say I'm crazy about San Francisco, and I don't think I should lose this extraordinary opportunity to work for Helen."

"Well," she said, "I'll tell you one thing. Helen's divine, and she has more sense than your silly friend, Whitney Warren." Because of their interest in the theatre and a great many other things as well, Ina and Whitney were great friends.

Ina said, "I know Helen will be nice to you, but you'd better get back to New York. You could live out here about two weeks, and by the end of that time you wouldn't be able to find anybody to talk to. These people are hicks, and you'd be bored stiff. Now, I've got a divine husband, and I'm very happy with him, but I could not work out here."

Thank God, I didn't pay any attention to Ina and accepted the opportunity to work for Helen.

Her house in Carmel was colossal! It had been designed by Gardner Dailey, and they were great friends. They had the kind of friendship that can only happen between two rich intelligent people who live in a small town, and he was to design the new apartment that Helen was going to build across the street from Whitney Warren in San Francisco.

So it seemed that suddenly like a bolt from the blue I was to be involved in helping these two enormously rich San Franciscans, Whitney Warren and Helen Crocker Russell, decorate their new apartments.

I think a lot of people were waiting for me to fall flat on my face because they didn't see how it was possible that I could successfully work for Helen and Whitney at the same time, but everything worked out perfectly well. Helen and Whitney were also great friends, and what they had in common was almost too much taste, but each one's point of view was entirely different. Whitney had inherited a great many beautiful things from his family, but Helen had inherited even more from her mother.

The Crockers were an interesting family and they had quite a lot of Indian blood in their veins, which they were very proud of indeed. Some time after I began working for Helen, she asked me if I might consider helping her brother, Bill, who was an adorable man but as weak as a kitten. Helen was adorable too, but about as weak as a stag.

Bill Crocker lived in Burlingame in a house that was called "Skye Farm." "Skye Farm" was built on top of a mountain and you reached it by driving up a long winding road that passed through the most beautiful grounds like a botanic garden in some great park. When you got to the house at the top of the mountain, you found yourself looking down over the surrounding countryside as if you were on top of the world. The entrance to this very simple country Spanish house was through the most beautiful doors, and you could look straight through it to another pair of doors, which were the ones you went through when you left "Skye Farm" and drove down the other side of the mountain. There was none of this business of going back over the same road you came up on, or of having to pass anybody.

Helen, Ina, and I were invited to "Skye Farm" for lunch and when we arrived I was introduced to Bill and a very attractive woman who was considerably younger than he. She was blond, had the best figure, was chic enough to die, and as cold as an ice pick. Her name was Elizabeth Coleman and she and Bill were soon to be married.

Ina was furious because she couldn't bear Elizabeth, and not over fifteen minutes after we had gotten there, she got me aside and again warned me that if I worked for Bill and that woman, she would never speak to me again.

Ina said to me, "She's just trying to marry him." We were having cocktails before lunch, and she said, "Look at poor Bill. She's making him not drink, and she's ruined that sweet old man's only fun because his only pleasure in life is having a drink. We're all sitting here enjoying our drinks, and he's licking his lips like a Pekingese." I must admit that what Ina said was true because Bill did have a fat little face, and his eyes, wild with boredom, were practically falling out of his head because he was not drinking. However, I saw that Bill had no choice because Elizabeth, the steel trap type with no sense of humor, was not going to have any nonsense.

After lunch, Helen, Ina, and I left "Skye Farm," Bill, and Elizabeth behind, but as events turned out, and in spite of Ina, I did work for Bill Crocker.

Bill and Cole Porter had been roommates and best friends at Yale, which was easily understood the minute you met Bill: even though he had gotten fat, and was never sober, for he had the most enormous charm. When Linda Porter, Cole's wife, sold all her furniture in Paris, Bill bought it, and had it shipped to California to the marvelous house that I was to work on.

The inside of the house was not pretty, and all of Linda's beautiful furniture had ended up on the third floor. It had been moved up there and replaced with hideous modern things. So I just went up there and got enough furniture to do the guest rooms and the master bedroom. Downstairs, I had all the good stuff recovered, got rid of everything that was not so good, and the result was more than pleasant.

Not so many years later I was amused to hear that Elizabeth Crocker had remarried and become the Duchess of Manchester, and I thought of Ina. Perhaps Ina was right, because as my life turned out I did not move to San Francisco, but I certainly would not have traded anything in the world for my experience of working there.

CHAPTER TWENTY-SIX

*. . . I have always felt that she was
amazingly feminine. I do not mean
namby-pamby.*

Not only do I think that the Wolcott Blair house in Palm Beach is the most beautiful one there, I also consider that the most beautiful house on Long Island belongs to them as well.

Mrs. Wolcott Blair was born Ellen Yuille, one of four famous sisters who had come from the South and were known for their great charm and style. They also represented luxury in the greatest sense of that word. Mrs. Blair's sisters were Burks Carstairs, whose husband was named Carol and owned the most delicious gallery where one could buy French Impressionist drawings; Melissa Bingham, whose husband was Harry Payne Bingham, a man of immense wealth; and Nancy, the Vicountess Adair, who lived in a beautiful house in Ireland.

Those four sisters had the most wonderful clothes sense, but I think that Burks and Ellen were truly outstanding. Burks really started the style of what the ladies called "separates." In other words, Burks would buy material, and I don't necessarily mean dress material, and then take it to her dressmaker where she would design and have made the most magical skirt. She would then wear with it the most incredible soft sweater or a blouse made of entirely different material which was beautifully cut, and close around her neck she literally *jammed* artificial jewelry.

Ellen Blair wore the most wonderful clothes as well, and many of them came from Hattie Carnegie. I recall one evening when I was having what to me became perfect evenings, dinner alone with Ellen in her Sutton Place apartment, and I complimented her on the blouse she was wearing. It was made of the most marvelous gossamer I don't know what, but it was a lovely thing to see, and Ellen said, "I'll tell you right now that this is a very old blouse but it's always in style because it was designed by your great friend Pauline Potter. I have a great many clothes that she designed when she worked for Hattie and I have never gotten more pleasure from wearing any others including all the ones I used to buy in Europe." Ellen then asked me if I would like to see some of the clothes that Pauline had designed and which she had bought years before. I did, and Ellen had her maid bring to us, in the living room, dozens of evening dresses and other clothes that had been designed by Pauline and it was true: the style of those clothes was timeless. Unlike her sister, Burks, Ellen wore no fake jewelry. Her jewelry was absolutely beautiful, just as her house was.

The Long Island house had a dining room in which there was the most remarkable dark, dark bottle green Chinese wallpaper, beautiful Chippendale furniture, and by the window, an immense sofa and some easy chairs where people sat after dinner for coffee. Ellen was one of the first to have the idea of having buffet service for dinner, and it was a wonderful thing to do because it made the service quicker. She had by far the number-one French cook in New York and the food was beyond any belief or duplication.

Her apartment in Sutton Place was almost entirely in black and white and was the epitome of the style of the 1930s. Ellen had enormous creativity and she used to love to come to see Mrs. Wood. I remember one winter day when she came to Ruby's office and she knocked us all out because she was wearing a perfectly beautiful new black Persian lamb coat onto which she had had Maximillian, the furrier, put quite large brass ball buttons. That was the first time anyone of us had ever seen that done.

Ellen was a contemporary of Wallis Warfield's; in fact, she went to school with the duchess at Oldfield, and there is no doubt that both of those women had some of the best clothes sense of their time. It is ironic as well as tragic that Ellen is now like the duchess in regard to her health.

Wolcott Blair, who had been born and brought up in Chicago, was one of the best-looking men in New York, and he was madly in love with his wife, Ellen. They had an only son, Watson, whom they simply adored.

Both the Blairs had very extravagant taste as far as color went, and when Watson was a very young boy his parents decided that little Watson's bedroom in their Palm Beach house was to be done in yachting flags with the suitable colors. This was quite violent for a little boy eight years old, and Watson reacted rather strangely to the whole Palm Beach thing. His doctor advised them that it might be a good idea to take off the glare of the primary colors of the yachting flags by having dead white walls and hopefully make him a little less nervous.

When Watson decided to marry, the Blairs were in a terrible state. It wouldn't have mattered whom Watson was going to marry because they adored him so much that they simply could not stand the idea of him marrying anybody, but Watson knew what he wanted and what he wanted was the best that ever was. He married Josie Cutting, who was from a matchless family and possessed wild charm. He was her third husband and she was considerably older, but never mind. They did the right thing because they're still exceedingly happy. They have a ravishing house on the property of Watson's mother on Long Island, and they also now live in Ellen's apartment on Sutton Place.

In the early 1960s I'd been having the greatest pleasure and a lot of work to do with my beloved Josie Cutting Blair. Her first husband was a charming man from Philadelphia called Alexander McFadden and he met a tragic death in a skiing accident. She had three children by him: two sons, and one remarkable daughter called Mary. From the first time that I ever saw her I could tell that Mary was brilliantly intelligent, extremely original in every way, and perfectly capable of competing with her stepfather, Watson Blair, whose age was not that far from her own.

Mary was not the kind of girl who was going to spend much time on the post-debutante stages of New York life, and she very quickly got a job, and also an apartment of her own. Because of what I had done for her mother, Josie, I found myself one lovely day in 1962 standing with Mary in the guest room suite of a beautiful French house in the upper Sixties of New York. I honestly scarcely felt that I knew Mary, but there I was discussing with her what was to be done to the lovely suite of rooms that was to become her apartment. Here there was one beautiful square room with two enormous windows, a beautiful Louis XVI mantel, plus a small bedroom, and plenty of space left in other rooms for her to make a dressing room, baths, and a kitchen.

I was rather surprised when she said to me, "Now of course this big room must have a beautiful bed in it, but it must not look like as though

Mary McFadden. (Condé Nast)

it were a bed at all, and I have found a *lit de repos* upholstered in the most beautiful red damask and also the most elaborate French valances. I am mad about the *lit de repos* and that will make the whole room. So, let us try to find something for the bedroom that doesn't look at all as if I'd slept in it, but that I could if I wanted to, and I'm insane about the Empire style."

So I said, "I think I can assure you a wonderful early-nineteenth-century French Empire bed for the bedroom."

Mary said, "I love rugs of that period with those beautiful squares of wonderful colors in yellows, dark greens, and beiges, and I think the two drawing-room windows would be marvelous in very dark green Empire velvet. I also think that it should be possible to find in New York, and if not, in Paris, a few pieces of really good Empire furniture that I could afford. With the addition of comfortable contemporary upholstered furniture, the drawing room will be a lovely room for me to entertain in. I expect to entertain in a very informal way, and I would like to be able to have two round tables that when set up would make eight people very happy dining. I've seen some very amusing portraits of the period which would look wonderful in the drawing room."

Every word that Mary uttered was true and possible and also spoken like the most confident business executive, but I have always felt that she was amazingly feminine. I do not mean namby-pamby. For even at that moment, she was about to have a wonderful job with Dior of Paris, really representing him in New York.

Josie said to me after I had been helping Mary with the apartment for quite some time, "You will notice that I've totally absented myself from any conferences which involve you and my Mary because I do not want to interfere in any way. It is her money and let her spend it the way she wants to." Mary and her two brothers, as well as Josie, had inherited colossal sums of money when Alexander McFadden was killed. Watson was concerned only with his own taste and we didn't have to consult him about his stepdaughter's taste or where she was going to live.

I have to say that when the job was done it was really very attractive. It was heaven to go there in the late afternoon in the fall and winter and be high up on the third floor with the branching arms of trees outside, and sit in front of the roaring fire and have delicious drinks.

Mary was doing extremely well with the Dior connection and in spite of that she found time to become engaged to one of the most attractive men around. He was enormously rich and worked for one of the South African diamond firms. Mary married him, went to live there for a while, and had a daughter by him.

Josie asked me if I would do the flowers at the house for Mary's wedding reception. The wedding itself was performed at St. James's Church and it was certainly one of the chicest performances I've ever beheld. Mary was like one tiny brilliant jewel. She was covered in brilliants from her headdress to the trail of her bridal gown. The bridesmaids were all dressed in the most lovely very ancient green and white satin, very stiff and rather Directoire in feeling, and wore huge floppy turbans of olive green velvet.

The Blair house was a nice tall one, so the scale of the flowers which I placed everywhere could also be very large, and in order to make the guests more comfortable we built a temporary outside staircase leading from the ground floor up to the drawing-room floor.

Unfortunately, Mary's marriage was not a success, and Mary divorced her husband. She tried marriage once again for the second time but that too failed, and she came back, free, to live in New York and begin her brilliant creative life.

CHAPTER TWENTY-SEVEN

"Nothing-at-all is better than second-best."

*I*t was a little unusual and almost overwhelming to meet Mrs. Paul Mellon as I first did, which was at a ball given in Virginia on June 16, 1961, to introduce her daughter, Eliza, to the world. Quote, "The taste of Mrs. Paul Mellon had become legendary," and everybody always spoke of Bunny Mellon with a slightly hushed breath; not fear really, but almost reverence. Certainly, her word would always be the final one.

Of all the many women of my own age whom I was lucky enough to work for, I can say through personal experience *she was* the only one who bought the land, took a major role in drafting the architectural plans, supervised the building of the house, designed the gardens and planned every horticultural aspect of them, and then did the decoration, which really came last, which is the way I think any serious decorator should think: i.e., architecture should always come before the decoration in planning a house.

The ball for Eliza was at Paul and Bunny's house in Virginia, where I had never been. The entrance to the party was through a beautiful red brick house, which was the house of Paul Mellon and his first wife who died, and which was copied in every detail and measurement from the famous great American house in Annapolis called the Hammond Harwood House. After Bunny and Paul were married, they knew she couldn't possibly live in the house because it was far too conventional and far too formal, and so she and Paul moved into the rambling farmhouse where they now live.

The night of Eliza's party, the first floor of the beautiful red brick house was stripped and simply used as a sort of reception entrance room where you left your coat if you had one, and then walked through the beautiful rooms and out into the garden into the lovely summer night. The garden side of the house had been entirely masked by a giant slipcover upon which was the drawing of a French château. It reminded me of the kind of thing that the Baron Niki de Gunzburg, who was at this party, did in Paris when he gave two famous balls there. The moment that you passed through the door and out into the garden, you entered the world of masquerade and saw that every single thing was there just for that night.

There was a ravishingly pretty dance floor surrounded by arbors, and a little separate pavilion where omelets were prepared. You went up to the omelet chef and in two minutes you had the best omelet in the world. There was a perfectly amazing little house in which there was a drawing room with fake painted boisserie where many attractive people of all ages sat and ate incredible food and drank wine. There was a fortune teller in another tent, and an orchestra in a quiet part of the garden for waltzing. It suddenly seemed to me that everything had been there for a long time, and you found yourself walking around in the marvelous atmosphere of the eighteenth century, but transformed into a wild lively result. This effect, you knew, was created after weeks and months of the most immense work on the part of a great many people. We left as the dawn was coming up over the farmland, and silhouetted against the sky were the horses.

As if that weren't enough, the next day all the people who were visiting were invited back to the Mellons' to a bang-up lunch. The whole neighborhood was jammed with overnight houseguests because most of the people who were invited to Eliza's party didn't go home until the next day. I stayed at a lovely old house with the Benjamin Kittredges, who owned the Cypress Gardens in Charlestown.

It was during this time that I really first became aware of the extraordinary quite subtle charm of my tall, calmly handsome hostess. I also had my first glimpse of Bunny's great efficiency, her enormous sympathy, her determination to accomplish what she was after, and her determination to settle for nothing but the best.

In the early 1960s I remember doing a guest column for Eugenia Sheppard's "Inside Fashion" in which I did an alphabet, about decorating, A through Z. For the letter N, I wrote: "Nothing-at-all is better than second-best. Never fill an empty space just to fill it. Second-best is expensive, while nothing costs nothing. First-rate is the best investment, and patience is its parent." Without qualification, I think my letter N represents to a great degree what Bunny Mellon is all about.

That day at lunch I remember I was clowning with that incredible beauty, Babe Paley. Babe was a great deal taller than I, and in order to compensate for that I stood myself on the edge of the orchestra platform. Babe stood facing me, but not on the platform, and at that moment we were the same height. It must have been a very funny sight because it was quite a hit, but it must be stressed that Babe with all of her great charm and manners was not being made fun of because God knows she wasn't. We were simply having a good time recalling an earlier ball that Babe and Bill had given in 1957 for his daughter, Hilary, in Manhasset. I had been responsible for the pink and white striped tent in their garden which had alternating stripes of flowers in different colors.

Several weeks after Eliza's party, I was asked by Mrs. Mellon if I would come and see her. To be quite truthful I had been rather surprised at being invited to Eliza's party because I was not really a great friend of the Mellons, and I thought it was the same old thing: I was the extra man, and the dancing man, and heaven knows — she saw what a good time I had had as did her husband, Paul, who misses absolutely nothing. So I was asked by Mrs. Mellon to come to Virginia to talk to her, and she didn't even say about what.

I can certainly say that I was wildly excited. To be blasé about Bunny Mellon should make you resign from whatever business you are in. Of course I went to Virginia. Of course I saw evidence of her extraordinary taste the moment I went in the door of the house. It almost looks like the house of a caretaker because it is so simple. It is an old house which has been added on to, and rambles around from room to room, and you can see that she has said, "Oh, I must have a little library here," or "I feel desperately in need of a lot of chintz," and so she built a room for it. Everywhere are masses of flowers that have been brought in from the greenhouse. They have been placed in the most personal way on the floors, on the walls, everywhere, and such examples of plants you have never seen: all simple old-fashioned flowers.

We started in immediately because what she had on her mind was the necessity of some things to be done in her greenhouse. The greenhouse, which has a most lovely architecture, is at the end of a rather formal garden opposite the house. The central mass of the greenhouse is crowned with a dome and lead decoration designed by the great jeweler Jean Schlumberger. When you get into that greenhouse, naturally it smells better than any greenhouse you've ever been in, and every flower is of the most extraordinary beauty, and they are loved and cared for by Mrs. Mellon herself.

You can't imagine how wonderful it feels to be in that house and in those greenhouses. You *know* that she loves every chair, you *know* that she feels tenderly about every single blossom, and you *know* that she rips out anything that she doesn't like, not with violence or cruelty but with the simple determination to eliminate it. Hers is a regime of no tolerance for the mediocre.

That day we began a long lovely experience that lasted throughout many years. We spent as much time and thought on finding the perfect cigarette box to doing an entire room, and every job was done with total honesty. She did say more than once, "Oh, come on, Billy. Let's take a chance. You aren't sure and neither am I." We did take chances quite often and naturally there were times when our choice was wrong. Bunny would just simply say to me, "It didn't work." We had both made a great mistake, and Bunny was always perfectly willing to be honest about any admission of failure, and ready to tackle the problem again. She is a very intelligent woman.

In addition to our professional relationship we began a friendship of long duration, which is certainly one of the great ornaments of my life. Working with Bunny makes you have an experience that is very much one of give and take. She knows an enormous amount, and she forgets nothing. She loves beauty more than anybody I have ever known. She really is subject to the outlines of a lovely little French table just as she is to the lines of a beautiful flower. She has the most wonderful sense of values, which she follows with great dedication.

My day in the greenhouse was many many years ago but I recall it as if it were yesterday. The central part of the greenhouse is an octagonal room in which are painted *trompe l'oeil* shelves, and on the shelves are painted garden implements. There is even a *trompe l'oeil* letter from Paul Mellon giving her permission to build the greenhouse. The greenhouse was not exactly in need of furniture the first day I saw it, but it was desperately in need of one thing, and that was a table in the middle of

Mrs. Paul Mellon. (Condé Nast)

the room. I felt it so strongly that I didn't say a word. I felt that I couldn't say a word until I found some way of backing it up, and in spite of racking my brain I could not think of anyplace in New York, London, or Paris that would have the table that I knew would be perfect for the greenhouse. So I just thought to myself, Keep yourself quiet, Billy Baldwin, it will come.

Five or six years passed and one day I was in one of the best antique shops in New York and I found what I had been looking for without even knowing that I was looking for it and that was a country Louis XV painted table which was considerably lower than the normal table. The height of the average table in the world is twenty-eight inches, and this was about twenty inches in height so that one looked down on it, and whatever would be put on that table would be seen slightly from above. I was so excited by my discovery that I could hardly speak, but I called Bunny in Virginia and told her I was sending some things down for her, and I also told her about the table which I was going to send.

I am so happy to be able to say that one of the incredibly rare qualities of this incredibly rare woman is her ability to empathize with another's enthusiasm, and she was overjoyed in her appreciation and enthusiasm for the table.

Her establishments in the world are run with perfection, a perfection which denies that there is any work going on whatsoever. There is one thing that Paul Mellon has wherever he is, and that is total at-homeness and comfort.

Their principal house is in Virginia and is surrounded by the most beautiful land. Paul Mellon's original brick house has fast become a sort of library, an office building, and has guest rooms of utter total comfort like an English house. There is a very handsome town house in Washington, D.C., that once belonged to Bunny's adored father who was a brilliant yachtsman and architect, and which is now used as a sort of guest house for entertaining visiting curators at the National Gallery. They own an amazingly attractive French town house in New York City, and a beguiling house in New England on Cape Cod, the garden of which only recently won a prize for being the best garden in the East for the summer.

Their house in Antigua is built of native stone and is completely successful in that it does not look like the rich man's house in the Caribbean. She has accomplished the remarkable feat of creating the most extraordinary gardens there in spite of the difficult circumstance of the lack of water. There is another miracle in that house and that is the food, which

Bunny in Antigua.

is a triumph because it is so delicious. Luckily she had her staff in Virginia to supplement her Caribbean one and she brought some of her beloved servants down there and they taught her staff in Antigua about cooking.

Bunny Mellon is very blue as far as color goes. That comes from her love of the country, nature, the sea, the sky, and the very air. She does not really like cities. She spends very little time in them and her New York town house is used more often by her husband. My work with Bunny on her houses spanned a number of years: I worked on Antigua in 1964, Cape Cod in 1967, Virginia in 1969–70, New York in 1970, and did additional work in Cape Cod in 1970.

Bunny has always surrounded herself with those who have reached the top of their professions, and there can be no doubt that because of her enthusiasm, support, and appreciation of their talents that she has helped them on their way. Jean Schlumberger, perhaps the greatest jeweler of our time, is one who Bunny has certainly patronized.

When I first knew Johnny he lived in New York's East 90s in a charming tiny white clapboard house which was totally freestanding with a quite big garden in the back, and surrounded by very big buildings. It was at the time when Johnny was at his greatest vogue in New York, and I'm happy to be able to say that Walter Hoving with his great ability as a merchant had had the wisdom to contract Johnny exclusively for Tiffany's.

Johnny was well established in France but not so well known here at all. He produced his work in Paris and it was sent to New York where it was displayed on the second floor of Tiffany's in a discreet office which was very attractive and done with great restraint by Van Day Truex, who was at that time waving his magical wand over everything at Tiffany's as its designer boss. The Schlumberger department was reached by entering an elevator where two guards stood in case of attempted robbery. In the few little cupboards that were in the Schlumberger office were kept the extraordinarily beautiful creations that Johnny had conceived. There were many watches, rings, bracelets, and feminine conceits: all made of the most extraordinary combinations of gold, silver, and platinum, and quite often he mixed semiprecious stones with wonderful jewels in his creations. He had the point of view that many designers had then, really for the first time, of mixing everything up, and Johnny was one of the first ones who did that. Of course, his workmanship was absolutely glorious and in no time his jewelry became known as the Schlumberger pin, or the Schlumberger bracelet.

There was a very exciting moment when an exhibition of Johnny's work was held at the Wildenstein Gallery. There can be no doubt that this exhibition was certainly one of the most beautiful things ever done in commercial New York. The installation of the show was entrusted to Gene Moore, the genius who was responsible for the joy of the Tiffany windows. I consider him to be *almost* the great genius of New York in the way of design. Gene has real integrity as well as an endless supply of ideas, and the Schlumberger exhibition was something that proved it.

The exhibition was very large and a great number of items were on loan. These were not jewels in the sense that they were to be worn by women, but they were objects very much in the Cellini idea. There were vases, candelabra, and all kinds of ornaments, which Gene Moore had had so superbly lit that their beauty shimmered. Bunny's loaned objects constituted a large part of the exhibition; however, it was easy to see that Ailsa Mellon Bruce, Paul's sister, had been led astray by the enthusiasm of her sister-in-law, Bunny, because there was a marvelous collection on display of all the jeweled objects owned by Mrs. Bruce. Today, it makes me extremely happy to know that Johnny still has his business in Paris and contributes his designs annually to Tiffany's.

Although it really does not mean a great deal to her, Bunny was dressed by Balenciaga, one of the great dressmakers of the world, but what does mean a lot to Bunny is perfect workmanship, and basic style. She does not hang on every line that she looks at.

Bunny is a great friend of Hubert de Givenchy, who is also a friend of mine, and in so many ways to me it is ironical that many many years before I met Hubert I visited the house in Paris that Hubert now owns and lives in when he is in the city.

When I was a very young man I was in Paris one summer, and also in Paris at the same time was Mrs. William Manley, who had been born Mathilde Keyser. Mrs. Manley was attractive, vital, bright, cruel, relentless, and had been widowed for quite a while. She had grown up in Baltimore at the same time that Harry Lehr was having such a spectacular part of his life before he went to New York and joined Mrs. Stuyvesant Fish as one of society's leaders.

The year I was in Paris was the summer after Harry Lehr had died, and Mrs. Manley strongly felt that due to the fact of the Paint and Powder Club friendship of Harry Lehr and my father, she should take me to call on his widow. Off we went to the biggest house I have ever seen in the Seventh Arrondissement of Paris and certainly the biggest house I had ever been in.

It cannot be truthfully said that Mrs. Lehr, née Bessie Drexel Dahlgren, was a woman of charm because she wasn't. She was very sour, very vindictive, and she had even written an account about her unfortunate marriage to Harry Lehr, which turned out to be a snow-white portrayal of their life together. It had been common knowledge at the time that even though Bessie was crazy about Harry, he had not so much as touched her even after their marriage.

It was quite a shock to my very unsophisticated American decorator's eyes to see all the walls of the first floor of the colossal house hung with black velvet in heavy mourning for Mr. Lehr, which was the custom in the houses of very rich people after a death.

Today my good friend, Hubert, lives in that same house and he told me that he would never be able to furnish the house because of its gigantic size. Because of Bunny's friendship with Hubert she helped him design and plan the gardens of his country house. There is an enormous variety in her work which can be seen in the design of the gardens for the Kennedy Library to her erection of a superb modern library building at her farm in Virginia. Bunny can really go from the most feminine to the magnificent scale of the National Gallery.

One thing that is very tantalizing about Bunny Mellon and which cannot be overlooked is her laughter. She probably has the greatest sense of humor of anybody, especially about herself. The expression of this humor comes out in a very pale but colorful ripple of laughter, which is very soft, but every now and then it does give way to an outburst of joy.

I know that I have often said of many people that being with them makes me be at my best. However, Bunny automatically *makes* me be at my best, and I cannot possibly imagine letting her down in any way.

CHAPTER   TWENTY-EIGHT

I said, "You must say nothing."

*A*fter going to the Schwarzenberg Ball with the Millers, I went
to Paris with them to continue my wonderful holiday. About a
week before, Gilbert said to me, "Kid, give your plane tickets
to my secretary because we are going to take you with us, and not only
that, but I want you to give her your engagement book so that she can
fill in your dates with us there."

Well, that was pretty nice, of course, so off I went with them in a
plane called the Viking, which was really one of the first jets. Kitty was
a brave woman because she was terrified of flying, but she had been
indoctrinated under the wheel of Gilbert, who used to fly every weekend
from London to Drungewick, their lovely house in the English countryside, and so she was fairly used to stormy travel.

We had a lovely time in Paris, and toward the end of my week there,
Kitty said to me, "Tomorrow, you are going to go with us to meet
someone whom you really don't want to miss because she is a famous
beauty, and a famous lady. Her name is Pamela Churchill, and I think
you'll find her charming."

The next day we went to the avenue des Etats Unis where Pamela,
who was separated from Randolph Churchill at the time, was living in
a flat. The flat was rather low, very full of sun, had a marvelous view of
the Seine, a great deal of beautiful Louis XVI acajou in the English taste,

Pamela Churchill. (Condé Nast)

and quite a collection of ostriches. She had grabbed any eighteenth- or nineteenth-century porcelain, plate, or vase that had an ostrich on it, and it was easy to see that her collection was worth a considerable amount of money. She also had some beautiful little almost miniature bronze ostriches which she later took to Washington with her.

It was one of those lunches that you never forget. There were only the four of us: Kitty and Gilbert, and Pamela and me. Pamela said to Kitty in front of me, "I hated to be such a pig, but that is what I am. I just wanted to meet your Billy, Kitty, and without a lot of others, because I've heard so much about him. I hear he has the best taste in America. I'm going to listen to everything he has to say, and I know that I will adore him."

So we did have a good time, and she was lots of fun, but it seemed to me that she laughed almost too much; however, she certainly did do one thing, she made you feel that you were the only man in the world or the only one that ever had been.

As we were leaving she said, "Now listen here, Billy Baldwin. You must come for lunch with Kitty and Gilbert next Thursday. In fact, I demand that you do because we're going to have some fun."

"Oh, that's too bad," said Kitty. "We will have gone back to London, but Billy will still be here. What are we going to miss?"

Pamela said, "You are going to miss three meals. You're going to miss Billy Baldwin with me, Rosie and Bill Gaynor, and Bill Paley with Babe."

The Gaynors and the Paleys were all in Paris having a real holiday. It was the height of the Fine French Furniture fever in New York, and everybody who had any money at all had to have a splendid piece of it; no matter what it looked like, and no matter whether they even cared about it. French furniture was a signature of taste, of fashion, and absolutely a must.

Bill and Babe had been doing quite a lot of work on their Long Island house and I had been helping them. My job with them was finished except that I was to help them find a French commode for the drawing room. I cannot say that it was a must. There really were plenty of pieces of furniture that we had seen in New York that would have been lovely, but Bill had the strong idea of collecting for a name, and he was determined to find what he wanted in Paris.

So the Paleys had come with the Gaynors to look. Rosie, it is quite true, had grown up with lovely French furniture, which had belonged to her mother when she was married to Mr. Vanderbilt, and she had always known a great deal about it and had a great deal of taste. Bill Gaynor knew nothing about anything except being about the best-looking man in Southampton and being a brilliant doctor.

I had made the most marvelous agreement with the Paleys. They had asked me to be their guest in Paris for a week in order to look for the French commode, and they wanted me to go with them every day. I agreed to be their guest and to help them, on the condition that I would not take a commission if we found the right thing. That way I could have the pleasure and the fun of freely and totally expressing myself, which I think is very hard for anybody to do honestly if money is involved.

Bill Paley had the strength of ten and it was great fun to go to all the terribly expensive and fashionable antiques shops with them and find everyone staring at Babe. She looked extraordinary that summer, and

Mrs. William Paley. (Condé Nast)

with her beautiful manners and that divine smile, the city of Paris was at her feet.

One day Bill said to me, "I think you, Babe, and I should go alone tomorrow afternoon. I've heard about a piece of furniture that I want to see."

So off we went in the late afternoon to a very well known antiquarian, and there we saw a black lacquer commode which was positively guaranteed to have belonged to Madame DuBarry. The price was absolutely staggering.

The dealer who owned it knew the Paleys, and had even been to their house on Long Island, and he said to Bill, "Mr. Paley, if you take that commode and put it in your salon, it will immediately make it the most important room in New York."

Bill said, "I don't doubt that. It is magnificent."

Magnificent it was, but I knew if we got the commode into their drawing room that it would look like a whore. It was much too elaborate, much too fancy, and it would not be right at all and because of my agreement with the Paleys, I was in a lovely position to say exactly what I thought the minute we left that gentleman's shop.

"Well," Bill said, "no, I can't see that, but the important thing is that I'm starving and I've got to have some herring right away."

"Well, darling," Babe said, "of course you must, indeed."

"Billy?" he said. "Do you like herring?"

"I love it," I said.

"There's only one place on earth that has really good herring and it's right here on the Champs Elysées," said Bill. We stopped at quite a strange restaurant, and it was true: I had the best herring I've ever eaten.

Several days later I witnessed a remarkable scene when we were shopping in Versailles. There was a woman who had a couple of lovely small houses filled with the most desirable furniture that one could ever possibly see; however, most of it was not for sale because it was going to be left to the Château of Versailles.

In the middle of her small salon there was a French commode that even I had to admit was to die for. She was known to be a prosperous woman and no price would she listen to. Onassis had been there and also Niarchos, but she would not sell. And there was Bill Paley literally down on his knees with tears in his eyes pleading with her to sell it to him, but getting absolutely nowhere because she didn't care and was not the slightest bit interested in him or in selling. Bill just couldn't believe it. Babe and Rosie would have given almost anything to own it, but it is now to be seen in the museum, and I think it is the most beautiful single piece of French furniture that I have ever seen.

The following day we went to lunch at Pamela's. It was the most lovely thing to be entertained by Pamela in the midst of all that hard work, and believe me that kind of antiquing is hard work! Her charm, her wit, and the great knowledge that she has acquired of French furniture made it a joy to be with her. The one thing that everybody did after lunch at Pamela's during this time was to drink lots of poire.

With the appalling passage of time Pamela came to America and married Leland Hayward, and because she was so nice to me, I saw quite a lot of her. It must be admitted that they bought a hideous modern house at Yorktown Heights, but she was able to create a wonderful garden there and produce beautiful flowers which were very necessary to her; in fact, all her rooms were filled with them.

Their very very bad modern house had been done by someone in a very English-lady-type way; however, Pamela built an addition, a very pretty room indeed, for Leland, and she also built the most luxurious swimming pool and swimming pool house that I have ever seen anywhere. The pool was lovely in that it was on the side of a hill that looked down into the valley. It was rather rustic, and there were many tall trees but not so tall that they would interfere with the sun. The house was so terrible that I cannot relate it.

It must be stated that in my experience no one can exceed her as a housekeeper. To spend the night in any one of Pamela's houses is an experience that you can hardly believe because of her concern for you as a guest. I stayed with her in Yorktown Heights and in Washington, and every kind of thing that you could possibly need in any way is there for you. There is the best reading light, the most marvelous sheets, the best breakfast — her food can't possibly be overestimated — in fact, it is as if she had a genie to fulfill your every desire.

Before Pamela married Averell Harriman, I had the pleasure of doing a tiny apartment for her at the corner of Park Avenue and 62nd Street. This was a real pied à terre in every sense of the word, and it was also the real height of luxury. The whole thing consisted of a sitting room, bedroom, and a terrace. We hung the walls of both rooms with a lovely fabric, and we were lucky enough to be able to take most of the museum-quality furniture from the big apartment she was leaving and use it in the little one. The rest of the furniture was to go on its way to the house that Averell had had for years and of which she was about to become the mistress.

It was really lovely to work for Pamela because she was always smiling and in good humor; however, she was also *very* demanding, but only when she was sure of her ground. Averell's house in Washington had had very little done to it because his wife, Marie, although she had been one of the most beloved and popular women in Washington, had not been interested in houses or housekeeping at all, and food had not existed for her; nor had it for Averell. Pamela said to me, "Now you are going to stick by me and we'll go down to Washington and get that house of Averell's decorated."

I knew the house because Averell had given it to Jackie Kennedy to live in after the assassination. I said, "I don't remember the house that well, but it's a very good Washington house and with your beautiful furniture it will be fine. There's a large garden that goes all the way through, which is unusual, and also an empty house next door which is wonderful for storage."

"Well," she said, "we'd better plan to go."

So off I went one afternoon in 1971 to meet Pamela at the Washington shuttle where we were to be met by Mrs. Graham's car and chauffeur. Pamela was spending the night with her, but I was to come back to New York.

Pamela had an absurd, silly romantic idea that I got out of her head as soon as I could. She did not want to see the house. She wanted to be carried over the threshold as a bride and I was to go and choose the bedroom because she did not want to have Marie Harriman's bedroom!

"Pamela," I said, "this is all lovely schoolgirl romance. No! I don't think it's a good idea at all." Mercifully, she agreed, but what she did was something I couldn't have done.

When we got to Washington, I said, "Don't forget this is not Chester Square, and this is not a beautiful London house. Georgetown never was famous for its fine houses, but it's full of charm, and you must behave. You must not run it down. You cannot. You have to respect his life there and his age. He was popular to a degree with her and you just play it low."

However, as we got out of the car in front of the house, she looked up and said, "I must say, I don't think too much of those doorways."

I said, "*You must say nothing.*"

The door was opened by Averell with his usual attractive manner, and he looked perfectly marvelous. I had seen him at their wedding in New York, and had also met one of his daughters, who said to me, "Well, I am so happy to know that you are really going to make my father comfortable. I hear that she is going to insist that he have a mattress long enough. At the moment his legs dangle beyond it."

The house was not beautiful architecturally and was rather awkward in many ways as those Georgetown houses are, but it had charm, and I could see that the magnificent French furniture would go perfectly well in it.

When we entered the first little drawing room, which was perfectly lovely, Pamela said, "We'll just rip that mantel right out."

I said, "Pamela, we will do nothing of the kind. That mantel is harmless. It's a good American copy of a French mantel, and we will leave it there and put on it your magnificent Louis XVI candelabra. In that way you will not have changed the house; instead, you will have added your things to it, and *you will not* make people think that you feel that Averell has been living in a dump, because he hasn't."

She went through the entire house *that way* but I loved her for what she did. On the third floor there was quite a big bedroom, another single room, a sitting room, and two baths, and she just made that into a suite for herself. It was high up and had a beautiful view and it was really charming. I would hardly have chosen it without her.

The house itself is not beautiful, but she filled it with lovely things, including some of Marie Harriman's pictures; the rest of which were sent to the National Gallery. Every space in the house had been covered with a fine Impressionist painting, none of which meant anything to her and which she didn't even like. Pamela urged Averell to give them as a memorial to Marie, and let her have some money to spend on the house, which is exactly what he did.

Averell must be the luckiest man in the world when you consider his age. She treats him as though he were a dazzling young boy and she a young girl. She is a marvelously active creature with beautiful manners who is polite and intelligent, and God knows she is a positive force as far as Washington political and social life is concerned. She is the kind of woman who after being married to Averell for practically no time at all changed his entire outlook on life. Very soon after their marriage, Pamela's son had a birthday, and Averell gave him an airplane for a present.

In the summer of 1971 I had the great pleasure of installing the Lawrences in "La Fiorentina." I had come into the most glorious experience that any decorator can have, really, that is I became the master decorator for a remarkable woman, Mary Wells Lawrence, who wished me to "do" — and "do" was the word she used — four places for her and her husband to live in. At the time I saw her first, she was Mary Wells, the president of one of the biggest advertising agencies in the world. She wanted to have a triplex apartment in New York City, a ranch in Arizona, a "house of my dreams" on the Riviera, and a house in Texas, "Dallas preferred," because she was about to marry Harding Lawrence who was the president of Braniff Airways whose headquarters were in Dallas.

The house in Dallas, which I did in 1970, turned out to be a wild success and I confess I did it in a taste that is not really mine at all: brilliant colors, American paintings, and good furniture both old and new. It also had colossal comfort primarily because Mary was determined to have a complete staff to run it as well as any other house she lived in. That was an absolute must. She had a total instinct for what was the best; of that there can be no doubt. We started with a staff of people who were already in love with the Lawrences, who couldn't work too hard, and who seemed to love their jobs before they even began them.

After we had finished the house in Dallas, the next thing Mary wanted to do was to find that house on the Riviera because she was determined to spend the first possible hour that she could there. Soon afterward I found myself sitting with them in a rather strange rented house in the south of France.

Mary said to me, "I want to do this attractively. I'm going to have the prettiest house, the best servants, and the most fascinating people as guests. It is going to be nothing but beauty everywhere I move. I know you can do it, and you understand what I want."

I said, "I do, I think."

I, of course, remembered "La Fiorentina." I had heard that Rory Cameron had been snooping around in Ireland looking for a house to buy if he could sell "La Fiorentina." I also knew that as he had no idea of selling its contents, it would be perfect for the Lawrences. I thought to myself that I had to find this out for sure at once!

I somehow got to a telephone because I had to call my secretary in New York in order to find his number, for I knew that he was also in the south of France. There was the most remarkable connection, the circuits worked, my wonderful secretary in New York gave it to me, and I called him at once and said, "Rory, this is Billy Baldwin. Is it true that your house is for sale?"

He said, "It certainly is. Why?"

"Because," I said, "I'm spending the weekend nearby, and I've got some people who are serious about buying it."

"Well," he said, "could I come there for lunch tomorrow?"

I said, "Where will you stay?"

He said, "Don't worry about that."

So we began talking and I said, "You know, I don't want you to come here. I want you to wait for us at 'La Fiorentina,' and I'll bring my friends to you there," and we both agreed to do just that.

So I then told Mary and Harding all about "La Fiorentina" and they said, "You won't believe what's happened. We've sailed by it in our little boat."

Mary said, "I told you in the letter I wrote you that first of all I wanted the dream house of my childhood. Now, I've seen it, and I'm sincere when I say that there's no point of my looking at anything else."

"Well," I said, "I'm sure that's probably true. I've seen it too, and I can think of nothing in the world more divine if you want that sort of thing, and it is for sale."

"I want to see it," Mary said.

So the next day we motored over and walked up the great flight of steps to wait for Rory.

Pretty soon, he appeared and, looking like an Apollo with a splendid tan, he came smiling up, and they presented themselves to each other, and we went through "La Fiorentina."

Because they were both hopelessly in love with each other, it was absolutely fascinating to see Mary go through the house with Harding behind her. The first room they went into was an enormous hall, and turning slightly, Mary said, "This is where the screen is to be placed."

I said, "What screen?"

"Oh," she said, "there will be a screen for that corner, and over here I'd rather have less furniture." She talked to Rory as though she had bought it. Mary went through the entire house that way and when we had finished our tour she said to him, "Later on we've got to talk about money."

We had been invited to a big dinner party that night, and Rory asked if by any chance we were going to the So-and-So's. I said that we were and that we would see him there. Obviously none of them wasted any time discussing the money because at cocktails just before dinner, he came scooting up to me and told me that the Lawrences had agreed to the price that he wanted and he was going to sell to them.

So the Lawrences bought "La Fiorentina" and I began this wonderful second thing with them. From that minute on we did nothing but talk about the furnishings for it and what I was going to do to it. Not one thing did they wish to see, and I was to buy everything in Paris, London, Rome, and New York.

Decorating "La Fiorentina" was the most divine fun and the nice part was that Rory lived in a very pretty small house on the property which was not for sale, and I moved over and stayed for the whole time that I was working there.

We got possession of "La Fiorentina" the first of November, and Mary said, "You've got to promise me you will get us in by the first of June for the season."

I said, "Now, listen here. How can I?"

"Well," she said, "You can."

"What about the costs?" I said.

"I want you to call me in New York when the big estimates come in, like the painting," she said.

So I did, and I guess I went abroad four or five times, and near the end of June I installed the Lawrences in the completely furnished house. It was the sensation of the summer that year and they had a large party to celebrate. There was no doubt about it that the house was a great success. I don't think everybody liked it because they didn't; it was either too modern or not decorated in a grand enough manner, but never mind, we got "La Fiorentina" done. Mary got the staff too. They were Italians who lived just across the border and they were marvelous. That was Mary's second full staff.

In 1973 I decorated her New York triplex apartment, and that too had an entire staff to run it. We had also done the ranch in Arizona. It still does not seem possible to me that within a matter of four short years Mary Wells Lawrence accomplished exactly what she said she wanted to do when she first met me.

. . . you sensed through her rather pale physical container that there was a character of great power, great strength, and determination which were not exactly conventional.

*J*t will never be possible for me to explain the mystery of Nantucket, but that is exactly what it has been to me from my childhood, when it took me and my family over twenty-four hours to go by every form of travel, except air, from Baltimore to the little town of Sconset on a far end of the island.

I was definitely a Southerner, so that everything I saw seemed quite foreign; especially the people who although perfectly normal seemed very odd in many ways. There was no dressing up, there was no fancy business, and there was really no social life in that place in the summer. It was just a nice, calm, peaceful, healthy life. The island was also quite overwhelming in its beauty, and although I was very young I appreciated it because I knew that beauty is always simple.

Among many of the special things on Nantucket was something known as the Hidden Forest; off the Polpis Road, inland, and in one of the most beautiful parts of the island, surrounded somewhat by cranberry bogs of great beauty and moorlands of remarkable strength, this peculiar thing existed. What it really was, was a valley in which trees had grown so that the tops of the trees were more or less on a level with the top of the valley; therefore on entering the forest you descended into it.

I had heard about the Hidden Forest for a great many years but had never seen it. There was a kind of mystery about it too; as to whether you could get permission to see it or not, and I was told very frankly by my family's friends that you couldn't. Consequently, I was never allowed to do anything about seeing it, but was very curious because I thought the name was so magical and tempting.

As a young man I had met another young man about seven or eight years younger who lived in Sconset with his mother and father, the David Grays, and he was David Gray, Jr. He was a romantic character full of violence, full of temperament, and full of talent which was seen later in his sculpture. His mother and father were people of great good looks who came from the West Coast and were supposedly very rich, and it is true that David's father had the great generosity and kindness to present the casino to the town of Sconset, and quite a few other things such as the flagpole. A little later he also presented them with a beautiful golf course called the Sankaty Golf Course because of its proximity to the Sankaty Light House, which is quite near Sconset. It was said that Mr. and Mrs. Gray decided that Sconset was getting too social. It could not really have been wildly social because it was a simple little place; however, they bought the most beautiful acreage on the Polpis Road to get away from society, and included in their purchase was the Hidden Forest.

I saw very little of David Gray, Jr. in those years; probably because of the fact there was an age difference. I suppose he thought that I was really too old, and I thought that they, meaning David and his friends, were too young for me, but he was a picaresque character, and as the years flew by and I was not always on Nantucket, I forgot about my childhood acquaintance with him.

Oh, so many years later, I went to a dinner party given by one of those wonderful people who go to Sconset in the summer. It was a party of not more than eight or ten people and just before dinner was announced my hostess grabbed me by the arm and said, "Come over here. I don't think you've met Mrs. David Gray."

Indeed, I had not met Mrs. David Gray, and somehow I had heard that David Gray, my childhood remembrance, had died. Sitting there, looking absolutely extraordinary, was his widow, Nancy. In a funny way she looked scarcely human. She was so silvery or gold or something, but certainly not flesh. She had the most marvelous pale pale hair, wore no rouge, was very fair, and very small. All those dull words like exquisite and ravishing are not right to describe her, but she *was* all of them, and she was more because you sensed through her rather pale physical container that there was a character of great power, great strength, and determination which were not exactly conventional.

I plunked myself down beside her and told her just exactly who I was; adding that I was so sorry that I had never met her, saying that her husband had entirely separated from my life and I from his. Oddly enough, the very next night, my friend Michael Gardine had asked me to dinner, and I was to meet Nancy again. He said, "You've got to meet my best friend, Nancy Gray." It seemed that Nancy and I were destined to become part of each other's lives.

Little did I realize that a couple of years later I would be visiting her in Santa Barbara where she took me to her ranch to spend the day. To my surprise, our arrival was not only greeted by the most beautiful countryside, but also by a very comfortable low ranch house which was furnished mostly with beds and very simple furniture. There was a kitchen, and you could indeed spend the night in the house in great comfort, but to me, the crowning glory of the ranch was a fantastic gazebo which had been designed and built by David Gray. It was architecture of the most extraordinary beauty, octagonal in shape, and quite a paradox: Chinese, but not at all; American, but really not at all. There were hammocks, and apparently they sometimes had cocktails there, which was a beautiful tribute to David really. Without doubt, it is one of the most lovely things that I have ever known.

That night at Michael's dinner party I said to Nancy, and not with any shyness at all, "Will you let me see you sometime? And I have to tell you that I am really almost more anxious to see the Hidden Forest than I am to see you."

Nancy said, "Of course. Why don't you come out to the house for dinner tomorrow night with Michael, and you can see it."

I had heard from somebody that Nancy lived in a totally fascinating house on the edge of the Hidden Forest. As I grew up, it seemed to me that every year my love for houses increased. It became the primary interest in my life and there was nothing else that even came close to touching it. That has been true all of my life, so it was with the greatest good luck that I went with Michael to Nancy's to dine where I was to enter one of the perfect houses of the world.

We got out there by daylight on a summer evening, and as we approached, the house, surrounded by an untouched lawn, really a meadow, suddenly came out of the earth; it was of no color at all except the color of the moors, as though it had been painted with the same palette as the moors themselves.

The house was very low, one story, very rambling, and had very definite bones; bones which were of great beauty and honesty, and which

were based upon the salt-box houses and the general classicism of a Palladian house. It was quite big, but never imposing. You drove up to it over a long drive which was really like a country lane, and you parked on the grass in front. There was no foolishness about anything, just getting out and walking in the front door.

Outside the front door there was the most beautiful bell which looked rather odd and you couldn't quite tell what kind of bell it was. Through the front door was a vestibule in the real sense of the word, and it was furnished with a pair of daybeds like sofas, a desk, many photographs, and quite a lot of memorabilia which was very mystifying. I couldn't imagine what the bell, photographs, and memorabilia meant, and I said to Nancy, "What is all of this?" She explained that it was the relics of the little railroad that ran for a brief time between Nantucket and Sconset. The bell was from the train engine.

Standing in the vestibule, you looked straight ahead and saw a long room at the end of which was quite a big group of furniture placed in front of windows. I suddenly realized as I stood there that this house spread from right to left, and forward and backward with the most beautiful movement or really without any movement at all, and, of course, I thought to myself, How is this curious thing happening?

Cold-bloodedly, I soon realized as I walked from room to room that most of the rooms could be used either as sitting rooms or as bedrooms. These were wonderful guest rooms, a couple of which even had sleeping porches off them so you could sleep outside if you wished. There seemed to me to be an incredible choice. The Grays had been their own decorators and they had had the brilliance of mind, strength, and determination to paint four bedrooms, a living room, dining room, several halls, kitchen, pantries, bathrooms, and sleeping porches exactly the same color, to use the same spatter-painted floor throughout, and to use only three fabrics. Because of the light from the windows, and the different dimensions and ceiling heights of the rooms, the painted wall color, which was exactly the same everywhere, seemed to be composed of the most marvelous varieties of color like the moors or like a remarkable sky. The house had an incredible atmosphere, and I felt when I was inside it that I was inside something like a mushroom which had grown up from the ground.

I thought to myself, What a lesson. This house should really be shown to anybody who is going to be a decorator or an architect *if only* to have them understand the importance of repetition. One of the materials which was on the wooden furniture was an English chintz with quail on it. The colors were of the quail's feathers and a lot of woodsy colors which were on a background of an almost gone dull red. You really had to look twice to find the birds. The large upholstered furniture was done in a lovely linen which was quite golden in color, very warm and luminous.

Do not for one moment think that this house was empty or bare because it wasn't. It was filled with things that were suitable, which went with it, and which seemed to have lived there forever. I can't imagine anything being brought in, and it seemed to me that the contents of the house must have just grown there. Its comfort was to a degree that was only realized after you had been in it. I have never seen anywhere such an extraordinarily beautiful serene natural achievement in my life. It is something that I shall never forget, and I never got accustomed to it.

I had the enormous good fortune of joining Nancy and being a fellow houseguest with Michael for several weeks in the falls of 1975 and 1976. She was terribly hospitable, and really liked people in a strange kind of way. She was enormously tolerant and gave from everything that she had to everybody.

I was so pleased one day when my friend Bunny Mellon said that she was coming to Nantucket Island from her house in Cape Cod with her houseguest, Hubert de Givenchy, and as Bunny's brother had been an intimate friend of David and Nancy's, it was perfectly possible for Nancy to ask them to come for lunch, and it was my wish that they did. It had nothing to do with anything social, truthfully, although they were all charming, very bright people. It was about *that house*. Of course, I wanted my friend Bunny to see my friend Nancy, but that wasn't really what I wanted. I wanted those people to see Nancy's house. I knew there was no casting of any pearls before swine in that case because Bunny has the love that I have for houses, and she spends a great deal of her time in the five she owns and has done herself.

Nancy arranged a perfectly beautiful luncheon, and she invited her great friend Michael, and also Way Bandy. The six of us had a lovely time, so much laughter, and of course, Bunny was charmed as I was by the house. Hubert, being French and analytical, got the whole point, understood it all, and loved it all. We all had a perfectly lovely moment and nobody had to explain anything.

Fog threatened, so Bunny and Hubert had to leave rather suddenly for fear that they might not be able to get away, and as they rushed to their car, we went with them to say good-bye, and we were met with a perfectly horrifying sight. Their car had been rented and was being driven by a very big black man. He had, suspended in midair, an enormous turtle which he was waving around holding on to by its tail.

With as much of a shriek as was possible, Bunny screamed at him to stop. It was the most horrifying sight and such a wild contrast to the gaiety and pleasure of the lunch and the beauty of the house. It was ugliness personified in the flash of a moment.

Bunny commanded the man to put the turtle down, which was almost the biggest land turtle I have ever seen, and he quickly dropped it. It must have come up from the Hidden Forest where it could have lived unbothered for years. We watched it crawl off into the shrubbery and liberty.

Nancy was a very good cook and she did all the cooking when she had a dinner party, which was often. You went down a long hall into a kitchen of marvelous efficiency, where you had local and extraordinarily delicious food served to you, which you took into the dining room. It was surrounded on three sides by solid walls of windows, and there you sat at a lovely table and ate, as though you were actually in the middle of the trees with a background of verdant forest. Almost any kind of conversation could follow after dinner, and almost any kind of surprise.

For example, the second time that I was a houseguest there along with Michael, Way Bandy was also there, too. It was late fall, early winter, and we were having a lovely evening after dinner talking away. Our thoughts went to where we were going to find ourselves in the spring, and I, as usual, shot my face off and said, "A place that I have never been and always wanted to go to is Haiti." I think it was Michael who said, "Why not?" Well, we all looked at each other and said rather quickly, "Why not?" Because of my business I had traveled a great deal and had a wonderful travel agent in New York, so I said that I thought I'd just better telephone him. So telephone we did and made complete plans for a two-week visit to the island of Haiti, which actually took place. I couldn't believe it myself, really, when I found myself motoring from the airport to the Grand Oloffson Hotel in Port-au-Prince.

Our trip was one of those absolutely lyrical experiences because we stayed in this most remarkable old-fashioned Victorian hotel called the Grand Oloffson. Nancy took a suite on the top floor, which was called the John Gielgud Suite, and Way, Michael, and I took the separate cottage rooms on the edge of the swimming pool.

Every night we would meet at the crowded little bar in the hotel where *tout* Haiti met. Nancy was always a little bit late, and she would appear looking like a spirit at the door at the long end of the room. She seemed, I thought, to be illuminated from inside and she *was* shy. She would float into the room and be seated pretty quickly beside a delicious daiquiri.

Many people spoke to us, and one was a very nice woman who was the wife of the American ambassador. She asked me if I was not who I was, and discovered that she was right. I learned that they were cousins of a great friend in Palm Beach, and she said, "We will call you for we want you for dinner."

It was awfully nice that they followed it up and gave us the most glorious evening at the embassy. We motored to the outskirts of town and shuttled up to the gateway of the embassy, which is a very beautiful white house of American design, and were greeted by two beautiful

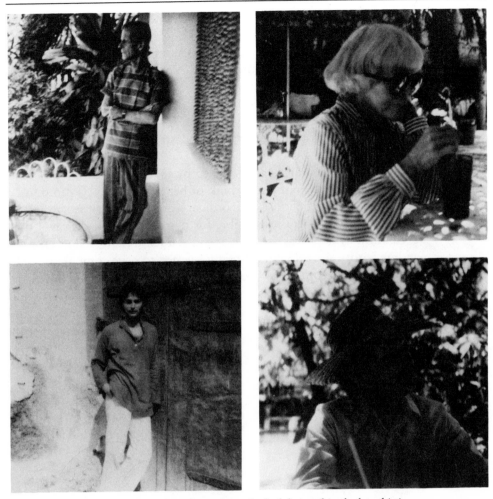

(Clockwise from top left): Billy wearing pajamas he had designed in the late thirties and wore at the Lido; Nancy Gray; Michael Gardine; Way Bandy.

black children in white uniforms who took us to the drawing room where we had wonderful rum cocktails with Heywood Isham and his wife, Sheila.

The big salon which was really big had its walls covered with abstract paintings by Sheila. We dined outside under a full moon on a carpet of grass thicker than any carpet you have ever known. Near us was a giant white frangipani tree in full bloom; there were no mosquitoes, the food was delicious, and the hospitality of our ambassador and his wife was not only charming but extraordinary.

Our time in Haiti flew by. One day was spent motoring to the coastal town of Jacmel, another at the iron marketplace of Port-au-Prince. Of course, the answer was that we all had fallen in love with it. I don't know how there could have been such laughter, pleasure, and joy as there were in those two weeks in Haiti. It was truthfully a strange extension of the atmosphere, charm, and strength of the house by the Hidden Forest in Nantucket.

Still, in my memory, I am haunted by that house. Although Nancy has since died, I cannot really think of her with sorrow. I can think of her with joy and the most extraordinary gratitude because she and her husband, David, were responsible for it and what it had in it. I don't even know what it was that it had in it, but its strength and its character and its beauty were so unique that it seemed to have come up from the earth or down from the sky and settled there. It also would never have surprised me if one day I had gone out there and found that it had quite simply disappeared.

*. . . "You're not an Englishman." I said,
"No, I'm not. I'm an American."
"Oh," she said, and looked as though she
had smelled something very unpleasant.*

I n *Country Life,* June 11, 1921, there were some extraordinary photographs of Althorp, the seat of the Earl Spencer. I was so impressed by them that I immediately clipped them out and put them into one of my favorite very special scrapbooks. On October 29, 1977, Arthur Smith, my former partner, who bought my firm, and I went to lunch at Althorp, and we were taken there by Hardy Amies, whom we were visiting in the Cotswolds for the weekend.

I have always felt that paradise on this earth would be to own and live in a house in the Cotswolds, and Hardy Amies has done exactly that. He bought an enchanting schoolhouse, smack in the middle of the village, and in no time at all created a garden, mostly for herbs, which looked as if it had been there since ancient times. A short distance away and an easy walk, there was a large barn, which he was converting at that moment into the most luxurious tennis house with several dressing rooms, a big party room, and guest rooms. Both the house and his additions are made of that incredibly beautiful gray Cotswold stone.

We hear so much about what is personal and how sad it is that so much is not as personal as it might be, that it is a great relief and a great treat to see that everything Hardy has done is a complete expression of his personal taste.

Arthur E. Smith. (Horst)

All the front yards of all the Cotswold houses were a mass of glorious blossoming roses. It was one of those late autumns where the roses just seem to be having the best time of all by being in bloom for the last time. We had motored out from London through the beautiful English autumn on a Friday, and we were going to be with Hardy until Sunday night.

From my bedroom window I looked down into the herb garden, which is very much in the style of the great Gertrude Jekyll. Hardy has been very sensible. It is really not necessary to gild the Jekyll lily, and Hardy knows and respects that, so what he really has done in his little garden is to make it exactly as though she had done it. It is a brilliant copy, and the smell which drifts up to the bedroom windows is something you can never forget, and God knows you don't want to. The air was so lovely that we took several long walks while we were there. The Thames so far away from London at that point is practically a tiny little beautiful brook, and has such a gentle quality that you really cannot believe it is the same stream.

We did not stay up late on Friday because we were going to have quite a day the next day, although there were many wonderful books in Hardy's great library to read and be amused by. The main part of his house is a very big room which was formerly the schoolroom and it is filled with ancient English oak and is very masculine indeed, and is eminently suitable.

Having slept in the most beautifully dressed bed I have ever been in, I awoke to have Hardy himself deposit upon my lap the most marvelous breakfast with the prettiest blue and white china, and the prettiest blue and white linen. His food is delicious and quite a lot of its great quality is because of the fact he himself cooks it.

We were not rushing, but as we were going quite some distance to lunch, nearly a couple of hours by car, we had to get dressed rather quickly and leave. Hardy had a lovely car and chauffeur, and off we went. He told us that we were going to a very well known house called Althorp and he pronounced it for us, and asked me if I had been there before, and I told him that I had not and that I didn't know the house.

So Hardy said, "Are you sure you don't?"

"Well, I know the name, but I can't quite associate the name with what it is like," I replied.

He said, "I will only tell you that it belongs to the Earl Spencer and that two of his daughters have been rumored to be engaged to the Prince of Wales, and he himself is a rather new bridegroom, having not so long ago married the ex-wife of the Earl of Dartmouth."

I said, "That's terribly interesting because I happen to have known them both when they were married and they lived next to Kitty Miller in London in that remarkable house which was once lived in by Mrs. Marriot. I'm sorry to tell you that I didn't even know they were divorced."

They had been so nice to me in London that I had had a note from Kitty the following autumn saying that they were coming to New York, and it would be nice if I could possibly have them for a drink. I decided to do my best and so I got hold of Miss Case and told her to just somehow get me four tickets to *Oklahoma!*, which was the rage at that moment. So I took the Dartmouths and Miss Case for dinner at Côte Basque and then to the play, and I will say that they were mad about all that Americana that they saw so beautifully done.

Raine, Lady Dartmouth, I had first met at a very attractive luncheon given by Peter Coats. She was a very pretty woman in a rather Gainsborough way. Peter's luncheon was on a spring day, it is true, but she sat at the middle of that city lunch table, wearing an enormous pink organdy hat. However, she was not at all what she seemed. When you first saw her you thought, "Good heavens, a typical kind of almost Edwardian Gibson girl with no sense." *Not at all!* She had plenty of sense, and from the time that I last saw her, she had had sense enough to marry the Earl Spencer.

It seemed as though we rode and rode but it was never boring because of the beauty of the countryside, which was really unbeatable especially on such a fine autumn day. At last we entered the gates of the enormous estate. The driveway went through flat but gently rolling fields full of cattle and beautiful trees, and eventually led us to the very extraordinary house; extraordinary because it had originally been built of a lovely pinkish brick, but one day in the past the owner had had it refaced entirely with gray stone.

Later, as we drove away, Arthur said, remembering that Ruby Ross Wood's favorite color was pink, that he was sure that years before when Mrs. Wood visited Althorp she had mentally erased the stone and seen the lovely pink brick.

Out we jumped from the car, very happy indeed to arrive. The enormous doors of the house were open, and I stepped into something that I simply couldn't believe. Althorp indeed! Althorp was the house from *Country Life* that I pasted in my scrapbook many long years before, and the room I was standing in was an immense entrance hall in which there were five life-size paintings of horses by John Wootton.

I said, "I cannot believe it." And as I uttered those words I was presented to the earl, who was absolutely beaming with pleasure and looking great in a marvelous tweed suit. I said, "I must tell you that I saw this in *Country Life* in 1921 and put it in my scrapbook. It is one of my favorite places in the world, but I had forgotten the association of it with its name, Althorp. However, I remember the photographs so well that I can tell you about that chair which is sitting in front of that wall." The earl seemed terribly pleased, but the overwhelming thing to me was the scale of the huge stallions.

We were taken almost at once into a long long library, which was a huge white room with huge fireplaces with beautiful windows opposite them and it seemed as though the room was composed of books on one side and glass on the other. The style of the room cannot even be imagined and the scale was colossal because the room was. Around each of the fireplaces were big groups of very comfortable furniture, and in front of one of them were a few young people. They were the earl's children by his first wife.

Then I saw my old friend Raine, now Lady Spencer, who was perfectly charming. She said, "What a thing! I couldn't believe it when Hardy asked if he could bring a New York decorator to see the house, and when he told me who it was, I said, 'Can you bring him! You can bring him and anybody else that you want.' "

There was sitting beside one of the fireplaces a person who struck me as a very odd note indeed. I took a second look and she seemed wrong in every way. I was taken over to be presented to her and she was Barbara Cartland, Lady Spencer's mother.

The name meant a little bit to me, but not much, and I did remember that she wrote tons of romantic tripe and that her novels were wildly successful. Before I was practically pushed down beside her, Lady Spencer said, "I'm afraid lunch is not quite ready, but there are several rooms that you might wish to see beforehand because I know one thing, and that is that you are going to be dead exhausted when you are finished seeing the rest of the house for we have miles of picture galleries and this is a very big house. After lunch I'm going to take you by the hand and show you my quarters, which I have just finished decorating, and after we've done that I want you to see our fair. Today is the first of a series of fairs that we have in the stables to benefit the house and to try and make it possible to keep it intact for us to live in and save for the nation."

There I was beside this lady. So down I sat and she said to me, "Tell me about yourself."

I told her that I was staying with Hardy, and she said, "Oh, he's a darling." Then she said, "You're not an Englishman."

I said, "No, I'm not. I'm an American."

"Oh," she said, and looked as though she had smelled something very unpleasant.

She was dressed in the most terrible clothes you could possibly imagine. She was a harmony of baby pink and blue, and she had a halo of white hair. I thought to myself that I have heard many English people criticize Americans, but nobody can take the place beside this woman for being the limit.

Then she said, "I know you know all about me and you know what I do, but what do you do?"

I said, "I am a decorator."

"You are what?" she said.

"I am a decorator."

"Well," she said, "I've just come from your California, and I hope to God you're not a decorator from California, are you?"

I said, "I have done some work there."

"Well, you better go back again," she said. "God knows they need some taste. Another thing you might do while you are at it is to tell your airlines to have a little manners. When I travel on this side of the Atlantic I've been accustomed to having at least two full seats because I am not a young lady and I get tired and it is very necessary for me to stretch out. So naturally, out of politeness and courtesy, I am given at least two seats and sometimes three. To my great disgust, the last time I came back from your country on your airlines they wouldn't let me have two seats, and I wanted three."

How can I possibly get out of this, I thought, and what am I going to do about this horrible creature? Fortunately, lunch was announced and I was mercifully freed. We went into a hall just off the enormous library into a normal-sized dining room, and we were: the Spencers, four or five children, Mrs. Cartland, Hardy, Arthur, and me. The children had beautiful manners and were perfectly enchanting.

Lunch was absolutely delicious. We ate something like a wonderful veal which was really good, and tiny peas about the size of pinheads. The children took over but in exactly the right sort of way. They were not annoying but just having fun. They were not shy or frightened looking. I sat on the right of Lady Spencer and on her left was Arthur. Next to Arthur was an absolutely adorable, very pretty girl called Lady Diana, who was full of charm, full of wit, and full of humor.

I had been told that her sister had caught the eye of the Prince of Wales, but that it didn't take, and now there was a sort of rumor that perhaps Lady Diana might be the one in favor.

I had not met the Prince of Wales but Kitty Miller had, and she told me that he was her pet. Kitty always had a pet in the royal family, and she had told me not too long before, in 1977, that she was absolutely stuck on the Prince of Wales. She said, "I met him at a party the other day and asked him right away to come to one of mine, and he said he would. He's got real charm and I'm crazy about him."

We had an enchanting lunch, and then Lady Spencer excused herself and said to me, "My dear, I have to go take one last look at the fair before I show you my apartment, and then you will see my bed." She absented herself for a very short time, and I waited for her in a suite of rooms off the family dining room.

She was soon back and we went to her rooms. The bedroom was a corner room and it was blazing, it was so nice, with the biggest bed I've ever seen in my life which was hers, and it had just been done in pale pink and pale blue silk. It was the most luxurious, the most comfortable, the most extravagant thing that I almost have ever seen. There were masses of flowers everywhere, and it was just like a bower for Titania in *A Midsummer Night's Dream*.

After my tour, we all got into cars and went down to the stable, which was very large and had a beautiful Adam room. There was an enormous courtyard with tables in it, and one whole wing had been turned into a glorious shop. Nearly everything had been given by the people who lived nearby, so the quality of what was for sale was like being in the most marvelous shop in the world.

There were very attractive ladies and gentlemen taking care of your needs and what you wanted, and good little cookies to eat and marvelous things to drink. It was certainly an attractive sight and I was one hundred percent impressed by the looks of the women. They were not chic women, but there were, however, many who had been beautiful and many who still were beautiful, and almost all of them looked very elegant indeed, dressed very suitably in slightly old-fashioned-looking fall clothes. They looked very tweedy, very wooly, and far better than if they had attempted to look like the fashion models of today.

The sound of their voices was very pretty and they had the most marvelous manners and real concern for you. Everyone asked if you were having a nice time, and they all wanted to know all about you. I was so happy to see that my ogre before lunch had somehow disappeared. I only hoped that she was trying to catch a flight and made it.

When we returned to the house a very attractive woman who was really the head curator took us through the miles of portraits which comprise the greatest private collection in England. We saw every single bit of that house and *finally* with the greatest sorrow we had to say goodbye to our perfectly divine host and hostess. Now, to think of that adorable girl, Lady Diana, who one day may be Queen of England, makes me feel very happy.

"When I hold this, I feel like fleeing."

J had been hearing reports about the house that Jacqueline Onassis was building in Chilmark on Martha's Vineyard. My interest, of course, was doubled by the fact that my great friend Bunny Mellon, who was also an equally good friend of Jackie Onassis, had been tempting me with tales about the beautiful property and what was going on in the way of the house that Jackie was building.

It is easy to understand my total pleasure when I received a postal card from her asking me to come and lunch and see what she and Bunny had been doing. She telephoned later at my house at 22 Hussey Street on Nantucket and told me that she would send a little plane to pick up Andy Oates, the guiding genius of the Nantucket Looms, our friend Michael Gardine, and me, and that we would meet in time for lunch with Bunny, who would be flying over from Cape Cod.

Off we started on a beautiful morning. My anticipation was like that of a small child on Christmas Eve, and I knew that to see Jackie again would be in itself a delight, but I also knew that seeing Jackie on her property and in her house would be quite frankly the realization of a long curiosity.

The flight was without any excitement except for what I had inside of me. I remembered so well the first time I ever saw Jackie, the weekend of November 16, 1963. I was on my way to the Mellons' in Virginia

Living room of Billy's house at 22 Hussey Street in Nantucket. (Condé Nast)

where I was to spend the weekend, and I was to stop at the house that she had bought for herself and her children to enjoy their life on horseback. The president didn't care one bit about the house, but it was a place for him to rest.

I arrived there quite early and was greeted by the most smiling little Filipino in the simplest possible way who said to me, "Mr. Baldwin, Mrs. Kennedy knows that you have been up quite early and therefore would like you to have some breakfast. When you are finished and are relaxed, she will see you." I thought of the many times in my life when I had gone places arriving at breakfast time and not been allowed to look at anything to eat until lunch. As I finished my breakfast in the sitting room, and was looking around at the house that really honestly had hardly ever been lived in, she came in wearing her beautiful jodhpurs. It is impossible to describe the intelligent estimate of her smile. She said, "You are very good to come down here to see me." It just happened to be one week before Dallas.

The next time I saw her was about three weeks after the assassination when she was living in Washington with her children in the house that Averell Harriman had very kindly lent her. This was a great gesture because it meant that her children did not have to go back to the White House, and they could stay there until they had a place to go to.

That day I arrived before lunch. A State Department car took me to the house and when I rang the bell the door was opened by a guard, with Jackie standing close behind him. She smiled at me and said, "Welcome, my friend." We had a little conversation and then walked across the street which was lined with people because it had gotten out that Jackie and her children were leaving that day for the Christmas holidays in Palm Beach with the president's family.

We went across the street to the house that Jackie and her children were planning to move into and which had been chosen for her with the greatest possible bad decision by her sister, Mrs. Lee Radziwill. It was just across the street, but it was absolutely hopeless because first of all there was no back entrance; consequently, the servants' delivery was also the front door. Second, it was high up on some steps, and had been designed for publicity. There was no possibility for privacy and in every way it was totally what she should not have had for those children; however, it had been bought, and it was up to me to get it finished enough for the children to move into with their furniture from the White

House bedrooms as soon as possible. However, before this was to be accomplished, Jackie decided that she could not live in Washington and moved to New York City.

Next *came* her marriage to Onassis in October of 1968 and that wonderful whispered telephone conversation in which she asked me if I could possibly come to Greece and help her. I went to Greece two days later, flying all night and arriving in Athens the very day that Onassis had come in from his island to finish up the purchase of three very important Irish oil tankers. The Greek newspapers had taken advantage of this to say Mrs. Onassis had left Mr. Onassis, and that the marriage was over, but of course, the marriage was not over. There was a mob of photographers in the hotel lobby, and I was literally picked up and taken to the car that was waiting for Ari and me to take us to his suburban house for lunch. When we arrived, Jackie, in the prettiest possible simple gray flannel dress, was standing on the terrace, backed by two very imposing Onassis sisters, and again, she smiled her welcome to me.

So there I was, sitting in a little plane going from Nantucket to Martha's Vineyard, knowing that I was going to be greeted once more by my friend. The very thought of spending a day with Jacqueline Onassis in her new house on Martha's Vineyard was enough to make you feel alive again. I had not seen her for quite a long time, and not for a very long time professionally, for the last time I had worked with her was when I had gone to Greece to help her with the decoration of a house for her children.

As a professional decorator for over forty years, one of the things I learned about my clients was that they could be divided into two categories, and almost immediately after I started a job I knew which kind of client they were. One had the joy and realization of their great good fortune in being able to execute financially the dream they wished to live. The other had the absolute absence of that quality and a workmanlike point of view of simply having a job to get done.

Jackie Onassis, in everything that she attempts, has that first quality to a degree that I have never seen exceeded. She is a romantic human being, and a room, a house, or a picture really becomes a romance with her. She is easily seduced by beauty, and I think she longs to be surrounded by it. More than anything is this quality applied to Jackie's feeling about words and poetry, subjects she knows a great deal about.

I don't think she is enormously experienced in houses and decoration because she really hasn't had a chance to be. Her house in Chilmark was the first time that she had ever built one except for the little house in Greece for her children: one that she built with a certain timidity but no less enthusiasm.

The gala excitement of holiday was certainly in the air as we descended in our little plane onto the island of Martha's Vineyard. There was automatically a lovely thrill on my part because to be welcomed anywhere in the world by Jackie Onassis is one of the most precious experiences that anybody can have, and also, quite frankly, I had never been to Martha's Vineyard before.

Jackie herself met us and drove us for quite some distance across the island to the entrance to her property, which was very much of a woodland. I knew that Bunny Mellon had done the landscaping from the moment we entered the driveway, which began twisting and turning in a most beautiful way past parts of the grounds that we realized had been there for centuries, and others which were obviously the result of Bunny's wand. There was an incredible give and take of vistas, which resulted in the remarkable sight of seeing something very briefly and then seeing it repeated again, and then suddenly the sea. Pretty soon we caught a glimpse of something that really was the house and then the barn, and the silo away from the main house that she had built for her children to use.

We went on a tour of the house before we had a wonderful lunch of lobster salad. I shall never forget a moment that occurred in her bedroom. I was sitting at her desk and we were discussing the arrangement of the furniture and the design of her bed. On a shelf below her desk was a beautiful red leather rectangular box. Michael was looking at it and Jackie said, "Isn't it wonderful. Would you like to see it?"

The object turned out to be a birthday present for Jackie, and it was Marie Antoinette's carrying case, the very one she had used to put her jewels in when she fled Paris from the Revolution. Jackie held it in her arms before setting it down before me on the desk, and said, "When I hold this, I feel like fleeing."

Our lunch was over too soon. We had had a glorious time and there was not a dull moment. Jackie drove us back to the airport. Looking out of the airplane window as we taxied down the runway, I saw her standing there waving good-bye to us. There can be no doubt that she is one of the mesmerizing people of her century, and I thought of the many people I had known over my rather long life, and came to the realization of something that I had never been fully aware of before. I have never cared about people who were dull and meant nothing to me, of whom there were many. No, I feel absolutely that life is too good. I think you have to give your best and expect the best of other people. I am quite intolerant in the sense that I really don't want and I never have wanted to sit around yawning, inside of me, politely. I can't. I haven't got time.

Afterword

AT THE AGE of seventy Billy Baldwin retired. On July 1, 1973, the firm of Baldwin, Martin and Smith was dissolved, and the tradition of the firm was carried on by Arthur E. Smith, who formed his own company.

To those who knew Billy it did not seem that he had retired, but rather that he had climbed to yet another plateau. It is true that no one in his profession had worked harder, been blessed with more talent, or been more dedicated, and he entered his new life with as much zeal, interest, and enthusiasm as he had exemplified in his career.

After his retirement Billy kept his apartment in New York, but he spent the summers of 1974 through 1978 in his cottage at the Chanticleer Inn in Sconset on Nantucket Island. His love for Sconset and Nantucket began at the age of nine and lasted throughout his life. The summer before he died I recall his great pleasure in showing to visiting friends the Sconset Casino where one distant summer he had played, costumed in his mother's chemise which was pinned with a safety pin, the part of the Happy Prince in a play based on the fairy tale by Oscar Wilde.

In 1979 Billy gave up his New York apartment, his Sconset cottage, and moved permanently to the town of Nantucket where he lived happily at 22 Hussey Street.

The ten years of his life after he retired, which he spent on Nantucket, found him actively involved in almost every aspect of the island's life, from volunteering at the Hospital Thrift Shop to draping the Pacific Club and the Pacific National Bank with bunting for the nation's Bicentennial celebration.

After another bout with pneumonia, Billy died on November 25, 1983, at the Nantucket Cottage Hospital. Billy's life on Nantucket was best expressed by one of his close friends who wrote after his death: "Billy's life and leaving us was all in the spirit and charm that he believed in. I admired him so the way he retired — not going down like so many who have led the type of life he did — hanging on to the same rhythm and people that after a time one does not want to keep up with — but gathering together his possessions and leaving the world of confusion behind and making a lovely new life on the island of Nantucket where his apartment was like an exquisite little house and he was surrounded by his friends who loved him and whom he loved."

Billy's instructions were always clear, and he had arranged that there be no funeral or any kind of service. He said that he had seen too many of his friends buried and realized what a charade funerals were. He did not want *some* people to attend, and he knew they would show up and be sitting in the front row. He was cremated and his ashes were placed at his family's gravesite in the Green Mount Cemetery in Baltimore.

This past summer Billy would have been extremely pleased to see that the menu of the Chanticleer Inn where he adored having lunch had his favorite hors d'oeuvre described thus: Vinaigrette de Poireaux Comme Billy L'aimait.

His vanity would have been gratified in the acceptance of some of his clothes by the Costume Institute of the Metropolitan Museum of Art in December of 1984.

He would have been thrilled to know that his many friends formed a committee and are in the process of establishing the Billy Baldwin Library and Archives of Decorative Arts.

In writing this afterword, I think of the words of Thornton Wilder: "All that we can know about those we have loved and lost, is that they would wish us to remember them with a more intensified realization of their reality. What is essential does not die but clarifies. The highest tribute to the dead is not grief but gratitude."

Michael Gardine
Nantucket, New York, and Key West
1985

Index

Note: Page numbers in *italic* indicate photographs.